# DESIRE

*Women Write About*

*Wanting*

Edited by Lisa Solod Warren

**SEAL PRESS**

For my children, who, whether they
know it or not, made me a better writer

For my sisters, who are the
best friends a woman can have

And for Michael, just because

Desire
Women Write About Wanting

"Writing My Way Back Home," from Seducing the Demon by Erica Jong, copyright © 2006 by Erica Jong. Used by permission of Jeremy P. Tarcher, an imprint of Penguin Group (USA) Inc.

Published by Seal Press
A Member of the Perseus Books Group
1400 65th Street, Suite 250
Emeryville, CA 94608

Library of Congress Cataloging-in-Publication Data has been applied for.

ISBN-13: 978-1-58005-214-6
ISBN-10: 1-58005-214-2

Cover design by Susan Koski Zucker
Interior design by Tabitha Lahr
Printed in the U.S.A.

# CONTENTS

## Of the Soul

*For the Real*

# Introduction

*D*esire, a thing at once ephemeral and yet so real that it can cause physical pain, palpitations, breathlessness, anxiety, depression, regret. Whether we give in to it, ignore it, or try to channel it into something we deem more appropriate, it is always with us.

Desire can spring from the heart, the groin, the soul, or some combination of all three; it is merely, and *not so merely*, an intense want: a want that can feel overwhelming, irrational, confounding, and even too large to imagine giving in to.

As women, we have been encouraged to subvert our desires, to deny their existence, or to fulfill them in ways that we think might not be so ... well, *desirous*. To fulfill them in ways more suitable, if at all. Many of us push down our desires so far that they become unrecognizable—but desire is selfish; desire is about *us*. And we're not supposed to think about *us*. At least not until we have thought about everyone else first.

Desire speaks to a privation, a lack, an emptiness in what *is,* and the knowledge that there is something out there that might well fill that space. Everyone desires something: a room of one's one, an Other, a place that feels real, independence (financial or otherwise), a way out, a child, an ideal, a thing one may not even be able to put a finger on.

If we never speak of our deepest desires, we still have them—we have always had them. Here, in this anthology, women who have agreed to reveal their desires are beginning a confession. But this beginning is just that. My hope is that you will read the essays here and some of them will resonate with your own desires, or at least inspire you to think about what some of your deeper desires are. I wish for these essays to encourage women everywhere to start speaking up about what they want.

Not that confessing or speaking up is easy. Some of the women I contacted to write about their desires demurred, even though their excitement about the project was palpable. One was afraid of what her children would say if they read her essay; another was simply afraid to put voice to what she really wants. Another, whose essay is in this collection, declined, after much soul-searching, to reveal a very personal episode in her life for fear that those reading it would think badly of her. Others struggled with their most real and honest voices, illuminating how they are so accustomed to putting their needs and wants in a perspective that others will not find offensive. But all of the women who write here were thrilled, ultimately, to confess, to finally be able to give public voice to what they felt they wanted most. They embraced their needs and wants and then spilled them out onto the pages. There is real and potent honesty here.

But interesting, too, is the fact that of the more than twenty women writing here, none of the desires are exactly the same. A few of them overlap (there is more than one essay about children, more than one about place), yet each is unique, which leads me to believe that we haven't even begun to tap our innermost wants. Even at this point, we are just skimming the surface.

When we women write fiction, it becomes easy to disguise our desires by placing them in the voice of a narrator who is not us. We distance ourselves. And historically, women's fiction was meant to be instructive. Even the classics, written by both men and women, tell us quite clearly that if we go after what we want, we will be punished. We will wind up destitute and alone, be disgraced, hurl ourselves under a train, or find other creative ways of leaving this earth.

As Nancy Armstrong points out in her groundbreaking 1987 work, *Desire and Domestic Fiction: A Political History of the Novel,* "The novel, together with all manner of printed material, helped to redefine what men were supposed to desire in women and women, in turn, were supposed to desire to be." When women wrote fiction, they often chose to disguise their personal desires by putting them in the mouths of other characters, or made those desires metaphors like wallpaper, water, escape. Recently, I spoke with poet Janet McAdams after a talk I attended as part of a conference at Washington and Lee University, and she pointed out that women too often write about the most intimate details and longings of our lives using "significant disguises." We make ourselves into third persons in order to write about things we cannot write about in the first. For good reason, too: The powerlessness we have felt during the previous centuries is palpable; power, if we got power at all, just made us damaged goods. Only a century ago, women were confined to institutions by fathers, husbands, brothers, merely for being independent, for talking back, for allowing that our children drove us a little bit crazy, for standing up for what we felt was right.

The essays in this collection *demand* the first person. These essays *demand* revelation, sometimes of things that might embarrass us or reveal more than we wish to reveal, or show a side of us that isn't quite pretty. Writing about desire demands putting aside the notion that others might judge us unfairly, or look at us as though we were aliens.

But that is okay. That is better than okay. If early fiction was used as a moral lesson to show us who we should be, then nonfiction, like the essays in this book, shows us who we really are. In expressing our desires straightforwardly and without self-consciousness or the need to disguise who we are and what we want, we become, rather than the Objects of Desire, the Ones Who Desire. We get to make the choices, rather than wait for someone to choose us. We get to decide if our desires are legitimate. Only then can we own our desires, and only then will we become braver and truer. Confession truly is good for the soul.

Recent memoirs by Nuala O'Faolain, Toni Bentley, and Jane Juska have continued a dialogue, a confession, a revelation begun by Maya Angelou, Rosemary Daniell, Erica Jong, Sallie Tisdale, and others. Now, finally, more and more of us are realizing that the stronger we are, the better we are and the more capable we are of real love and happiness—love and happiness based on our most true and best selves, not on someone else's ideal of us.

The desires expressed in this collection run the gamut from the sexual to the actual to the imagined. But they are all fully sensuous. Whether we desire motherhood, a home of our own, a private space that others are let into only by invitation, work that empowers us, freedom to be who we really are, or even the ability to transcend our own selves, the answer to Freud's age-old question is answered here. What do women want? We want everything.

*Of the*

*Body*

# Still Horny After All These Years

*S. S. Fair*

*Y*ou can read all you want about the nature of desire, its will-o'-the-wisp–ness, its deranging effect on a well-regulated social life, its seismic emotional shifts that level the sexual landscape into a desolate trailer park of unrequited love. But you can't know desire till it smacks you upside the head and catapults you into a different ozone layer where the only thing that registers is the person standing in front of you, bathed in light. Desire unleashes a choir of ululating corpuscles that soon explode into ten thousand ear-splitting death-metal guitar solos drowning out the halting, reedy voice of sanity.

Desire has its own circulatory system, too, coursing at warp speed, and as long as you're upright and breathing, you're riding its eternal loop of lust and satiation. If death is nature's way of making sure you slow down, then desire is Homo sapiens' way of goosing you into procreation—the better to perpetuate human folly and ensure that, for generations to come, no one learns anything useful from their elders or pays any mind to cautionary tales of lechery gone amok. Even when desire isn't bound up with procreation, it's the heart of a biological imperative to live until you die.

And this is the scary part, the part that everyone recoils from as they picture it in their imaginations: *Desire like this, sexual, roller-coastal, liberating, and mad, does not diminish with age.* Wrinkled, stooped, stone deaf, and feeble, you never lose the urge to merge, even if it's a physical impossibility. So there it is: Old people are horny.

Deal with it.

Young people find desire in old people (which means anyone older than they are) disgusting. This repulsion is an offshoot of the inability to picture one's own parents copulating, but you know what? Tough. As I head into dotage—I'm not being dramatic here; I really am getting older, even if *you're* pretending you're not—sexual desire has not abandoned me. It hovers over my daily routine and hops into bed with me right after Stephen Colbert. It's like a perfume's *sillage*, trailing after me as I empty the garbage, file my nails, pass through passport control on the way to . . . wherever. Even if I'm not actively looking for a roll in the hay and don't live near any hay, and wouldn't want to lie on hay even if I knew where to find some, desire somehow drapes its badass self across my lascivious latitudes and languorous longitudes whenever a person of beauty or soul or incandescent joy shows his face.

The accidental brush of a body on a busy thoroughfare can trigger Technicolor fantasies. As I lumber inexorably toward the slow lane of seniority, the fantasies really do suffice—a sign, no doubt, from the indifferent universe that even though the flesh is weak, the spirit enjoys some good soft-core porn now and again. Aging means life occurs more and more in introspective mode, but it also means that polymorphous perversity is no longer quite so perverse: Every organ, muscle, sinew, the vast ocean of skin, becomes exquisitely tuned to pleasure. Desire is all about foreplay anyway, and foreplay is all about desire. Once you get down to the nitty-gritty, people can actually finish up by themselves. But foreplay? Can't do it yourself; it's like licking your own tongue.

Where wham-bam sexuality was once center stage, now there are soft, gauzy close-ups, whispers, frissons, lowered eyes, and half-smiles that compose the better part of erotica and its multitude of orchestrations. The world may no longer take notice of me in my comfortable shoes and control-top knickers, but inside, where it counts, I'm baying at the moon, drinking Love Potion #9, and waiting for Godot—with his fly open. Though invisible to shop clerks, straphangers, and construction workers (yeah, like I miss that), there are those rare encounters with other polymorphous perverts to sustain me as I head into the mystic. Though I've shimmied through the tunnel of menopause and been marginalized by fashion dictators who insist on accenting the midriff and other body parts I've no intention of ever exposing again, there are men out there who are quite susceptible to my life force, which still rages on high fritz, but without all the static.

I've got one great sexual attribute. Okay, two. A been-there-done-that detachment that intelligence bestows on age in compensation for gravity and liver spots. And a sense of humor. And nothing stokes desire like detachment and a suggestive little knock-knock joke. So, though I picture myself above the trials and tribulations of courtship and the mating game, and do so with aplomb and a dreamy smile, I am, in fact, nothing more than a dirty old lady. And stop saying "ew"— it will happen to you one day, too. If you're lucky.

A wildly unpopular French prime minister in the 1990s, Édith Cresson, once claimed that one in four British men was gay because they never looked at her. The sexuality of British men is a subject we'll cover at a later date, but for now, let's just bet that Édith Cresson never ever got down and dirty in her life—she was so busy keeping score of which men were on booty patrol that her own sexuality dissolved into a pool of narcissistic slime.

Me, although I'm part of the Woodstock generation that hoped to die before we got old, we were fibbing just a tad. As I head into my sixties, I'll be damned if I'm going to slip into Birkenstocks too quickly. I know now that desire, hot-to-trot–ness, whatever you call it, acted on or not, doesn't fade. I'm enjoying the revelation that animal magnetism still holds sway and that those veiled messages I'm sending out still captivate the ready, willing, and hopefully able.

Case in point: Not long ago, I attended a very posh dinner with some putative wine experts, celebrity chefs, and members of the press. A man got up to say a few words about what wines we'd be sampling and how they'd pair well with this food and that. It was all intriguing, but not as intriguing as the speaker: personable, witty but not slick, and yup, tall, dark, and handsome—clichés are always clichés because they're true. It was hard to take my eyes off him, and, as he had the spotlight, I ogled to my heart's content, happy to sit in the shadows and enjoy a lurid fantasy or two. But to whom do you think he addressed all his remarks?

Me. The hound dog at Table #4.

Was I sending out some sort of uncontrollable sexual radar? Were red rings circling my head in neon? Were large, flashing arrows pointing at my genitals? God, I hope not. He was just watching me watch him, alert to the possibilities, doing a bit of ogling himself, steering my pleasant daydreams toward reality camp. It was ridiculous, he was half my age; it was unseemly, he was standing in front of a very savvy group of people; it was awkward, how was I supposed to respond?

It was great. And then it was over. Applause, lights, clinking of forks.

I went over to his table during the meal; his back was to me, yes, but somehow he knew I was behind him. I leaned over and said in his ear: "Can we talk later about those unibrew beers we had as aperitifs, since you didn't mention them in your speech?" He started to rise as he heard my voice, but I put my hand on his shoulder and said, "Don't get up." He responded instantly, sitting perfectly still, awaiting further orders, which he'd no doubt obey. Suddenly I knew him intimately: what he liked to do in bed, in what order, what position, the way that thin film of postcoital moisture would tickle his back and smell like amber, musk, and vanilla. He turned around slowly and looked up at me, whipped a business card out of his suit pocket, and said: "I'd be glad to tell you anything you want to know. Anytime."

I didn't need his number. I already had it. And of course I didn't call. The connection wasn't going to get any louder or clearer. The moment the sparks flew and the ignition rolled over, I saw the green lights and all the highway's curves and dips. Baby, said The Beatles, you can drive my car. Moments like that are my warm milk at night, or they juice me with untoward energy during the day. Half my age; I mean, really. The flattery of that, the little ego-stroke . . . oops, shouldn't mention "stroke" and "old people" in the same paragraph. And though there was no way I would ever go commando in that guy's presence, in his absence everything was permitted.

Case two: the auto mechanic. My car springs a leak in the suburbs near Philadelphia. I drive it into a friendly-looking place; a man sitting in near-darkness in a small office hears me out: the symptoms, the damage, etc. He has a delightful voice, gentle, reassuring, He will fix the car and I will stay at my brother's house until the job gets done. His name is Joe. Of course it is. I barely see his face but I know he's a nice guy. I have no sexual fantasies about him, since I am at that point fulminating on the new James Bond. The car is tip-top in a few hours; when Joe calls, we drive down to the garage. Joe comes out in the full-on sunlight. Joe is gorgeous. He has black hair, real teeth, cerulean blue eyes that don't quit. He's gazing at me steadily as he talks, and I can only hear his eyes and taste his words in their sweetness.

What's a poor old lady to do? We shake hands; I drive off and think, *To hell with James Bond; I've got Joe what's-his-face and he's got a couch inside that office and I wonder if he's married.* And then all I can think about is this: *Joe doesn't think me invisible; Joe has restored me to the land of the living, merely by looking at me in a certain way.*

And here's me, responding, even though I've given up my high-heeled sneakers; even though my waist disappeared somewhere between childbirth and the last time I smoked a cigarette under a tree on Bainbridge Island near Seattle on a rainy July morning.

The French say, *"Plus ça change, plus c'est la même chose."* The more things change, the more they're the same. And speaking of that, I met a great man on the rue Cler in Paris last month, buying blood oranges and fresh chèvre, holding a yellow umbrella. We shared a bottle of Chassagne-Montrachet and had a midnight snack. So this is what one old lady has to say: The best sex of your life is yet to come.

# Where Sluts Fear to Tread

*Rachel Kramer Bussel*

*O*n my thirty-first birthday, I gave my boyfriend two blow jobs. It was an unexpectedly sunny Friday morning, and I'd woken up bright and early, ready for a brisk hour-long stroll to work, where, for once, I might even be on time. I'd gotten up before him, had gotten dressed in a new, low-cut, soft lilac top, flowing blue silk skirt, and fishnets. I should've been out the door already if I wanted to walk versus cramming onto the subway, but I paused when I saw my boyfriend naked, fresh from the shower. I simply couldn't resist the temptation of his body splayed out before me.

I pressed him back against his tall bed. He hoisted himself up and lay down while I leaned over and took his soft cock into my mouth, sucking lightly until he became hard. It felt like its own form of love-making and gave me an inordinate sense of pride that I could turn him from flaccid to fuckable in mere moments. There's a different energy to swallowing a soft penis; it's a kinder, gentler form of cock-sucking, if you will.

The truth is, anyone's mouth would probably have had the same effect, but mine was the one doing it. We didn't have time for pro-longed teasing, but I made sure to do a more-than-perfunctory job. I think blow jobs should be voluntary offerings, not strident demands, and I knew that he wasn't expecting it. If he had been, I'd have been much less inclined. In fact, I found myself getting aroused as I took him down my throat, enjoying the sounds he made and the senso-ry overload of the situation, not to mention the fact that I was fully dressed and therefore even more in control of the situation. When he came in my mouth, I swallowed, then rinsed off in the bathroom, but I couldn't wipe the smile off my face.

It was only much later that night, when the hour meant we'd of-ficially left my birthday in the past, that I started to have my doubts about whether giving a blow job, never mind a second one, had been such a wise move. The nighttime blow job was different, less a perky wake-up call than a post-fucking "please come" message. He gave me instructions, which I dutifully followed, but the longer it took, the more I doubted my ability, gauging only from his grunts and groans whether I was on the right track. Afterward I nestled into his arms, and when he said, "You're a really great blow job giver," I smiled. But I also squirmed.

It's not that I haven't been complimented like that before. Per-haps I shouldn't brag, but I do pride myself on my ability in the deep-throating department. Yet his words gave me pause. I moved my lips from the crook of his neck to his more distant shoulder, averted my eyes from his gorgeous face. Was he wondering how I got to be that good at cocksucking? Did the ghosts of blow jobs past haunt him and taint his feelings for me? His statement lingered in the room; I couldn't think of a suitable response, so I resorted to nonverbal contact, nuzzling him. But his comment also made it abundantly clear that he knew I'd had plenty of practice, and, for one of the first times, I started to question the sexual MO I'd employed for most of my life. I didn't feel guilty, per se, just unsettled. Should I be *that* experienced? Does that make me a worse girlfriend? Does it mean I'm not marriage material if I've not only given many blow jobs, but enjoyed most of them as well? Was his comment a compliment or an insult? I couldn't bear to ask.

I realized that, although I may think I'm as sexually liberated as a girl can get (I did, after all, write a column called "Long Live Blowjob Nation" defending the beleaguered BJ from the likes of antifeminist Caitlin Flanagan's disparagement), there remain demons lurking in the far reaches of my mind, waiting to label me a slut. But sluttiness isn't so much about a given set of actions as it is about a state of mind. (I am all for the reclamation of the word, too—think riot grrrl and alt porn, as well as the four-letter word's more traditional epithet overtones.) And as for blow jobs, there's a reason why my blog, Lusty Lady, comes up second in a Google search for that word. I write about them when they're in the news (sadly, I was not yet a blogger during the Monica Lewinsky scandal), and because I find the word and the act incredibly arousing. I don't mean porn shots of girls choking on cocks that seem disproportionately large, or guys who think that just because they possess dicks, they deserve to get them sucked anytime, anywhere. I don't mean I've enjoyed every blow job I've ever given, or that I'm always in the mood to contemplate them, let alone give them. I don't mean that anytime I meet a guy, I'm imagining what his cock would feel like rammed down my throat, or that I even think about blow jobs on a daily or weekly basis. But I do mean that when I'm in bed with a guy I'm hot for, having my mouth anywhere near his lower half makes me unbearably horny. To me, it's an all-in-one sex act: giving him immense pleasure, turning me on, and letting me take control of something I'm both good at and enjoy doing. If either one of those last factors weren't in place, a blow job could very well feel like a chore.

Yet, for all the truth to the above statements and my wholehearted belief that more women (and men) like to suck cock than we give them credit for, something about my guy's pronouncement, perhaps because it was said after the fact, rather than in the heat of the moment, or perhaps due to his word choice, made me feel iffy, if not icky. I couldn't enjoy it as a simple compliment, because it seemed to have a silent follow-up, the next logical thought being that if I'd done it with him, I'd certainly have done it with other guys. Putting it down so bluntly makes me feel like a hypocrite; how can I advocate for sexual freedom for everyone in my writing when I can't even own my lusty desires? The problem is that I still care about what my lovers think of me, and I want them to see me as a whole person, one who just so happens to like sucking cock when she's turned on.

I have good reason to be concerned. In Sherry Argov's *Why Men Marry Bitches* (the follow-up to her ultra-successful *Why Men Love Bitches*), one of the male tidbits of wisdom she quotes is: "If a woman gives a fantastic blow job the first time you are together, and she does it without hardly batting an eyelash, he'll be thinking, 'Where the hell did she learn how to do this?' If you seem like a pro, you might be a 'ho.'" But a woman's penchant for lip service is just one of the ways in which we're tested in the modern bedroom. With some guys, it's three strikes and you're out if you don't put out, while for others, first-date sex is the ultimate taboo. It gets confusing, and, no matter how much we might advocate or believe in sexual equality on principle, it's next to impossible to blithely date and sleep with men (or women) and remain unaffected by these concerns. Women I've spoken to have gone to ridiculous lengths to avoid being labeled a slut: writing in marker across their stomachs before dates (to prevent them from giving way to temptation) or sleeping with exes so as not to up their "number."

This was not the first time I felt like a slut. Nor, I suspect, will it be the last. I recall a law school morning-after, not its sexual specifics, but the way sex with a man almost twice my age had made me feel: hollow, empty, and awful. The next day I was beside myself, hating what I'd done, even though in the moment I'd been enjoying myself. I felt like a slut, with all the shame, degradation, and self-loathing that the word's traditional meaning implies, because I'd had sex mostly because I wanted to be more worldly—not because I was overwhelmed by lust. I had cast aside my many misgivings about that particular man, only to have them boomerang back to me the next day. I felt slutty not simply because I'd had sex, but because I'd done it with someone I wasn't sure I even wanted to have breakfast with, let alone allow to dine *on* me.

Sluttiness of this sort isn't about giving in to a lover's pleas, because we can always pass that off as bad judgment, the other person's fault, a fatal flaw. But it's harder to do that when you're the instigator. In other words, it's not the blow jobs, per se, but the fact that I was the one who initiated them. That morning with my boyfriend, had I not done the initiating, he'd have gone about getting dressed, while I'd have arrived at work on time, rather than twenty minutes late. But something drew my mouth to his cock, and, if I'm honest, I must say that in this instance, it was not pure, unadulterated lust (though desire played a role). I am something of a blow job queen and usually find the act a surefire route to get me horny and primed for intercourse. I find going down on a guy intimate in the extreme, a heady (pun intended) overload of sensations, a way to get lost in my lover and get to know him intimately. And it usually makes me incredibly turned on in a way that few other sex acts can rival. But the motivation for that morning blow job was different. It wasn't for power or pleasure, but because of the knowledge that I could, if I wanted to, with just my mouth, make us both late for work, take him away from whatever thoughts or plans he had for those precious morning moments, and make him focus on me me me. His dick was almost a challenge, a way to prove myself as a girlfriend, as well as a way to spice up my day and leave me wanting more later on.

It wasn't a chore in the same way photocopying a stack of papers is, but still, I went about it with a specific goal in mind. Feeling him get hard, and knowing I was the cause, turned me on; it was part physical thrill, part womanly feat. I felt sexy, attractive, strong, and secure in my role as girlfriend. (He wouldn't break up with a girl who could suck his cock like that, right?) Leaving his place after washing my face and kissing him goodbye, strolling down the unusually warm November New York City streets with a simple shirt and skirt and cheeks red from blushing, I had the unmistakable look of a woman who's just been up to something naughty. Maybe my recent cocksucking wasn't written all over my face, but I felt somehow different from the women pushing their kids in strollers on the way to school, even though they may very well have engaged in the same activity I had that morning.

Pride, power, prowess, and prudishness: what a combination.

While part of me wondered if, instead of settling down with a "great blow job giver," my boyfriend would rather have, for the long haul, a girl who's a little less lusty in the sack, there's no real gentle way to bring that up. Sexual expectation can't really be stuffed back into Pandora's box. And giving blow jobs is like bike riding: Once you know how to do it, you don't forget. I don't think I could fake being an average blow job giver if I tried. Yet what purpose and whose comfort would that serve? Certainly not mine, and if I start worrying about being too slutty, I may as well not even have sex.

As I grappled with this awkward mix of feelings and emotions, I felt ashamed about worrying too much about what my boyfriend thought of me. Hadn't all my feminist training and years of exploring gender issues meant that I was past all that? I got into the sex-writing business in good part to escape the endless layers of shame I'd accumulated around sex. I knew I liked it, when I was with someone who fully appreciated me and all that my body could offer (not the guy I slept with in law school who responded to my request for oral sex, after I'd gone down on him, by saying that he just didn't like to do that).

The truth is that no matter how much sex I have already had or may have in the future, I never know what to expect when I get naked with someone, even if we've done it before. That is why sex is so endlessly thrilling: There's so much to discover anew. I'm like a virgin, and not; I'm not worried about understanding the basic mechanics of sex, but I am eager to see how the countless variables and ways two people can connect will play out. Will we talk dirty to each other? Will I hold my breath or start panting? Will I bang my fists and scream or silently tremble as I climax (*if* I climax at all)? I may fantasize about a certain kind of fucking in the abstract, but sometimes what I actually do in bed, what turns me on in the present with one specific lover, is completely different from what pops to mind when I'm in solo fantasy land.

So when I'm with someone new, I give all of myself to that moment. I am not thinking about how his dick or her breasts, his kiss or her ass, are different from or similar to those of past lovers. I'm not drawing up a size chart in my mind so I can compare body parts. I'm not pondering anything except what my lover and I are doing in that moment, or what we're about to do. It's a very private, special cocoon, the erotic equivalent of an extra-hard hug where my lover is the one embracing me, blocking out the rest of the world. That may sound incongruous, to consider my sex life private even as I write about it, but to me, writing doesn't take away from the highly interpersonal nature of sex. It's usually only after sex has ended that I start to question whether I was "too much"—too loud, too horny, too good, too voracious.

The same fear provoked by the blow job compliment cropped up one day with the same boyfriend when he was squeezing my nipples. Whereas before he'd given them gentle twists and tugs, this time we'd collapsed onto his bedroom floor, too impatient to actually make it to the bed. He pressed my nubs between his thumbs and forefingers, almost flattening them, and I gasped. "Is that too much?" he asked.

"No, keep going. I want it to hurt. I like it when it's almost too much." I don't know if I'd ever articulated that, but it was true. My nipples have always been extremely sensitive, and if someone's going to just gently lick them, they might as well not even bother. I want to feel that special soreness the next day, when putting on my bra can become an erotic act. But by telling him how much I can take, I was also saying clearly that I'd been there, done that before, enough times to know just how far my body can be pushed, how much pressure my nipples can stand. And it's true—other people *have* tweaked, stroked, pulled, pushed, nipped, bitten, and clamped my nipples. They've been pinched and flattened and sucked on by many other lovers. But by telling my boyfriend that I wanted it to hurt a little, I revealed a small but potent fact, allowing him to treat my nipples more roughly than he'd have felt comfortable doing otherwise. I promptly forgot about my fear as I succumbed to his touch, and apparently he did too, if he ever shared any of my concerns about my experience level.

After the birthday blow job statement, I realized that I really didn't want to talk about it after all, because I didn't want to have to think about where I'd learned to give a good blow job in the first place. Not only because I can't credit any one teacher with my oral education, but because it's not something I go around bragging about or would ever put on my résumé; it's not even something I think about being good at . . . save for when I'm actually doing it. Then my perfectionist streak comes out, and I want to be the best he's ever had. I want to leave him a little breathless, knocked out, and do something for him I know he can't do himself. I want him to think about my lips wrapped around his cock at random times during the day, the same way I do, and get excited about the next time we can do the same thing.

I'm not totally sure what to do about all this, but I do know that the only way things will every truly change is if we women start with pursuing what we really want out of sex—not to the exclusion of our lovers' needs, but keeping both parties in mind. What's funny is that, even as I worry about whether I'm too forward or slutty, I really don't care how many other girls have sucked his cock, as long as I'm the one he's thinking about in the here and now. I know I wouldn't want a lover with no experience. What if he didn't know how to get himself off? Or, worse yet, didn't know how to get me off?

If I had to do it over again, would I have settled for one birth-day blow job? I'm not sure, because even though his words made me hesitate, I was still pursuing what I wanted to do in bed, on my terms. Ultimately, I don't want to be with someone who can't handle the fact that I'm a woman with both a brain and a libido. I've been there and done that, with men who seemed like perfectly "nice guys" on the surface but secretly harbored some very old-fashioned notions about women and sex. Saying I like giving blow jobs doesn't mean I'm on my knees, waiting to suck any random cock that passes by.

When I was in my twenties, I would've been proud to call myself a slut. Now I feel that I have to qualify that statement. I can get off on being called a slut or a whore in the right context, as long as it's understood that in the real world, I don't think of either of those as epithets. I want to be slutty *in my own way, with my chosen lover,* but I don't want to feel like, or be made to feel like, a slut on anyone else's terms. I want to be celebrated for my open mouth and spread legs because the person I'm with knows that he or she is lucky to have me. I want my lust to be sought after, not questioned. I want to be a blow job queen on my own terms, and someday a blow job–giving mommy (and even grandmother). In my mind, the two aren't mutually exclusive. And most of all, I want to figure out what it feels like to live in a world where I don't have to second-guess my sexuality and can instead just enjoy it, no guilt or labels attached.

# The Ketchup-Lid Skirt

*Vicki Hendricks*

As a child I always felt odd, singled out for my inability to fit
in, even before I could attach words to that feeling. I remember day one of first grade, when each student was given a pile of tiny
paper letters from which to pick out the alphabet. I hadn't attended
kindergarten, there was no *Sesame Street,* and when time was called, I
had found A and was looking for B. Dunce of the class.

I was a misfit in many ways. I often sat down in church when
everyone else knelt, or stood when everyone sat. I had to pay close
attention in order to make the right moves, whereas others my age
seemed to know by instinct. It was a mystery. Of course, I could never
pay close enough attention.

I was "butter-fingers" when I played any kind of ball game,
and "butter-toes" in tag. I couldn't dance, for lack of rhythm, and
still can't. I'm one of those people who can never remember which

direction to turn when exiting a room, unless it's in my own house. You get the picture.

Not long ago, I heard John Waters, who's much odder than I, tell how he once heard his parents in another room, discussing him, when he was a child. His father was worried and wanted to do something to make him more "normal," but his mother, an enlightened woman, stated, "He's just an odd duck." Waters, upon hearing this, took it as a justification to "be himself" for the rest of his life, and that certainty has allowed him to exercise his unique imagination and become a major success in the film industry.

"Being myself" hasn't worked quite that well for me. However, by adolescence, I'd pretty much given up trying to fit in. And so, as far as I can remember, I came to think of being wild as my way to shine, despite terminal geekiness, although I had no idea how far down on the scale of "wild living" I really was, being insulated by a Catholic all-girls school until my third year of college.

Mostly, I think what those Catholic-school years did was intensify the delicious allure of sin. Poe dubs this instinct the "imp of the perverse." Love him. Bad boys like Hemingway, Bukowski, and Harry Crews attracted me, too. Extremes, the forbidden—I built up an appetite for them as soon as I realized their world existed.

If I'd had money, I might have found interesting outlets for my attraction to danger, but it wasn't until my first novel was published that I could afford to get wild in adventurous ways: scuba diving with sharks, dog sledding, skydiving, and, recently, having my first trapeze lesson. In my poor college and teaching-only days, I was limited to sex, alcohol, and ensuing relationships, the least expensive of "wild" opportunities for women. These experiences became useful as foundation material for writing that novel. With my oddball imagination, I exaggerated and contrived to make the book far more interesting than my real life.

This essay is about real life, however, so I'm stuck with reality (for the most part). As such, I've happened upon a trail of memories chronicling my early stumblings along the wild rutted path that somehow, eventually, led to my writing noir fiction in the first place. Those first instances were also the contributing factors in any other wild adventures I have had since.

My first tickle of sexual understanding happened at age eleven. I was young for my age, so even "tickle" is too strong a word. It was summer in Cincinnati, where I grew up, and I was at dinner at a restaurant with my parents, my aunt and uncle, and my cousin Johnny, five years older than I, who in later years would answer only to "Jack." They were our "wealthy" relatives, and Johnny was a smooth, blond Ivy League type, shirt tucked, maybe even a tie, the epitome of clean-cut in the early '60s, when that style was still politically correct. I realize now that he had what are called "bedroom eyes," and although the word "cool" was not in my vocabulary, I felt it oozing from his clear skin, like honey or perfume. A tease already, Jack knew how to prick my bubbles and enhance his charm.

"Why do your socks slip down under your heels?" he asked that evening, as he did every time I saw him.

I had no answer about the socks. My thin white anklets always disappeared under the heels of my strapped black patent leather

shoes, unlike any of my friends'. I was a fair-skinned blond, cursed
with an intense blush mechanism, to Jack's enjoyment. He tormented
me for years, until kneesocks came into style.

Jack would never remember this incident, of course. I was wearing my favorite dress at that age, shiny cotton, purple and green stalks
of flowers on a white background, with cap sleeves and a scoop neck
that might have dipped two inches below my collarbone, if that. Despite the girlish style appropriate for my age, I had a sense of languorous beauty in that dress. The skirt was gathered, but not full, and fell
just below my knees, exposing my shins: toothpicks, I'm sure, bruised
in matching purple and green from hurried exits from the neighborhood swimming pool, all above those disappearing anklets with white
lace on the cuffs.

I can't recall the entire dinner, but I know coleslaw was served,
because afterward, unnoticed by me, a tiny clump of slaw poised itself
near the edge of the scoop neck of the dress. Jack missed nothing.
He pointed it out to the whole family in a loud voice: "I thought it
was some kind of pin, a piece of jewelry," he announced, laughing as
if it were the funniest thing that had ever happened. He was always
laughing. He laughed and laughed and the whole family joined in.
My face and neck went hot and red, mostly from embarrassment, but
also from the knowledge that his eyes must have lingered on the coleslaw perched so near my bare skin and the flat, bony space that would
eventually grow a breast.

Years later, at nineteen, I was in my junior year of college, my
second semester in the dorm at University of Kentucky, after the two
years of Catholic all-girls college in Cincinnati. My father had died a

few days after my graduation from high school, and it had taken me that long to throw off the parental control of my mother and save up enough money from my summer jobs to transfer. At the dorm, I quickly learned the pleasures of Ripple, Boone's Farm apple wine, and, for fancy occasions, Mateus rosé.

Two of my suite mates, Pam and Fooshoo, who were "ag" (agriculture) majors hoping to get into vet school eventually, came up with a daring plan to see the Kentucky Derby, some hours away in Louisville. It was daring because Pam had no permission to take her car on a trip, and we had very little money for gas or food, not to mention bets. Somehow we were able to afford a cooler with jugs of Bloody Marys.

We wanted to arrive in the early morning, so the five of us packed into Pam's Corvair in the middle of the night and took off, stopping only to get gas, to go to the bathroom, and, in the chilly morning around dawn, to buy a box of doughnuts. After months of dorm life on the prepaid meal plan, I remember the excitement of being on the road. My custard-filled doughnut tasted luscious with freedom.

We arrived at 8:30 AM and lined up to get in, with our cooler of Bloody Marys and lots of blankets so we could lie around on the crowded grass infield, drinking through the day until the Derby race at the end. By afternoon, the Bloody Marys were gone, but they had done their job, necessitating a lie-down between each race. After we rested we would, still dazed, rouse each other to jump up and watch the horses rumble past. At some point I took a walk around and found my way to the mint julep line.

"Hey, Vic!" I turned. There was Jack. I was always Vic to him, even though we hardly saw each other. I had attended his wedding a few years before, so I knew he had a wife and a little daughter now, but he was alone. I felt titillated and giggly. I was a drunken teen and here was my "cute" older cousin, calling to me, in a city where neither of us lived. He had to remind me to call him Jack, since family members still referred to him as Johnny. I first understood his preference for the name Jack over Johnny at that moment, tough and aloof, rather than somebody's baby. We talked only briefly, as he said he had friends waiting, but there was no mention of his wife. I got my watery-bourbon julep and stumbled off, but I couldn't stop thinking about him, wishing my friends had been there to see how cute he was, wishing I'd made more and better conversation.

The chance meeting must have reminded Jack that I was alive and able to reach Louisville, because when his friend Pete threw a "Hairy Buffalo" party at his farm outside town a few months later, I was invited. "Hairy Buffalo," which I have since heard referred to as "Jet Fuel," at the World Freefall Convention of skydivers, and "Fet Juel" after a few cups, was a mixture of fruit juice and all types of liquor, glugged by each guest, bottle after bottle, into a shiny new aluminum garbage can.

At nineteen, I was thrilled to be included among married people in their twenties, the cool people who were Jack and his friends. It was summer and I was living back home in Cincinnati, dating Big Dan, a six-foot-five redhead who was seven years older than I, divorced, and rode a motorcycle. Of course, my mother disapproved.

"Are you sleeping with him?" she asked.

*Sleeping?* I thought, reflecting on the time spent in Dan's bed. "No, I've never *slept* with him."

Of course, I had dozed off.

I'd eagerly given up my virginity earlier that year, a late bloomer for sure. Catholic guilt spawned nightmares—me in bed with two men, tossing back and forth, unable to push them out, my mother walking in horrified, or, worse, my father—but I got over all that.

The garbage can was nearly full by dusk when Dan and I arrived at the rustic wooden farmhouse. Rumor had it that several quarts of 150 proof Everclear grain alcohol lurked tastelessly in the sweet, fruity mixture.

Jack's friend Pete showed us around the farm, which had no crops or animals but did have lots of grassy fields and no neighbors, the perfect party setup. I was feeling decadent for sure, out of town with Dan, wearing my ketchup-lid skirt for the first time. This was an original creation I had fashioned from the discarded white-metal caps from Heinz ketchup, three hundred strong, most of which I had collected over the two years I worked at Lum's restaurant. I have no idea why I collected the caps, but the skirt was quite a conversation piece. I had linked the caps together with metal rings and the use of a seat-cover tool from the hardware store, and laced the skirt up the front with a red cord that matched the red letters in "Heinz." It was stiff, so I couldn't sit down. I wore it with a red body stocking, a thin stretchy shirt made like a leotard with a snap-shut crotch, a popular clothing item that provided some coverage, since there were gaps between the lids. It was armor with hundreds of chinks, by design, an un-chastity belt. The perfect apparel for flirtation.

Much of the evening is a fog. I was in the kitchen for a while with Big Dan, eating, talking to Pete, his wife, Jack's pretty and petite wife, and others. Wood cabinets, a table and stools, bowls of half-eaten chips and salads, paper plates with hamburger remnants, baked beans, and chewed-off corncobs, my paper cup of ice and pinkish liquid—those are my lasting impressions. The light was bright and the night was warm, so the doors were wide open, letting in mosquitoes. Nobody cared.

After a while, Dan and the other women wandered off for more drinks, and Jack smirked into the kitchen. He always had that look on his face, the one that says, *I know something you don't know, and it's about you.* Pete faded into the background, looking amused.

Jack acted intrigued with the ketchup-lid skirt, walking around me, appraising it slowly in his sly manner.

"How do you get it off?" he asked.

I pointed out the lacing of the tied drawstring, feeling the heat of my invariable blush, blotches coming up on the exposed skin of my neck and chest above the scoop-neck shirt. He noted the holes between caps, and the red fabric underneath.

"Body stocking," I said.

He squatted down and fingered the edge of the skirt, as if it were exotic beaded finery. "Isn't it uncomfortable to sit on?" he asked. "Those caps cutting into your skin?" Chuckle. Chuckle.

I knew he was visualizing red circles cut into my ass by the insides of the caps. My face radiated heat. This was all the attention I'd asked for, and more.

"That's why I'm standing," I said. "I brought jeans for when my feet get tired."

"What in the world made you think of this?"

I shrugged and drank my drink. I couldn't admit it was an adolescent plea for attention. I probably didn't even know that. Jack knew. With his superior knowledge of women, he was enjoying every second of my discomfort.

After that, I remember sitting, in jeans and jacket, among a group of people in the dark, on wet grass behind the house. It seems we were in a circle, but there was nothing in the middle. Was it a game of spin the bottle? I don't remember a bottle.

Then, an incident with no beginning: Jack and me kissing deep, entwined, uncousinly kisses; long, searing kisses with tongues; fingers wandering under my jacket. Me, pushing my body against him, holding tight. I recall guilt and anxiety, too, but not enough to stop the electricity that flowed over me or the tension between my thighs.

It was the hottest grappling I'd ever done. People were watching, perhaps. I didn't care. I didn't know them. My first cousin. A married man with a child. This was clear in my mind, but it didn't matter. Was there anything I would stop at? Not adultery? Not incest? I'd learned in sociology that incest is taboo in every culture. Or at least that's what I remember thinking. But my conscience was detached from my body, soaked with Hairy Buffalo, living out an unconscious childhood fantasy.

Jack's wife loomed into my face, her dark hair bouncing as she yelled something bitter and dragged Jack off. I realized how beautiful she was. I have no doubt that she saved me from myself, before any thought of open grassy fields could occur. The two of them seemed to be heading for the car, even though it was a long drive back to Cincinnati in the middle of the night. I sat there, disgusted with myself. The air got cold.

I woke up in my jeans and jacket early the next morning, on top of the bedspread in a child's room, found the bathroom, and puked. I roused Big Dan from the living room carpet, where he was stretched out along with several people I didn't recognize. I insisted we leave before anybody else woke up.

The following year I transferred to Ohio State University, and by chance I never saw my cousin's wife again. Never heard a word about that night. The next thing I knew, she and Jack were divorced. Jack was remarried before I saw him, years later, then divorced and married again. Selfishly, I felt relieved when I heard he was divorced the second time, since I could be a hundred percent sure I had nothing to do with that.

As for the ketchup-lid skirt, the symbol of my guilt, it disappeared. I woke up one morning, years later, and realized it was gone, probably left under a bed where I'd kept it in some apartment, then taken to the dump to rust away, a twelve-story roach motel, home to a thriving population.

The last time I saw Jack, middle-aged, still compact, smooth-cheeked, and long-lashed, he mentioned the white anklets and how they always slid down under my heels. I cringed inside but rolled my eyes, refusing to let him know that he could still find my sensitive spot. It helped that I was wearing a turtleneck sweater. He has never mentioned the ketchup-lid skirt or that party. A few drunken, slobbery kisses with his silly cousin probably didn't even register on his wildness meter. If he ever reads this, he'll think I made it up.

If this were fiction, I would either have had to learn my lesson to stop drinking and save myself from a life of dissipation, debauchery, and ruin, or else I would have resigned myself to a life of suffering with my "imp of the perverse"—in a "loss of a last chance to change" story, as writer Rust Hills would say. But this is nonfiction, and I've mentioned skydiving and my other wild links to excess, so there's no such neat ending. No ending at all, I'm happy to say.

# Younger Than Winter

*Jane Juska*

*I* have decided not to have my vagina restored. Or to correct anything else on me that calls out for the rejuvenation promised by cosmetic surgery. One could argue that, at seventy-four, I would do well to avail myself of the wonders of modern medicine; surely, just about everything on me needs it, especially if I want to remain young—well, not *remain* young, but *look* young(er). What, other than money, could keep me from it?

Vaginoplasty, it's called, and while they're down there, they offer a specific procedure: hymen restoration. After a lapse of only fifty-two years, I could be a virgin! However, I'm not sure I want to repeat my First Time, not that I can remember it very well. I do recall that it happened in the backseat of a 1955 Chevy, and that there was no blood like what I read there was supposed to be if you were a virgin. Right then I wondered what was wrong with me, and why I hadn't had an orgasm (a word unspoken in the '50s), which is *supposed* to happen if you're engaged to the boy who popped your cherry, right? Well, I was *almost* engaged: Why else would he be doing this if he didn't want me to bear his children?

Maybe at that point I should have inspected my private parts to see if anything was amiss. The very idea made me shudder. After all, they wouldn't call them your privates if they weren't. No one, absolutely no one, was allowed to see Down There, with the exception of the doctor who would deliver my babies in the not-too-distant future, which, when I thought about it, also made me shudder.

That is why I skipped the part of the women's movement that encouraged group exploration: the part where you met with friends, one hopes, in someone's kitchen, hauled up your peasant skirt, climbed denuded from the waist down onto the table, and your friends brought out a mirror, put it between your legs, and glowed while you Became Acquainted with Yourself. *Eeeeeeuw.*

Fast forward to the year 2000, in which I turn sixty-seven. I am on the seventeenth floor of a New York skyscraper, being introduced to a young man who will do the publicity for my book *A Round-Heeled Woman,* in which I tell all about meeting men and sleeping with them at the advanced age of sixty-six. He loves the book: "totally courageous," he calls it. "Do you know," he says, raising his hands in surprise, "there are some women who have never ever seen their vagina?"

"No, really?!" I exclaim. I choose this response over the truth: "I'm one of them."

"Oh, yeah," he says, "have you seen *The Vagina Monologues?*"

"Yes," I lie. I seek to remain sophisticated and worldly in the eyes of this kid who holds my publishing future in his hands. But I feel a stab of guilt. Why haven't I seen myself down there? Why haven't I looked after it just as I've looked after my blood pressure, my lungs, my eyes, teeth, feet? What do I think awaits me? Floppy labia in need of repair? Maybe if I just poke around when I'm in the bathroom, maybe I can tell if the answer is yes, you flop. But then what? Do I really want to return to my pre-pregnancy state, thereby—and it's apparently guaranteed—increasing sexual gratification for both my partner and me? If your answer is maybe, Google "vagina restoration"; you will find what you need to know *and* there are pictures.

This kind of repair or restoration is the latest in the rage for Eternal Youth, which seems to have this country in an iron grip, especially heavy on both coasts and in Miami, where it is a sin to *look* old. One must Keep Up One's Appearance and not Let Oneself Go, which is what happens if you don't go to any lengths necessary to look young(er). These lengths are exhausting, expensive, and exploitive. And we women do it to ourselves; no one forces us to look at all those Before and After photographs. Even if our husbands or our lovers, or both, tell us they like us just the way we are, we know different. We know that with each passing day our secret becomes more visible to the passing parade: We look old. Because we are. So what's wrong with that?

Now, I will admit that if one makes one's living based partly on how one looks—Hollywood comes to mind—then plastic surgery is the price for keeping one's job. If one is a woman. The furrowed brow

of George Clooney, the creases of Humphrey Bogart, the pouches under Brad Pitt's eyes serve only to make them more desirable: In their
cases, signs of age add character to slickness, depth to the vacuousness
of youth. Jennifer Aniston had better watch it, though. She's reached
the upper register of her thirties, so a nip here, a tuck there are absolute necessities to maintain her looks and her income. Same in New
York, where, it seems to me, every professional woman who hits sixty
goes into retirement or hiding, although maybe they just get their
own private offices. Let's hope that's the case. But if it's true, they're
keeping the shades down.

"You don't look seventy-four," I have been told. I answer, "Yes,
I do, this is what seventy-four looks like." What they mean is, "You
don't look old." *Looking* old is the sin. *Being* old is okay, because then
they can ignore you, but *looking* old? No, because then old age stares
them right in the face and says, "Not long from now you're going to
look like this and then you'll die." Dying is forbidden in a culture that
worships youth and beauty. So is thinking. The solution to both is:
Don't do it. Get yourself made young and then you won't have to die
or think, and, even more important, no one has to watch you do it.
Those who look younger than we do can continue their lives as lotus-
eaters, feeding off images of women and men, all young or at least
looking as if they are. Everybody looks young! That's what counts. It's
safe, at least until you think about it. So don't do that.

Let me give you an example of what happened when I went in search
of youth, sex, and cerebral anesthesia: I was fifty-four and, lucky for

me, I met a nifty man, a musician somewhat younger than I, who could last the whole night through. He was an amazing lover: kind, generous, forgiving of my middle-aged body, and appreciative of my middle-aged mind. So why couldn't I have an orgasm? What was wrong with me? I decided it was my breasts.

My breasts grew too early and too big, beginning when I was ten and continuing into my teens. Would they never stop?! For without the support of a bra, they drooped. I believed the horrible song "Do Your Boobs Hang Low?" was about me. "Can you tie them in a knot? Can you tie them in a bow?" I answered a silent *yes*. I was ashamed of what had happened to me: becoming a woman. Forty years later they still drooped, only now even more than when I was young. My shame prevented me from climaxing; I was sure of it. So I got cosmetic surgery: I had a mammoplexy, a breast lift, and celebrated my new self by cutting the underwire out of every bra I owned, an act I would soon regret, for, sure enough, before even five years was up, they began their downward slide. Not at first, though. I tumbled into bed with my lover, confident that I was as sexy as any twenty-year-old. "I like your breasts," he said, and proceeded to do his part. As for me? Nothing. Still.

Six thousand dollars poorer and eventually wiser, I had to face the fact that my breasts—perky or plummeting—had nothing to do with my failure in the bedroom. It had everything to do with my emotional history, unrevealed to me until psychoanalysis forced me to think. After that? Well, sometimes I had an orgasm, sometimes I didn't. But not with my excellent lover who fled the scene soon after I tried to fake it. He was wasting his talents. I had none except that my breasts were pretty spectacular, though not what you'd call an actual talent.

You might argue, as so many fans of cosmetic surgery do, that surely I felt so much better about myself after the surgery. Of course I did, though not for long and not about myself. About my breasts, about looking good, I felt terrific. I should have gone porno; I could have made back those six thousand bucks in an industry where climaxing, if I could learn to pretend, was not obligatory. Alas. I went into hiding, sexually, for many years—until I learned from analysis to read myself, not my breasts or my nose or my tummy or my thighs, but my Self. Then I came out of hiding and went to town, my body structured by age, my mind shaped by understanding. I felt good about my Self, and the rest followed.

Still, I find myself wondering: Would I have cosmetic surgery if money were no object? Where would I start? Everything, starting with my face and ending with my ankles, is heading south or has been there for some time. If I had just my eyes done, then what about my tummy? Would I be satisfied with the rest of me? Well, okay, let's just do a tummy tuck and an eye-lift and, come on, what about my underarms and, while we're at it, my entire face, not to mention my inner thighs? Maybe, if I had bought into this culture in which looking young is prized beyond all else, maybe if I had done that earlier, then logic tells me that by this time, my age, I would not need the whole works, just a bit of firming here and there. But that's not really true. How long do the results of these procedures last? Five years? More? Less? And then you have to undergo the whole thing again. Either that or you can watch yourself not only *get* old but *look* old. Pretty horrifying.

Not necessarily. Not if you do it gradually. Not if you look in the mirror at age fifty-five and see those lines around your mouth as something less—or more—than a reduced income or death's approach. Not if you see them as signs of a life worth living, as signs of a person who has lived and is living life without shame. Not if you see the lines at the corners of your eyes as laugh lines, signs of a happy engagement with life, not of the relinquishing of it. Your face, your body, finally are worth reading. Without tampering with our looks along the way, we reach an age when we not only *look* interesting but *are* interesting.

The marks of living a full life are right there for everyone to see, despite the fact that people desperate for youth don't want to see us, don't want to read the book we have become. Too bad. For they might learn something from us; they might even be delighted by our appearance, so different from the smooth faces, unwrinkled brows, taut bellies, firm thighs of young women who look not so much young as alike. Can you tell, really, Britney Spears from Paris Hilton from Jessica Simpson from Christina Aguilera (when she's blond)? Do you really want to spend the time trying? Unless you're thirteen and think you need a role model of how to look and act, those women are boring. Unless you wonder what real-life plastic looks like and your Barbies have disappeared.

But I know, even as I knew when I began to write this piece, that in the end, despite all arguments to the contrary, we will allow ourselves to be sliced and diced, cut and pasted, in order to remain desirable, to retain, to strengthen, our strongest attachment to life: desire.

And the object of our desire is a man. We want to be desired by him, to be selected and bedded by a man of our choosing. No man, we believe, will go to any length for a woman who looks old. Occasionally, we find ourselves wishing we were gay; women seem to be more generous with other women than we assume men are. That's not necessarily true, of course, but it is certainly a powerful part of the propaganda that makes up our female competitors' campaigns in the war for men. So off we go: As the field narrows, the competition gets fiercer, the chances of success fewer. However, win or lose, the desire remains. We are stuck with it; at the same time we will not let it go. For if we lose it, we lose life; with it, we remain very much alive. Further, if we are fortunate enough to find a man whose desire matches ours, we become young again, and the distance between ourselves and death becomes greater.

But even if no man comes to claim us, desire remains; we cling to it, often at the expense of the quietude of old age promised us by the same people who named those years the Golden Years. No longer fooled by labels, by images of fluffy clouds that scud across a bright blue sky, of sunsets and rocking chairs, we recognize a truth within us—desire—and we welcome it.

So we give up the notion of being *tableaux vivants* for our grandchildren, of providing real-life lessons in the stages of life. Besides, what's a little surgery? We've probably had some already, just not on the outside where it shows. Really now, wouldn't it be easier and safer for us to drive our cars if we had just a little lid-lift? And liposuction is much safer now, isn't it? Could we start with a bit of Botox? Is it too late?

For heaven's sake, this is America, where it's never too late to try, so why not? What have we got to lose? We would do only a *little* bit, right? Never a vaginoplasty, never anything that would alter an essential part of us. Besides, a vaginoplasty costs a lot of money, between $5,500 and

$6,500. On the other hand, ALL MAJOR CREDIT CARDS ACCEPTED: What could be more American than that?

Still, it's never too late to grow up. We could look our age. We could act our age. We could stand before the mirror, look ourselves in the eye, and ask: "Mirror, mirror, on the wall, who's the fairest of us all?" And when the mirror answers back: "Not you, not anymore," we could wisely and generously step aside to make way for the young who wait their turn. We might accept our place in the natural order of things. We might even be happy. It's worth a try. That, too, is American.

# The Ring

*Rosemary Daniell*

*"Madness takes its toll. Have exact change ready."*

—Unknown

*"Give me the keys!" I demand at the top of the stairs of my Victorian flat in Savannah. He's come in drunk once too often, and I'm through. "Bitch!" he mutters, swaying a moment before throwing them at me, then staggering down the stairs . . .*

I breathe what I think is a sigh of relief and then turn to my daughter, Lily, who is visiting. "Now he's gone," I say, betraying my sadness and suggesting my favorite cure-all: "Let's go out and have a drink."

A few minutes later, as we walk toward River Street, alongside the Savannah River, toward a favorite pub, we see him lurching along the cobblestones, even drunker than before. He doesn't see us, and seeing him that way tears at my heartstrings. "I want to go home," I say, no longer into our outing.

When we get back to my second-floor flat, there he is in the bedroom, sprawled on the bed and snoring roundly. He has rappelled up the back wall of the house, come in through a window, and gone to the haven he still assumes, with his usual sense of entitlement, is his.

It's not the first time I've tried to get rid of him, nor will it be the last. As a country-Western song goes, "He's a hard dog to keep under the house."

Flash forward five years. I didn't want to wear a ring in the first place. I didn't even want to get married, but, as women often do to men, Zane had given me an ultimatum—marry him or lose him and his beautiful body, the passion to which I have become addicted. Because of the Marlboro-man grooves he has already accumulated around his eyes, and the lines etched beside his sensual mouth, I called him my sharpei puppy—despite his being fifteen years younger than I. He looked like one of the muscular angels on the ceiling of the Sistine Chapel, I think, mistakenly assuming that also meant he possessed a certain sweetness. He was so cute that I wanted a stuffed, life-size him, complete with red pubic hair, to lie beside me in bed on the nights when he wasn't there.

When I finally succeeded in throwing him out because of his drinking—after he'd thrown my television set out a second-floor window, barely missing my neighbor's Mercedes—I gradually started seeing him again, missing our good times and his body. But I still refused to marry him, even when he offered me a new life at a base near Venice, Italy. (A natural warrior, he was in the army back then.) After I succumbed to the ultimatum, I tried again to get out of it. My sister Anne came from Atlanta to sit on the bed beside me as I told him over the phone that no, I was not going to marry him that weekend, as we had planned. He had called to ask about putting me on his bank account, and upon hearing my words he slammed down the receiver. Later, he appeared with two dozen red roses, and for the rest of the two weeks that were to be our honeymoon, he said nothing more. Two months passed before he threw the ultimatum at me again: The army was demanding that he make decisions about where he would be stationed next, he said. And this time I gave in. Without knowing it, I was agreeing to marry a master manipulator.

Going to the health department for the blood test required for the marriage license was like going to the guillotine, my heart sinking closer to my feet with every step. After we signed the prenup I insisted on, saying I wouldn't be responsible for his debts, he was so furious that he stomped out of the lawyer's office. And when my little Fiat stalled out near a bar on our way home, he rushed inside to swill three martinis, his drug of choice.

The day we got married in the probate judge's office, Anne, who had come to stand up with us, predicted to me in the ladies' room that it would last one year, and I concurred. *I'll show him,* I thought. Little did I know that I'd still be with him twenty years later.

"And what does it matter if you're married three times or four?" Anne continued, referring to my previous marriages. Indeed, thinking back on the previous three—the wild crazy boy who tried to drown me on our honeymoon at Jacksonville Beach; the boring architect who rode the bus downtown each day wearing button-down shirts and little black wingtips; and the Northeastern Jewish prince whose family felt that he had married down—I agreed with her again.

Leaving the courthouse, we ran into an attorney we knew, who said, "Call me when you're getting a divorce." That day, at our wedding luncheon at Elizabeth's on 37th Street, Zane raised his water glass to Anne's and my stems of chardonnay: "Alcohol will never touch my lips again in front of my bride," he said.

When we had gone to Service Merchandise to buy the rings—yellow gold for him, white gold for me—I felt my heart sinking again. Wearing a ring—any kind of ring—would be like wearing a ring through my nose. "You could never afford a ring I would wear," I told him. I meant that I was the kind of woman who would prefer nothing to something I considered inelegant (or, as we say in the South, "tacky"). Was I deliberately, if unconsciously, providing a wound that would later be part of his repertoire of hurts, one that would fester over the years to be brought out during the moments when he would accuse me of "classism"?

Yet how many over-the-road truck drivers like him would even know to use such language? That was one of the reasons I loved him and would continue to love him for such a long time. He could look over something I was writing and zero in, in a moment, on what was wrong. Though he was more visually oriented (read: He was also a man) and a lover of what was new in TV, rock, and film, he could nevertheless switch to reading J. M. Coetzee, William Trevor, Cormac McCarthy, or Albert Camus in a heartbeat, discussing them with a freshness of insight that enchanted me: me, the high school dropout who lived for words and ideas and had finally published my first book at age forty. Never mind that he showed his love of poetry (during a reading in my living room—two gay men, a drag queen, and us) by throwing a guy who wouldn't stop talking during the poems down the stairs of my flat, sending his backpack after him. At times he burst into poetic soliloquies that sent me searching for a pen, or comic riffs that left me in stitches. It was these things, plus his steel blue eyes, his rosy penis, his honesty, that riveted me.

That I felt more at home on a plane than in my own house didn't threaten him. We were both natural travelers who preferred being elsewhere, preferably alone. Yet we both liked and sought out spurts of intimacy. (When I read Vivian Gornick's essay on what maintaining her independence by remaining alone had cost her, I shuddered. Despite being empathetic to her reasons for doing so, I still wanted to be with a man.) Then there was our mutual love of adventure, of sensation, even of sleaze—as in one of his favorite credos, "I've gotta have sleaze." This inclination led us without hesitation to a live sex show in Hamburg, to the red-light district in Amsterdam, and to NCO clubs—where soldiers and their German women hung mesmerized over slot machines, and three separate discos featured Latino, country-Western, and rock music—in Europe and the United States. After nights like this, he would slip a $50 bill into my stocking top in the cab on the way back to his quarters, pretending that we had just met. It was the same attribute that had led him to jump from airplanes over three hundred times, unable to imagine why not everyone might want to do such a thing.

And there had to be something good, because so much of the rest was awful. He was the original, the little boy with a curl in the middle of his forehead; when he was good, he was very, very good, and when he was bad, he was horrid. By the time we had been together twenty years, all the signs that he was not "good husband material," as my Grandmother Lee used to say, had come to fruition. Especially after he was in Desert Storm, those signs ripened into more of the drinking, depression, rage, and penchant for running up credit card debt that had long alternated with his charm. The fact that he was near death after a quadruple bypass and a subsequent staph infection, during which his open heart was left exposed for a week, only endeared him to me further, and then enraged me when he didn't stop smoking, much less have the wake-up call I expected such an ordeal to bring on.

Added to that was his seemingly inexorable drive to "motherize" me, a term I had created in one of my books even before I married him. That was back when I had been wise enough to have concluded that the two things a smart woman most needs are economic and sexual freedom. I had used the expression to describe a man's drive to turn his wife into his mother, which in our case meant buying a house with a yard and a garage. The garage was a priori, he said, a place to park his Buick Turbos, though the first month we lived there, one was stolen from our front yard and used in an armed robbery. That had never happened when we lived where everyone parked their cars on the street.

It also meant moving away from Savannah's historic district, where I could walk everywhere, even to my favorite bars. But I gave in to him, again feeling as if I was going to my own personal guillotine. I even found the house for us, complete with the yard and garage he wanted. And, horror of horrors, despite my telling him that I loved a wild English-style garden, I was soon seeing my sex *objet* not only doing yard work but struggling to turn our new Eden into a replica of his mother's pristine, flat green rectangle in North Carolina. As it turned out, my adventurous paratrooper husband, who had application papers for the French foreign legion when we met, had an unexpected suburban streak.

Then there was the mortgage that went with the house, which weighed on me like a stone: It had been one thing to have him living with me in my little flat, where I still felt I could kick him out at any time, but it was something else entirely to have our finances entangled via property. And even though it was his mortgage and I was half-owner—he had given me half the title as a "love gift"—separating those strands would be no small matter.

But worst was seeing myself falling into the same pit of frustration, the same hysteria and tears, as my mother, who was imprinted with the Southern propriety that led her to suicide. She believed in the values that tell women, "It's up to you to save a bad man through your prayers." She sought to deal with my Valentino-handsome, but drunken and gambling, father by those methods. Indeed, I had been set up for this roller-coaster ride by the two of them, becoming the perfect example of how intermittent positive reinforcement is more addictive than consistent behavior.

Though I was more intellectual than Mother and had done things she would never have allowed herself to even imagine, I was now scarfing down books like *Men Who Hate Women and the Women Who Love Them,* by Susan Forward, and *Change Your Life and Everyone in It,* by Michele Weiner Davis. I was also devouring any Al-Anon literature I could get my hands on. And while our house may have been crammed with books filled with the wisdom of the ages, I had long since stopped setting them out in hopes that Zane might actually read one—I knew the chances were nil.

On my better days, I was writing edgy poems against marriage, citing the women of San Cristobal, Mexico, who use the word "suicide" as a synonym for marriage, or quoting Shakespeare, who said, "A husband would have to be a very good husband indeed to be better than no husband at all." I frequently cited my AA theory of marriage: "One day at a time." And I told myself and others that being married many times is not unlike never having been married at all.

Often, while in conflict with Zane, I would recall a postcard with the message, "Having you gives me the strength to deal with the problems you bring me." If nothing else, he kept me at the top of my game.

But most of the time, I felt like the *New Yorker* cartoon in which a woman tells her lover, "I want our relationship to be like it was before we met," leading me to ask myself over and over how I—a rebel, a leader of girl gangs, a kid who had gotten into fist fights and imagined taming wild animals—had gotten into this fix with yet another man.

"There's only one person in this world you can count on, and that's yourself," Judith Thurman cites Colette's mother, Sido, as telling her daughter in Thurman's biography *Secrets of the Flesh: A Life of Co-lette.* Thurman goes on to say that for Colette, "a man really worth loving would have been an invitation to perdition." And before I met Zane, these had been my sentiments. When a friend said she had finally found a man "worthy of her," I looked at her, puzzled by a goal that had never even entered my mind. I was more like a traveler with a taste for danger and difficulty, creating my own Rough Guide to men, a Wonder Woman of love and art, determined to prove my strength, my mettle, through bonds that said, *Yes, I can handle this, and all the rest.*

Indeed, had Zane been willing, I would had, like Aline Kominsky-Crumb, wife of cartoonist Robert Crumb, a "second husband" to balance what Zane was not. As humorist Jill Conner Browne wrote, "A woman really needs five guys in her life: one to talk to, one to dance with, one who can fix things, one to pay for things, and one to have great sex with. The Good News is that all but one of these can be gay!"

In fact, becoming monogamous after years of sexual freedom was the hardest thing about being married again. Like a cat that had once been feral, the wild boy, the hidden penis inside me, symbol of my own oft-unseemly aggression, was still alive and well. What had been my secret shame as a child had become my pride, my hubris.

Some women still feel embarrassed by what, in retrospect, they call "promiscuity"—by having had too many sexual partners. But I felt the opposite. I had learned to separate sex and love, as men are said to be able to do, consuming them like Godiva chocolates with no thought of tomorrow. And the act of seduction was one I adored.

"Watch Mother," my older daughter, Lulu, said to her roommate from NYU as we walked into a Savannah bar during a visit home. "She can pick up any man she chooses."

As a writer, I was controlled, self-disciplined, even obsessed, but in sex, I sought something else. What I wanted from men was relaxation and fun, and when I was single for the first time in my life after my third divorce, I carried a little daybook in my purse with X's on the days I had sex—and the more X's, the better. "Many women carry their genitals as though they're sealed in an envelope," wrote memoirist Nancy Mairs, who described her own struggles with faith and sexual fidelity. But, as in the cliché "You can't be too rich or too thin," I couldn't have too many lovers.

I scoffed at Judith Rossner's novel *Looking for Mr. Goodbar,* because I felt its message was that women shouldn't take risks like men do—go to bars alone, meet strangers—and that, in the end, such a woman is always punished.

"Mother, you have a slightly sociopathic streak and a strong drive toward novelty-seeking," Lulu, now a psychiatrist and one of the most brilliant women I know, told me when she read an earlier version of this essay. Her comment made me laugh, given her own handsome (and sometimes unruly) blue-collar boyfriend, and her penchant for horseback riding, shooting on an open range, and traveling to whatever foreign country she hasn't yet visited.

Being my daughter, she also knows that I live to resist convention, to scrutinize any given; in that respect, she's not unlike me. When she was growing up, I was much like Oscar Wilde's mother, who said, "'Respectable'! Never use that word here." Censorship of any kind had been verboten within our walls; we all kept journals, which we tossed casually around the house, and told our most intimate dreams at breakfast.

Starting when I was a child, I saw what happened to women around me when they got married: They became diminished, keepers of an ideal rather than of themselves. The best a traditional woman could hope for was many marriages within the same marriage to one man, but that requires a flexibility that many men don't seem to have. As a psychoanalyst once told me, "Most men would rather lose the woman than lose their image of the woman."

Thus, from an early age, I was as desperate *not* to conform as my mother, aunts, and grandmothers had been to do so. (True, this hadn't stopped me from getting married for the first time at sixteen, but that had as much to do with my need to escape my boozy, abusive dad, and to become an adult, with an adult's freedom of choice, as anything else.) My second marriage, to the boring architect, was also an exercise in survival, a submission to the imperative to marry. Nineteen years old, with a baby in tow, making $40 a week as a secretary at Emory University—and living with my still-weeping mother, who had just had her first breakdown and who herself was living with Grandmother Lee—I listened for once to my grandmother and aunts, who glowingly called my new suitor "good husband material," meaning he had a job and two degrees.

By the time I met my third husband, the Northeastern (and thus exotic) Jewish prince, I was well into choosing men with the tempestuous, headlong part of myself, the part that wanted passion, adventure, and the excitement of breaking class boundaries. Long gone was that part of me for whom mere survival was enough. And into the midst of this heightened freedom came Zane.

Twice in my life, my unconscious sent me messages that I wasn't made for the chador of propriety. And once, walking in the city dump behind my paternal grandmother's house at age eleven, kicking at the empty Jim Crow bottles and broken-down couches, deep in my own thoughts, I was suddenly suffused with a golden haze, in which I knew that someday I would do something different from my grandmothers, my aunts, and any of the other Southern women I had known—perhaps even something great.

The vision came again when, as a twice-married mother of three, I sat with my conventional young husband in our suburban backyard, watching our kids on the swing set. Again, a delicious reverie slid over my brain, filling it with a vague yet exciting future. I was flooded by the certainty of a life filled with art, many different people, and travel to unknown, exotic places. And, though it was nonspecific, this time my fantasy was decidedly more erotic. My mind swam with faceless, unknown men (and women), who floated through my brain again in the shower the next morning while I removed the diaphragm that was part of married life's drudgery. ("Put it in every night before you go to bed, just like you brush your teeth," my gynecologist had recommended.) When I saw a therapist at the end of my second extramarital affair, he asked me to draw a man and a woman. I drew a man carrying a suitcase, and a woman deep in thought, pregnant with poems—the very person I am today.

Recently, still married to Zane, I went to sleep reading Esther Perel's *Mating in Captivity,* in which Perel quotes motivational speaker

Anthony Robbins as saying that our capacity for passion has every-thing to do with our ability to tolerate anxiety. She also cites Stephen Mitchell as saying that the fantasy of permanence may trump the fantasy of passion, but both are the products of our imagination.

The next morning, I woke up thinking of the period in my life when I lived in a beautiful, if roach-infested, flat, had $500 in the bank, went out dancing at least three times a week, and slept with whom I pleased, in between writing and teaching poetry to kids for the National Endowment for the Arts. I recalled spending the last of my minute savings for a trip to Guatemala with some edgy people, where I met other edgy people much like myself. "You were so happy then," Anne said one day as we talked about that time in my life.

When I first started writing, the publishing industry conspired with my carefree attitude by sending me off on periodic book tours in which, given the climate in publishing back then, I was driven around in chauffeured limos and stayed at five-star hotels. "You'll never have to think about money again for the rest of your life," my editor told me—as my first memoir was being printed in five hundred advance reading copies, complete with full-color covers—in one of those charming but misguided statements that finally make one realize that editors and publishers don't know any more than we do. But for the time being, I floated on a cloud of freedom and fearlessness, the part of my brain that screams, *Security! Money in the bank!* not yet activated. The cloud only began to dissolve well into my relationship with Zane.

Needless to say, other things began to happen during my years with him, things that were even more intense and challenging, things that put whatever was going on between us on the back burner. I was dealing with the sanity- and life-threatening chronic illnesses of two of my adult children, a situation that would consume most of my psychic energy for almost two decades. (Ironically, and increasing my attachment to him, Zane was the one person in my life who helped me most during these crises.)

Using what Lulu explained to me as "cognitive dissonance," I could easily make up a story, as people frequently do about a difficult but life-changing experience, about why this was the best thing that ever happened to me. But I'll say only that these realities created new grooves in my brain, a new respect for stability, for life beyond pleasure. Though that wild boy inside me can still flare up in a moment, I now know the truth of the Spanish admonition "Take what you want, but pay for it." I also know that if I want to stay at a Park Avenue hotel, I'll have to pay for it myself.

As often happens when a woman is independent—living alone, with lots of boyfriends, the perfect apartment, the perfect work life, for once happy and solvent—a man will step in to fill what he sees (but she doesn't) as an absence, a vacancy. As though she is a challenge to his manhood, he will do whatever it takes to insert himself into her life, at center stage. And the prouder she is, the more subject she is to this phenomenon.

In contrast to the animal world, in which the more docile female chimps, the least sexual ones, make the best wives, as they are the most monogamous, in the human world there are men who will go up against nature, only to later become frustrated with their mates. In research that revealed "The Wifebeaters of Kabale," as *Time* magazine called chimps that were discovered using sticks to beat other chimps, most of the attacks have been directed at sexually active females.

When *Esquire* ran a questionnaire for men to determine how big their balls are, I realized that, as a former football player, paratrooper, and participant in barroom brawls (with fights "with more than one person at a time" receiving the highest score), Zane was right up there with Russell Crowe and crew. Because of the challenges he presents, he has also provided endless raw material. Toward the end of my memoir *Sleeping with Soldiers,* I wrote as if I were describing the end of our affair (au contraire—it had barely begun). Later he appeared—the macho man incarnate—under my byline in *Harper's Bazaar, Self, Mother Jones,* and *Men's Fitness.* Parts of this essay came straight out of one of my notebooks, written during yet another period of frustration, proving once again that it's rarely ease that drives us to art. Perhaps best of all, Zane's above-mentioned cojones also mean that he doesn't give a damn what I write about him.

My cat, Principessa, was once feral, living beneath our house; my taming her enough to be my special pet, despite her skittishness, has made her gray fur a magnet for my fingertips. In the same way, Zane's goal has been to possess me, and, in a way that seems almost magical, he has done so. Every time I've thought of leaving, it's as if he's read my mind. Over the years, I've received more flowers, boxes of chocolates, and silky things from Victoria's Secret than would seem possible. Once, as he came up the steps bearing yet another vase of roses, I asked, "What are those for?"

"Don't you know?" he replied.

"You want me to do something I don't want to do?" I said, throwing out a guess. "No, it's our anniversary!"

And, more nights than I can count, he has insisted on my pleasure, leaving me too weak for anger. Indeed, my very slipperiness and standoffishness have added to his passion. He is the gladiator struggling for victory, and I am the prize.

For my part, I've been intrigued by the mystery of rubbing up against a person different from myself. My bad taste in men is no secret. But in truth, I considered it an animal's protective coat, designed to shield and ensure the safety of that wild boy inside me. I thought that by choosing a really impossible candidate, someone with whom I was unlikely to stay, I was ensuring my freedom. "Good husband material" had not been what I was looking for.

And now my shame, my black hole, was that I had once more let a man take over my life.

Or had I really just been a dummy, giving up and giving in to what felt like the inevitable, the imperative to marry, as I'd seen so many women do? Would I end up like my friend Kathleen's mom, Elma, who had married her charming, bipolar husband three times? Or Francesca, a poet who wrote a brilliant credo against marriage, then suddenly, at the height of her beauty and power, became engaged not to one man but to two in quick succession?

Or had I truly come to love someone despite, or because of, the problems he brings me? Yes, the unconscious has its own reasons, and one of them—dare I say it?—may be love.

Fast-forward to last month: a full twenty-five years since Zane and I first met. We both happen to be in the same city, and he and I sit at a truck stop, where I've come to meet him for lunch. The tension on his handsome face makes his anger and self-pity clear. Thinking to cheer him, I quote Thomas Carlyle, saying that we're often the spot on our own sunshine, then add that Carlyle was able to say this despite the story that a maid had trashed his entire manuscript of *The French Revolution,* forcing him to rewrite the whole book. But, as usual, I see that my homily only fuels his bad feelings, and we part with a chilly kiss.

A week later, I wake thinking for the thousandth time that I *have* to live apart from him. I've long relegated my wedding ring to a dresser drawer, though he still wears his. Whenever I broach this subject, arguing in favor of our living apart but still being lovers, he refuses to listen and instead gives me his stock answer: "I guess we'll have to get a divorce, then."

After noon, I come in after a morning of errands to find him still sitting at the dining room table, cigarette butts at his elbow, the TV on—in other words, exactly what he was doing four hours before, when I left. Except that now he's also flipping through the sexy pictures of me that he's collected over the years. "Can't you do something constructive?!" I yell, irritated at the sight of a grown man titillating himself at midday, and thinking about all the things around the house that need doing. I've long since given up on nagging him about the novel he began five years ago that now languishes on a shelf.

But as I sit down, he shows me the less graphic ones he's selected for me, the ones in which we are together, looking undeniably happy and, yes, beautiful—in Paris, at parties, in bars and hotel rooms. Then he begins a rap about how his one goal in life is to take care of me, provide for me, and my heart—so easy, always so easy—softens.

That evening, in the kitchen, he makes me laugh with one of his comic riffs. Later, we go out to dinner, then dancing. My hand on his strong back, my nose in the oh-so-familiar masculine scent of his neck, I float to the country-Western band, wondering who this man, this delicious stranger, is, and how long he will be in my life.

# Makeup and Mud Puddles

*Daphne Gottlieb*

*Y*ou could blame it all on *Porky's,* that '80s tittyflick with the shower scene, if you wanted to. I think I did for a while. That was the movie that I asked Hannah* to go to with me. We were thirteen, on the verge of needing adult women's products but unable to see adult women's breasts on the big screen. Go figure. Hannah and I had gone to the movies before, but this time, somehow, was different. For me, anyway. When I looked at Hannah, with her long dark hair, something happened to me. It was like the rush I got from putting on the makeup I wasn't allowed to wear yet in the mall bathroom. She was forbidden, made my breath come a little too fast. It wasn't just that she was a girl, but that she was an exciting girl, an adventurous girl, a girl who went to a school I thought was much cooler than mine, who knew how to tweeze her eyebrows. She listened to NPR. She was so sophisticated. I wanted to kiss her. I wanted to touch her. Past that,

I wasn't exactly sure of the specifics. Just speculating made me a little squeamish, but I was still intrigued, enthralled, captivated. I wasn't sure what wanting her meant, but I wanted her.

We had prepared our stories for the movie bouncer. We didn't drive, so we didn't have licenses. When he simply waved us into the movie, I could breathe a little easier. Except when I looked at Hannah. I took our easy entry as a sign, a sign that she wanted to be with me, too, that she wanted to kiss, that maybe there was something between us. When the movie theater lights went down, I imagined that I could feel the heat from her hand near mine. That was as close as I got to touching her.

I don't remember much about the movie, but it came into play about a year later, when I came out to my mother for the first of five times. I don't remember much of that conversation, except for my talking to her about seeing *Porky's*. I explained it to my mother like this: "So, there's a girl and you're looking at the girl a certain way because you have to because that's how they made the movie. You look at her the way they filmed her, like a peep show, only you don't get a choice. You have to see her like that. You're *supposed* to want her." My mother seemed perplexed by this, not because of any rock-solid conviction about heterosexuality but because her entire experience of desire was one of a desire predicated on difference: Me and the Not-Me. Tab A and Slot B. Electrical outlet and electrical plug. She didn't know what to say. And I didn't have the language yet to talk about femininity as a fetishized commodity. The conversation between me and my mom sort of petered out. I didn't notice, as I was swaddled in my head with the smell of Hannah's hair, the heat of her hand nearby. *There is no gender to hands,* I thought, as my mother made dinner.

Soon after that conversation with my mother, Hannah and I fell out of touch—summer had ended and we went back to our normal social circles. Hannah had never figured out that I wanted her. I was both sad and relieved, and pretty clear on the fact that I was queer. I continued to be clear on my queer desire through my high school crushes on girls (which reflects not at all on my then-boyfriends), and through my college tussles and grapples, and through my first real girlfriend, a girlfriend who wasn't a one-night stand or experimenting or curious.

In a small town, there aren't many girls who kiss girls. Finding the girl was more important than what she wore. She was gorgeous, with perfect lipstick and lacy panties, and she liked me. We looked more alike than different, but we never haggled over who was going to be the tab and who was going to be the slot. We figured it out as we went along, the way queers in small towns did before the Internet and support groups, that girls were for us and small towns were not. She moved to a big city and I moved to San Francisco.

As a recent transplant there, I emerged into a giddy relationship with Delia, the older sister of a college friend of mine. She talked about Central America and the unionization of the peep show she worked at, and I knew I'd arrived. She could talk politics and kick ass in her platform heels. And we started hitting the town, and suddenly everything around me looked different—I was squarely in the middle of a butch-femme culture. Until San Francisco, I'd never seen a butch my age—in my small town and in the media, butches were represented largely by plaid-wearing, broad, gruff, unpleasant types with bad haircuts. But in San Francisco, the butch women had James Dean rising and they walked like John Wayne crossed with the dorky guy from your sixth-grade math class. I started dating butches with a familiar short-breathed, giddy anticipation. It wasn't that I stopped *liking* girlie-girls. It was that the butches asked me out. But even as I rode the high that this new frontier of too much pomade and boxer briefs offered, a sudden, strange shame colored my entire history of dating women. I realized that all my life, I'd been doing it wrong. I mean, I knew I'd been doing it wrong to begin with—dabbling in the same sex as well as the opposite one—but now I was really, really wrong: I'd been dating the same femme gender when I should have been dating the opposite butch gender. Or so looking sideways at other couples would have had me believe.

Without even knowing it or trying to, just two weeks before, I had propositioned a girl at a club, a girl with shimmery lipstick, a dress with sequins like magic coins, and punk-rock hair. I was talking to her, tucking one fishnet-clad leg behind the other and lowering my eyes. I said, "Maybe," and then, peeping back up at her from under my eyelashes, continued, "maybe you want to get some fresh air?" I wanted to sink against her, feel the way she pressed back, wanted to—my knees were bending, sinking toward her as her laugh cascaded gently, not unkindly, toward me. "Not now," she said. "Maybe later." "Later," of course, as in "never." I dragged myself home and hid in my bed, sure I was repulsive, untouchable. Less than a month later, I understood. I had asked the wrong girl. I was doing it wrong. Femmes weren't supposed to hit on femmes. Butches and femmes. I didn't know you could do attraction wrong. I was so ashamed. Now I knew. I had to do it right from now on, now that I knew. I wouldn't talk to or think about or want girls like that. Not anymore.

When I met the love of my life, a gorgeous butch thing, I was so nicely acculturated into butch-femme life, I didn't really notice my girlfriend was butch. I didn't think much about my desire for femmes or wanting femmes or what my attraction to other femmes meant. Well, yes, there were a few femme anomalies—the dalliance with the hot thing in the skintight PVC skirt in the nightclub bathroom; the car makeouts with the belly dancer who moved like smoke made by thighs rubbing together. To some extent, my extracurriculars had a theme. And because these women were femmes, because I wasn't looking for a relationship with them, fooling around with femmes was socially sanctioned, a "Why not?" party conversation, a fan-club chorus out on the town—*Oh, yes, she's* gorgeous, *who* wouldn't *jump on her?*, a sort of *mmm-hmmm: Of course she's hot. And of course we feel that way. Look at how she's putting it on! We're supposed to.*

For almost a decade, femmes were a side dish, playtime, a kind of sex play that was nonthreatening to my partner or someone else's partner. And then one night, single again, I was out with a date. My lover introduced us. I want to tell you that I couldn't stop my knees from shaking, or that I was so wet from just the sight of her that I grabbed her and kissed her or something awkward or romantic, but really, I was confused.

A couple of years before I met Callie, I'd written a poem called "the frightening truth of desire" that went like this: "i don't know/ whether i want/to be/her, fuck her/or borrow/her clothes."

And this is exactly what I felt when I saw Callie. I didn't know which I wanted. Or, rather, I wanted all those things. And I wanted to be *with* her. I was single and was thinking about things like flowers and violins and roaring, bellowing, unfeminine sex. To my shock, when we ran into each other a few weeks later, we exchanged numbers. And we started dating.

It had been a long time since I'd dated a femme, and certainly never anyone like Callie, who would show up for pizza and a forty-ouncer in the park wearing a leopard-skin coat, high heels, and a tiny red slip.

I was diesel femme, she was retro drag. She wore spike heels; I wore combat boots. She wore sheer, vintage, Cuban-heeled stockings; I wore ladder-ripped tights, decimated to spiderwebs. And I loved all of this about her, and I wanted her because of all of this, that it pleased her, that she dressed with her tongue halfway in her cheek, that she played the girl as much as she was every inch girl. Her brain, her comportment, made me as hot as—or even hotter than—her looks.

I think that's why I suddenly found myself so worried. Was there room for both of us to be fabulous? Would people think that I was "the boy," since I was taller, older, broader, far less glamorous? Or, worse, would people suddenly think I was butch? It might be worse to be misunderstood than unseen.

And the world didn't seem to see us, either. After a couple of weeks, seeing the reactions our coupling garnered, we joked about making T-shirts that said 2 GAY 4 U. Because suddenly, we were too gay—so gay, we were impossible. We were like-meets-like, and you just don't *do* that (at least not in San Francisco). In the "real" world, we were seen as just two women out for the night, our hand-holding seemingly a mark of our girlish affection. Our relationship was invisible, disrespected. In the queer world, we were seen as two femmes out for the night. Callie got sly propositions, offers of walks and fresh air from sweet young butches. I stood back and watched, invisible and disrespected. The world didn't see us, and neither did our "home."

The world didn't see "us," a couple on a date, but they sure saw Callie walking into a room. It was an uncomfortable pleasure as I watched every head turn: She was with *me*. Everybody wanted to be where I was. A second later, I felt ashamed, as if this somehow collapsed Callie to her looks, made her valuable only because she was a knockout. I didn't believe that, but I was afraid she might suspect me of such beliefs. And worse, she *was* a knockout. Was I wrong to enjoy the way she looked? Wasn't I supposed to look at her that way?

It turned out it didn't matter—because of changes in her primary relationship, we stopped dating. But we remained close. There were more worries, but I would start working things out on my own.

Things like this: They say that opposites attract. Check. Women are from Mars, Tab A, and all that was covered in Coming Out 101. But even in butch-femme, there's a polarity being played out—one of "female masculinity" and one of "female femininity." The roles and expectations have already been cordoned off, and everyone expects that the butch, with vague similarities to the man in traditional heteropatriarchal structures, is supposed to pick up the tab (unless the femme does first or they go Dutch), and the femme will get on her back (unless the butch gets on hers first). There are standards to be upheld. These codes, both in compulsory heterosexuality and in the queer world, give us our cues, tell us how to behave, help us transmit our wants and needs.

But on a date with another femme recently, everything became a process of negotiation: Would she open the door or would I? How stupid would I look bringing her flowers if she was already bringing some to me? And even worse: What if she treated me like a butch or a boy? Because, inevitably, there have been girls who do. Girls who have used against me the coded behavior of butch-femme they've learned. It's like being shot with your own hot-glue gun. One minute you're a girl with a girl, and the next minute she's treating you as if you're her older brother's best friend: embarrassingly horny, not to be taken seriously, and likely to pull her pigtails and burp, but still throw down your coat so she can safely cross a mud puddle.

The last femme I dated was Fatima, willowy and pale, black hair framing her face. Everything about our first date was perfect: the low lights and her soft bed, her half-closed eyes and her mouth tasting like a country I had always wanted to see but couldn't afford to visit. I wanted her, achingly. I wanted to know the curl of her ears with my tongue, wanted to know how warm the soft curve of her neck was, and if she'd shudder as I breathed softly over and against it. And still, I was uncomfortable. But I didn't know why. I tried to shove it down, make it go away. After all, it was the first time we were fooling around seriously. I willed the thoughts away while the music in the background swelled and swooned, and we rolled over and over, kissing and tangling like snakes in heat. And then things got serious: She got up to turn something off or on or adjust something so that things would be even more perfect—I don't remember exactly—and that's when it happened.

She removed her sweater and lingeringly let it slip from her fingers, staring me in the eye, not breaking eye contact as she slid her skirt down her thighs, onto the floor. She looked amazing, expensive, pink, lacy lingerie highlighting everything nature did right. Fatima leaned over the bed and began to crawl over to me, just like you'd see in a porn flick. Humorlessly. Intensely. Halfway across the bed, she paused and flipped her hair.

It was enough to send me right into the mud puddle, desire first. Dirty is great, but this kind of muddy can be fatal. If you're a femme. Let me say this: Any guy who saw what I did would be the luckiest guy in the world. But, still, I *wasn't* a guy. And I didn't want to be pandered to like that, in that way that smacks of what guys think girls do in bed, rather than what they do. In a way, it was the opposite of the Callie problem, *Am I still a girl if she's a girl?* With Fatima, it was *Can I still be a girl if she plays me like a boy?*

And really, the two questions are different facets of the same issue: identity and attraction. Can you be her, fuck her, and borrow her clothes? Sometimes. And it's complicated. It depends on whether your categorical identities and codes of behavior can mesh, how much visibility in the outside world affects you, if you can figure out who's paying for dinner and who holds the door open for whom. There you both are. And you look so scandalous together, tramping hand in hand into the mud puddle, flinging handfuls at each other, giggling and screaming and shouting until your mouths close over each other's and footing slides away and there's skin and squirming and you are not boy or girl; you are boy and girl and you kiss and you kiss and the desire won't stop. When they ask *Who's the boy?* you don't stop to answer.

*Names and other identifying details have been changed. A lady never tells it all, right?*

# Two Cups Orgasm,
# A Measure of Taboo

*Connie Baechler*

*I*t's Tuesday night, I'm in bed with Regular Guy, and I already know what's for dinner. Meat. Potatoes. Meat. Potatoes.

The head of his penis prods me in a familiar, been-together-long-enough-to-know-all-the-right-moves way as I raise my hips to meet it. Safe sex served medium-well in predictable portions satisfied me for a long time, but lately my mouth is set for rarer delicacies.

Long ago, I had fantasies about Regular Guy, too, but the time we acted on them was a debacle. I endured the event every woman worth her leather bustier tries to avoid—the dreaded Bed Disaster. For variety, I decided to leave the four-poster and take Regular Guy on an adventure, wearing four inches of black spandex and a smile. Instead of throbbing against my thigh, he couldn't stop worrying that other people would see us in the park where I groped him at midnight. Yes, that's the point, I said, there may be voyeurs. Let's be so hot for each

other that we don't care. We can invite them to watch. As I coaxed
him against a tree, he eyed the swing sets like a skittish horse and
said nothing. When I unzipped his pants and slid his T-shirt over his
navel, he yelped and yanked it down.

Yelping is not sexy.

The trouble is, Regular Guy exists only in the world of the real—
he doesn't translate into fantasy. I don't hold it against him; in fact, I
love him. But I still desire strangeness. My imagination doesn't oper-
ate on the meat-and-potatoes level. It hungers for exotic and heady
aromas wafting from silver chafing dishes.

As Regular Guy serves the meat, I shut my eyes and submerge
myself in the opulent dining hall opening in my mind. It's my delicious secret, my seven-course meal arranged on steaming trays by
impeccable staff. Once I taste the first course, I can't stop myself. The
truth is that I'm no longer paying attention to this Tuesday night dinner with its ordinary seasonings. I'm focused on the exquisite banquet
behind my eyes—a banquet that would probably amaze the man who
lies above me.

I walk through a series of rooms lit by round lanterns whose light re-
fracts and illuminates warm orange walls. Each room connects to the
other in a honeycomb whose hive is the nude people buzzing inside. A
woman in a red silk robe approaches and takes my hand in her own red-
nailed one. Inhaling rose petals and sandalwood, I follow her past rooms
of people caressing in the shadows just beyond the lamplight; I glimpse
breasts, legs, and buttocks writhing in mesmerizing figure eights.

The woman in red leads me to an anteroom filled with gold flowers, a gold chaise, and a cluster of crystal glasses on a gold tray. Each glass holds a gem-colored liquid that glints burgundy and emerald. Before I can ask questions, she unbuttons my shirt, eases it from my shoulders, and, slipping her fingers between fabric and waist, undoes the top button of my jeans. I slide them down, my heart thudding with anticipation of what may come. When I'm nude, she smiles and pushes me back on the chaise before leaving in a rustle of silk and roses.

My nipples peak in the cool air as I study my pubic triangle and the soft rise of belly above. Just as I am about to touch myself, the door opens and a man enters. He's wearing a white sarong that sets off his striking chest and abs, and he gazes at me with hunger in his pale green eyes.

"I am Javier," he says. "And you are beautiful."

I quiver as he approaches and touches my breasts with great reverence, bending over to take first one, then the other, nipple in his mouth. His hair, pulled back in a thick plait, falls halfway down his back.

He smiles, brushes his finger across my lower lip, and crosses to the tray of glasses.

"And now," he says, "you must choose a drink."

I sit up as he brings the tray closer, kneeling before me in the lamplight.

"But I don't want to take drugs," I say.

"What you choose liberates." Javier strokes my cheek. "It is not a drug but a release of taboos. You will taste your own desires as a woman who is free."

Freedom: the ultimate aphrodisiac.

I select the fourth glass from the cluster and sip. Almonds and vanilla lace my tongue.

Javier smiles as I lie back on the chaise and feel my legs fall open. He kisses me and takes me in his arms. I expect romance novel–style lovemaking and wonder if I should swoon, but before I know it he's carrying me outside, leaves crunching under his feet. Crickets serenade the evening breeze as he enters a small clearing and slides me into the hammock swaying between two trees. The group of men standing in a rough semicircle at the edge of the clearing causes me to throb with anticipation.

Lying in the hammock, I want three guys at once, but they must wait for my fancy. I touch myself and dangle a leg over the side of the thin mesh as the gentle sunset draft teases the nape of my neck. The watching men shift their weight and clear their throats below my moans. A wolf howls in the woods.

I have slipped on a white shirt, unbuttoned but knotted at the waist, to cover some of my nakedness. Below, I'm nude and open to their eyes, but not their bodies—not yet. I insist on their waiting and make them crazy with my own lust as I teach them how I like to be touched. So many men are prone to diving in and starting to grab and rub things. My motions are deft and light, an encouragement of the flesh, rather than an insistent tapping into some suspected sap.

Regular Guy buries his face in my neck. The beige cotton sheet bunches up under my ass, and I grab the bedpost for leverage. Then I close my eyes again as he groans, "Oh, baby" and "Oh, yeah" into my ear. The noises remind me of the time we roadblocked at the cheesy porn that got him hot. Those women, with their fake "ohs" and cookie-cutter "ahs," weren't anywhere near coming. My own orgasms are interior events, not public spectacles resulting from the insertion of Tab A into Slot B. If I wanted to be a slot machine, I'd go to Vegas.

After my hammock interlude, Javier leads me reeling back to the hive and shows me to a changing room. The woman in red appears, fragrant with honeysuckle, and drapes me in a nightgown that shimmers silver like the sea in winter. Then she leads me to the threshold of a chamber, and three steps later I'm in bed with my friend—the one who's off-limits in daily life because he's happily married, though that restriction doesn't stop me from drooling every time he appears. Now here he is, naked among the white pillows and squeezing my nipple like it's an ordinary pleasure. I put a hand over his.

"Wait," I say, though I don't want to. "What about your wife?"

"She doesn't mind."

I look down at the foot of the four-poster and find his wife lying on her side with an expression of casual indifference.

"Go ahead," she says. "I'm taking the day off."

Unable to believe my luck, I tremble to think that such long-coveted fruit has fallen into my hand. Reaching for his penis, I squeeze hard; he rolls over to mount me as I have longed for him and his bedroom eyes to do ever since we met five years ago. Curved and thick, his penis opens up some space on the floor of my vagina that I didn't realize existed. It's as if I'm a new sphere, spinning in the telescope, and he's the heat-seeking missile headed for my solar system, glittering and otherworldly.

I could come that second, but he slows his strokes until I beg him to speed up. He knows how to make my flesh rise with a deft rhythmic shift. The giddy thrill of access to this long-tabooed body floods me, and he rides me rough as I throw my legs high and pound out my pleasure on his back in a staccato of surrender.

I'm thinking of changing positions to woman-on-top, but Regular Guy seems to be having fun up there, so I stay put. Nothing wrong with a little missionary meat-and-potatoes sex when a girl's having so much fun under the surface. Besides, I know this position buys me more time before Regular Guy climaxes. He used to get grumpy when I didn't come from his oh-so-glorious penis inside me, but I handed him *The Clitoral Truth* and a notepad. Since then, he seems perplexed but soldiers on in spite of the confusion. I bite the inside of my cheek against the laughter welling up within, and open to my interior world again.

Wandering out of the bedroom where my taboo lover reclines satiated among the sheets, I pad barefoot down the hall to shower. The soap smells like lemongrass, and I slip a sliver of it between my legs. Javier appears to dry me in a white towel softer than those at a five-star Hilton, and the red-dress woman kisses my cheek before leading me to a room with a black leather curtain draped across the doorway. She lifts the leather on a tableau of man on top of woman on top of man—the trio together on a large round dais lit by candelabra. The woman keens and shifts her weight as the man on top steps back and raises a small flail, which he brushes, like a promise, down her back, where she glistens with oil.

I press my legs together at the spectacle. The flail brings possibilities to mind. Next to me, on a black beanbag, a man with shaved scalp and pierced eyebrow reclines and touches himself. Despite the erotic threesome undulating so close, I can't take my eyes off his hand in motion—so deft and sure. His breath catches as he moves, and then I hear the smack of flail on flesh and turn to see the woman working the back of the man below her, his cheek pressed into the pillow as he groans. When I return my gaze to the pierced man, he's watching me and smiling; it's clearly an open invitation to join in. I want them all and turn in a slow circle to see the group at hand.

Then someone cups me close between my legs. I smell musk, sweat, and forest and know it's a man. He lifts my hair and licks my neck, sending me swooning backward to where he presses hard against me from behind. Hands come around my breasts from underneath, and long fingers tug at my nipples.

Nothing between us but breath and rhythm until I try to turn my head. He tells me not to move an inch. As the pierced man touches himself and the trio bucks together, biting each other in their frenzy, he strokes me slow and languid, standing there. I pulse and shake, but he stops when I'm on the cusp of coming. I moan to feel his hand over me where I radiate heat to melt the thickest iceberg, but he doesn't move. Onstage, the woman comes—a lioness growl—with a man below and beneath her. Her head thrown back and wild hair cascading make me ache for touching, and at last the man behind me whispers that I must move myself against his hand. And if I do it right, the way he knows I like it, he'll let me finish before the pierced man pleasing himself on the floor. If not, an hour of the flail stroked soft across my body. I writhe against his hand while he slips a finger inside me and pulls me close against him where he is carved granite. His other hand slides around the back of my neck and squeezes hard.

The pierced man looks up and sees me held there, a nude offering for his voyeuristic thrill, and I strum myself against my holder's hand with intent to finish. But the pierced man spasms, his "Oh!" an arc across the silence of my sweat. The man at my rear removes his hand. Come back, I moan, but he brushes my shoulders with the flail and says, You know the rules. I cry, Yes, but let me come and then you can tease me all you like. You can have me kneeling on the floor, but please touch me where I need it.

He pulls my hands behind my back in response, still not allowing me to turn and face him, and slips a blindfold over my eyes. A moment later the flail strokes my legs, and then two sets of hands run over my breasts and cheeks. I step forward but touch no one; moving back brings me only air. The hands remain, holding me pinned. I have become the woman I was watching.

I struggle to touch myself but find I am tethered with soft cord and can only wait until, at last, my legs are opened and I am penetrated by them both. The feel of two men against me sends me over the threshold of what I thought were boundaries. I taste salt and oranges on my tongue and cry out at the fullness, coming between them and hearing myself keen—a woman in her power and shape shifting—so I feel their bodies as part of mine for a breathless moment. When they come it's an afterthought, my body slick with its own juices, contracting and swelling: dark pink pearls stranding across the throat of a jaguar.

Regular Guy breaks a sweat but manages to keep pace with my bucking beneath him. I savor the taste of salt in my mouth as I bite his ear. After a startled pause—we don't usually bite—his thrusts speed up and make the bedsprings squeak. I sense him trying to hold back his orgasm until I arrive at my own centerpoint and dive back into my pool of images so as not to disappoint.

My body open and loose, I follow Javier and the woman in red down a narrow corridor—into the rearmost catacombs of the hive. A warm moment of waiting before the woman in red pulls back a curtain of amethyst and gold beads. A single round table swathed in white linen sits in front of a spotlit stage. Javier pulls out my chair for me as the music starts. I realize I'm wearing a short white dress that stops mid-thigh, white leather boots, and no panties. Crossing my legs, I watch the stage and sip from the champagne flute Javier offers.

A man steps into the spotlight in a tailored gray suit and a black fedora. His small mustache suits his fine-boned face, and I glimpse dark eyes under the hat brim as he rolls his shoulders and croons into the mic. I tap my foot and savor the champagne fizz as lights strobe overhead. The singer locks eyes with me and descends the three steps leading from stage to floor. He really knows how to move his hips; I can't help but notice as he approaches the table with a confident smile. Taking his hand, I rise to meet him.

Before I know it, the beat shifts and we're dancing a tango, while Javier and the red-dress woman watch from the back of the room. He's an elegant dancer, and old school in his kissing of my hand as he pulls me close, then twirls me around. My white dress flares out as I spin, and I'm a modern-day Marilyn. It's something past elegant to dance with him. I'm mesmerized by his eyes on mine and the planes of his face set off by the fedora.

When the song ends, he leads me back to my seat and leans in to kiss my cheek.

I lay his hand on my thigh just at the edge of my dress and the chair. He gasps and slides to his knees in front of me. Both of his hands slip under my dress, and he strokes my legs, silken in the strobe lights. He opens me to his fingers, slipping in where I want them. The fedora falls to the floor. My hand plunges into his hair and discovers a cascade of golden waves pinned close to his scalp. Unpinning him, I cup his chin in my hand and see that the man is a woman.

Regular Guy throws his head back. The cords of his neck strain as he grits his teeth. I know he's thinking of checking sports scores, paying bills, washing the car, anything to keep from coming too soon. He is always polite with his penis and its emissions.

I smile as she sees me seeing her. Our eyes hold for a long moment under the spotlight, and neither of us breaks the spell. The enchanter is enchanted. Following the crook of her fingers inside me, I stand as she slides a hand under my buttocks and positions me against the table's edge. Then she kneels. A moment later, my neck arches in bliss at her quicksilver tongue. She has skills beyond drag-king vamping. Skills to make me shake and moan.

I am no longer this collection of nerve endings sheathing a soul. I am light and laughter and music. I am red lipstick on a curved mouth. I am diamonds on black velvet, steam rising from fresh coffee. I am my own translucent crystal glass; the wine, uncorked, waits to fill me. Kiwi and coconut scent the air and the trees. Pressure, such pressure, stomach clenching, short panting breaths. No time here, no time, outside of time, sprinkling the thin sand line of being and not being.

Give me your songs. Your suit and your slicked-back hair. Offer me that rose, the hothouse pink, but most of all, bring me the water in the vase, all the available water, as I find myself on the shore, waves lapping over my heels and toes and arches, as we watch, held in place by the gentle susurrations of the sea, the larger waves waiting, and I walk as if hypnotized, a somnambulist seeking the dream of completion, sinking into hip-high water, to experience the lapping of the water, the deep midnight liquid that surrounds, encircles, slaps against me, intent on entering, on bringing the waterfall as well, the waves' crescendo, unbroken by surfboards, carrying me higher, each time the highest yet, and I can cry out to the sky at this elevation, only to lift ever higher, balancing on the jagged wild glass, crying, Take me, please, take me there, raw voice from the opening of all that is possible at this threshold crossing, at the closeness of the waves, and at last the merging, the waterfall within me spilling into all women who desire: how we gleam in the sun, how we shine, how we spurt high, grand in our ascent, gleaming in our furls and magnificent trajectory.

A net of silver fish writhes in flowing water. It's a glistening knot of slipperiness with no true center, only the movement of our breath and the iridescent fins of the fish swimming to and fro. The fish wriggle and gasp as the first one slips from the mesh to freedom. The others follow, widening the gap through which they slip like deft saboteurs, as our bodies, too, respond to the unfettered wild motion and we arc up, up into the gleaming water in a dozen pirouettes among the fish, which swim around us like a nimbus of silver light within the unknowable blue.

"Oh, baby, I'm gonna come," Regular Guy moans, and my eyes snap open.

For a moment, as if awakening in an unfamiliar hotel, an unknown bed, I don't know where I am, or what the hell this man is doing on top of me. Then he kisses me, a groan deep in his throat, and I gasp in recognition. His penis pulses as he comes deep and hard, and I welcome the feeling: It's like being washed from the inside with a dozen Jacuzzi jets.

A beat. Two. Regular Guy collapses on top of me, his heart thudding against my chest. Stroking his back, my eyes fill with hammocks, oceans, and silver fish.

"Oh, baby," he says. "That was the best yet."

"Yes. It was."

He raises up on an arm, gazes adoringly at me, then rolls off. A gush of semen spills out, and I contemplate getting a towel. Maybe the frayed orange-and-white-striped one.

"I mean, you were right there with me the whole time," he says. "It's like we were the same person."

I smile and think about how I am always sovereign in my own wild lands. My sensuality tucked inside my body like a flag unfurling. A marker of my own conquered territory, the endless banquet of my imagination.

"It's really a union, isn't it?" he asks. "I mean, sex between two people in love."

"I do love you," I say. "Very much."

Regular Guy lies back against the sheets, satisfied, and my skin tingles in all the best places as I sway to the bathroom, filled with pleasure and thrill.

# At Odds

*Julia Serano*

The thing that I remember most vividly about my junior high school years isn't my classes, hanging out with friends, extracurricular activities, or teen crushes. Rather, it is lying in bed, trying to fall asleep but not being able to. I had a monster case of insomnia—most nights it was at least an hour and a half (often longer) from the time when I first slipped under the covers to the time I would eventually drift off to sleep. Having been raised Catholic, I couldn't help but think of the time I spent each night ravaged by my own thoughts as a form of penance. I was being punished by my thoughts, for my thoughts. And as much as I wanted my nightly torture to stop, I didn't dare tell anybody about my insomnia. It was but one of many secrets I kept. My secrets were like Russian nested dolls—secrets within secrets—each one merely a shell that protected the secret just underneath it. And all of the secrets were designed to hide my most private, innermost core secret, the one that gave rise to my insomnia and my secretiveness in the first place: I wanted to be a girl.

Admittedly, "wanted" isn't really the right word. It's not that I consciously wished that I could be a girl, or that I felt that my life would be better or easier had I been born female. No, it was that, for some unknown reason, I simply couldn't stop thinking about being a girl. Like sleepiness, hunger, or thirst, the feelings I had about it would just flood my mind from time to time, without any warning, and despite countless conscious attempts on my part to ignore or repress them.

Initially, when I first became aware of these thoughts, I followed them. I indulged them. I would wrap curtains or blankets around my body as if they were dresses, and stare at myself in the mirror, impressed by how much I looked like a girl. Or I'd act out stories in my bedroom, in which the boy protagonist would suddenly be transformed into a girl, who would then go off on her own adventures, solve her own mysteries.

One day, after having enacted stories along these lines for a number of weeks, I paused for a moment to ask myself the one question that I had been avoiding the whole time: *Why do I enjoy pretending to be a girl so much?*

The world seemed to stop when I asked myself that question. I remember sitting on the edge of my bed, my body slowly growing cold. I had to admit to myself that this wasn't merely innocent exploration, like all those other times when I pretended to be a doctor or an animal or a character from *Star Wars*. Pretending to be a girl didn't quite feel like pretending. It felt real. Too real. A moment earlier, I had been just another kid playing make-believe, and now suddenly I was harboring a dangerous secret. And I felt very, very alone.

In the aftermath of that realization, I was consumed by all sorts of emotions, but the two that stood out most were fear and embarrassment. My fear came in many forms. I was scared about how devastated my parents might be if they found out, or how badly my friends and classmates would tease me if they knew what I was thinking. I worried that my thoughts about being a girl would never go away, that they would haunt me for the rest of my life, that the anxiety and restlessness they had inspired in me would never cease. But the thing I feared most of all was how God might judge me because of my desire.

The fact that I turned to God at this point in my life had less to do with my upbringing than it did with the fact that I felt as if I had no one else to share my secret with. Since God was supposedly omniscient, I didn't have to come out to him—he already knew what I was thinking and doing. And because I was eleven years old at the time, and had no access to any information related to what I was going through, the idea of turning to someone who might be able to solve my problem was immensely comforting. I would pray to him every night, begging him to turn me into a girl. I fantasized about simply waking up one morning as a girl and having no one in my life be surprised—they would act as if nothing had changed, as if the memories of me as a boy had been suddenly purged from their minds. Or I'd imagine that, during a routine doctor's visit, the pediatrician would realize something wasn't right with me. He'd order all these tests, and when the results finally came back, he'd say that there had been a mistake, and that I had really been a girl all along.

Of course, none of this ever happened. And as time went on, I started to seriously consider the possibility that maybe there hadn't been a mistake, that maybe I was supposed to be a boy after all. Maybe that was what God intended for me. And if God wanted me to be a boy, then my dreams of becoming a girl were no longer innocent fantasies. They were sins. I began to cultivate a preteen paranoia that God was testing me, like he did in those Old Testament stories about Abraham and Job that the nuns had taught me. And if God was testing me, then he obviously wanted me to resist this temptation, to sacrifice my own wants and desires as an offering to him. So, instead of praying to God to turn me into a girl, I prayed that he would stop the thoughts altogether. I tried to bargain with him by refusing to indulge my fantasies about being a girl, by spending my insomniac hours reciting rosary after rosary, by whispering the Act of Contrition to myself every time the girl thoughts popped into my head.

But nothing changed. If anything, denying the girl thoughts seemed to only make them more intense, not less. Despite all my prayers and begging, God never intervened. And the silence was deafening. I was desperate. Exhausted. Angry. Rather than continuing to confide in him, I began to ask myself what kind of God would purposely torture a young child like this. What kind of God would allow me, an isolated, frightened preteen, to become so consumed with the fear of burning in hell for all eternity that I couldn't sleep at night, that I couldn't concentrate during the day? I decided that I would not follow a god who required blind worship, who played cat-and-mouse games with children. I stopped praying and gave myself permission to experience the girl thoughts, to indulge them to a certain extent.

While I still felt that it wasn't safe to share my secret desire with others, I convinced myself that anything I did within the privacy of my own room wouldn't hurt anyone.

It took many years—even decades—for me to begin to dismantle the overwhelming sense of embarrassment that I felt about my desire. This wasn't simply embarrassment about wanting to change my sex; it had more to do with my wanting specifically to be a girl. Although I grew up in the wake of the feminist movement of the 1960s and '70s, when it was common to hear sound bites like "Women and men are equal" and "Girls can do anything boys can do," I found that such comments often had little bearing on the world I inhabited, where teachers and parents frequently expected boys to outperform girls at most tasks; where schoolchildren relentlessly teased young boys in gym class whenever team captains picked girls ahead of them; where the cartoons I watched typically featured male superheroes and relegated female characters to the role of damsel in distress. For all the explicit talk about equal rights at the time, young boys were still expected and encouraged to adhere to two unspoken rules: Do not let girls beat you at anything, and do not appear girlish in any way or under any circumstances.

And I was way beyond girlish; I wanted to *be* a girl. Even after deciding that it was safe for me to act out, behind closed doors, my fantasies about being female, I still wasn't able to move beyond the shame that I felt about my desire. In many ways, my embarrassment was exacerbated by being brought up as a male. While girls my age had to manage blatantly sexist attitudes in an immediate and tangible way, at least they were sometimes able to partake of the relative safety of all-female environments and receive positive messages about femaleness from the women role models in their lives. As I would learn many years later, the very experience of living in the world as a woman necessitates that one develop self-defense mechanisms and self-empowering attitudes in order to deflect all of the demeaning antifemale and antifeminine sentiments one encounters regularly.

But back then, I was still living life as an extremely closeted boy who wanted to be a girl. As such, I had no role models, no script to follow, no one in my life whom I could ask questions, no one to offer me empowering advice. Nobody ever took me aside and told me that who I was and what I wanted were okay. Instead, I was thrown to the wolves. Without any support or protection, I was left exposed to the blatant misogyny that exists in many all-male spaces. I remember wanting to simply shrink into nothingness whenever I stepped inside boys' locker rooms, where junior high (and later high school) boys regularly tried to outdo one another with their crass, sexist comments—everything from preschool sentiments like "Girls are stupid" to adult-male clichés like "Women are only good for one thing." Every demeaning quip stung me like a barbed needle. As a female-identified child, being forced to endure boyhood felt like bleeding to death from a million small cuts.

Somehow I had to reconcile my deep, subconscious desire to be female with the unceasing stream of messages I received that insisted that women were the lesser sex. Some women who have been taught to feel ashamed of their own sexual urges will sometimes turn to rape fantasies—imagining themselves being taken against their will—as a way of exploring their sexual desires without having to feel guilty about them. Perhaps for that very same reason, my early teenage fantasies about being female always began with my being turned into a girl against my will. I would be kidnapped by some imagined nemesis or random psychopath, who would turn me into a girl as a way of punishing or torturing me. During the precise moment of my transformation, I would always feel a strange combination of both humiliation and elation. Since I was not able to transcend the shame that I felt at the time for wanting to be female, I found ways to incorporate it into my fantasies. Like most coping mechanisms, it wasn't particularly healthy for my self-esteem, but it at least helped me to make some sense out of all of my contradictory feelings, and to survive the most isolated period of my life.

As I moved through puberty, I began to incorporate love interests into these fantasies. Rather than my being abducted alone, the villain in my fantasy would also capture a girl whom I happened to have a crush on. Then he would offer me an ultimatum: He would threaten to kill her unless I agreed to be turned into a girl. Of course, I always gallantly chose the latter, and afterward, the girl would fall in love with me, despite my female anatomy, because I had just saved her life. These visions were twisted transgender takes on fairytales, seamlessly combining sex change with chivalry and living happily ever after. In retrospect, what amazes me most about my fantasies is that they always ended both with my getting the girl *and* with my becoming a girl—an inventive plot twist, considering that it would still be a couple of years before I would hear the word "lesbian."

Ironically, it was my attraction to girls—a rather mundane desire given the fact that, physically speaking, I was a teenage boy—that confused me most. I had been dealing with the girl thoughts for about two years before my sexual attraction kicked in. And while my desire to be female was inexplicable in many ways, at least there seemed to be some sort of precedent for it, based on what I had seen on TV. Granted, this was in the late 1970s, when TV depictions of transgenderism were highly distorted and blurred all distinctions between effeminate gay men, transvestites, and transsexuals. But at least the shows I had seen suggested that some men did choose to live their lives as women, and that the main reason why they did so was that they were attracted to men. While I definitely didn't want to be "gay"—which, unlike "lesbian," had been tossed around the school yard as an insult since I was in second grade—I logically assumed that my desire to be female was a sign that I was going to end up being attracted to boys. And while TV images of gay men who became transsexual women may have been nothing more than inaccurate and unflattering caricatures, at least they offered me some kind of template that I could work from. As weird as it may seem, those images offered me the remote possibility that I might someday achieve a semblance of gender normalcy.

But once I began developing crushes on girls, my gender seemed to become doubly convoluted. Not only was my girl identity at odds with my boy body, but my sexual orientation was at odds with my desire to be female. These conflicting desires seemed to create two disparate paths for me, each leading toward an unfathomable and inadequate future. Either I could explore my attraction to girls by passing as a straight boy (which would require me to remain closeted about my desire to be female), or I could indulge my desire to be female by running away and starting a new life as a woman someplace else (which seemed to foreclose any possibility of meeting a girl who would be willing and able to fall in love with me). Both desires were strong—irrepressible—but at the time it seemed as though I could only choose one.

I think I went back and forth on this issue for quite a while. Then, when I was fifteen, I went to my baseball league's all-star game with a handful of my male friends who also hadn't made the team. We were sitting in the bleachers when three girls came over and started a conversation. Next thing I knew, the boys and girls were chatting in a teenager-flirty sort of way. Everyone except for me. I just sat there. Silent. Observing. From the outside, I must have seemed very distant and removed from what was happening. But on the inside, I was totally consumed by what was going on. The scene inspired in me one of the most intense feelings that I had ever experienced—an intuition. A *knowing*. It seemed so clear to me right then that I should have been on the other side of that conversation, standing with those girls. I should have been one of them. And as those girls walked away, I remember thinking that I was going to have a sex change when I grew up. I didn't even know what that was, exactly. It didn't really matter. All that mattered was that I would get to be a girl. While the very phrase "sex change" sounded bizarre, foreign, alien, I figured that it couldn't be any more surreal than how I felt every day of my life—always pretending to be a boy and simultaneously imagining that I was a girl.

However, the profound truth that I experienced that day slowly began to give way to the realities of my day-to-day existence. Puberty began to reshape my body: My voice got a bit deeper, hair started growing out of my face, and I became more muscular without even trying. The girl thoughts never went away, mind you; it's just that my own biology seemed to betray me. Like gravity, my body seemed to keep pulling me back down to earth.

My junior year of high school, I asked a girl I really liked to the prom. The following year, we dated more seriously. She was my first love. While she didn't end up becoming my happily ever after, we did have a lot of wonderful times together. For the most part, I was ecstatic about being in a relationship with someone whose company I enjoyed so much—although sometimes, when the girl thoughts were strong, I would be overcome by sadness, because I knew what was happening. By default, I was choosing one of the two paths. And for better or for worse, this was the path of least resistance. It didn't involve sex change operations or sharing my dangerous secret with anyone. It was the safer path by far. But as much as I enjoyed exploring love and sexual attraction, I couldn't help but feel, with each step I took, that I was leaving a part of myself behind.

Fast forward roughly fifteen years, to the fall of 2000. I'm in a Mexican restaurant in Oakland, California, sharing chips and salsa with my fiancée, Dani. I'm telling her about the two disparate life paths that I had always envisioned for myself when I was younger—one that led to a relatively normal life, with a wife, a decent career, close friends and family, and so forth; and the other, where I ran away to live as a woman. She smiles and says, "And then what?"

"What do you mean?"

"After you became a woman. What would happen then?"

"To be honest, at the time, I never really thought about what would happen after that."

"That's ridiculous. Being a woman isn't a life path."

We both laugh. Shortly afterward, a waiter approaches us and says, "Hello, ladies, are you ready to order?" Dani subtly rolls her eyes at me before ordering, as if to say, *Again?* This has been happening more and more often lately, even though my appearance hasn't changed much. I'm still wearing the same sweat jackets, T-shirts, jeans, and sneakers that I've worn most of my life. It's just that I am no longer censoring myself. And as I have become more comfortable just being myself, and less concerned about what other people think of me, I find that people no longer assume that I'm a straight guy. Instead, they pick up on my femininity and assume that I'm a gay man, or they read me as a tomboy (as the waiter was apparently doing now).

There was a time in my late teens and early twenties when I would have been mortified by the very idea of strangers' reading me as female. I would have taken it as a sign that my secret—the one I worked so hard to keep hidden—was leaking out for everyone to see. Now it doesn't bother me. I've finally stopped pretending to be male. While I haven't become a woman, per se, I am calling myself transgender. For the most part, Dani is pretty cool with it all. Granted, sometimes it can be difficult for her to be in a relationship with someone whose gender is in flux. But the idea of my becoming more feminine, or even female, in itself isn't really a problem for her, as she's identified as a dyke for most of her adult life. Ironically, we met shortly after she had begun to call herself bisexual.

I remember staring out the restaurant window, thinking about my teenage years, back when I believed that openly expressing my gender and spending my life with someone I loved were somehow mutually exclusive desires. Yet here I am, sharing my deepest and most dangerous secrets with my female life partner. Sometimes we do that to ourselves—we pit our desires against one another. We insist unnecessarily on seeing one aspect of our personality as being at odds with the rest of ourselves. Earlier in my life, it never occurred to me that I might someday fulfill both desires simultaneously.

Dani and I continue talking and eating, neither of us quite aware that one day, not too far down the path we now share, I will make the decision to transition. I will tell her this late one rainy night as we lie side by side in bed together. She will squeeze my hand when I tell her, and we will talk through the morning. I will tell her that I've imagined myself becoming female millions of times before, but this time will be very different. There will be no dreams about running off to a faraway city where nobody knows me, no fantasies of being forced into femaleness against my will.

For the first time in my life, I am able to imagine myself transitioning, right here, in Oakland, with her by my side. I picture all of it happening for real, in the life we share. And somehow now, it finally just seems right.

# Women Writing Desire

Ruth Knafo Setton

*"I have come to the heart, thinks Gaby, of the heart of my heart. A new country. I don't remember this hotel, café, street of blue torches. I have been in this city a thousand times: I have never been here. I say words I must have said before, but they blister my tongue and ache between my teeth until I utter them, raw and unformed: a new language."*

—The Road to Fez

*D*esire: The man trembles, the woman cries out, her beast skin bursts into flames. It is too late to turn back, to retrace the myth to its original point, when the goddess approached the man's cottage on all fours. It is already too late to restore her animal skin and allow her to exist simultaneously as beast, woman, and god—undissected, unfragmented, undiminished. Too late to slam shut Pandora's box, ignore the wolf (to omit "wolf" makes the sentence meaningless) in

93

the woods, refuse to bite into the poisoned apple. In that infinite moment of revelation and dread, desire lives and breathes. The language of desire carries the memory of the original primal woods, the scent of our fur coverings, the cry of the beast goddess at being torn from her essence. With almost painful intimacy and clarity, it makes us relive that moment when we were both more and less than human, the moment before we shut the door on memory.

When a woman writes desire, does she remember the metamorphosis from beast into human? Does she enter a new country? Create a new language? What *is* the language of female desire? How does a woman sound when she wants sex? When she wants to touch and be touched? Are the words she speaks Victorian in their reticence? Coarse and crude? Delicious as a frothy comic romance? Dark and brooding as poor Lucy Snowe in *Villette*?

In my writing I explore the song of desire as both men and women sing it. I approach both voices with excitement and trepidation. Perhaps oddly, the male voice comes naturally to me: easier to imagine myself as a man in the throes of passion, perhaps because the male voice expressing desire is more familiar. Desire in a woman's voice is more difficult, especially the challenge to keep it true. Sadly, a woman's voice is easy to falsify. When I examine women's voices, I can't help but return to my mother's voice, the first female voice I heard.

I consider myself very fortunate: My mother has always been unfailingly generous, not only with her time, but with her dreams and memories. She was my first muse. Night after night, we lay awake in this new country of ours, America, while my father worked night shifts and my little sister slept. Huddled in my bed, both of us afraid of the foreign night sounds, my mother told me stories about Safi, the small town in Morocco where I was born and where she grew up. A born storyteller, gifted with an amazing memory and the art of creating suspense, my mother re-created the wildly eccentric seaside town and breathed life into it. It wasn't until years later that I understood the urgency in my mother's tales, the need to communicate her past to me, to make me *see* the Jewish world in Morocco that had vanished, except in her memories. And in mine. By transferring these stories of people and places—now gone—she imparted a sense of responsibility to me: to never forget where we came from; to remember the martyrs, mystics, and musicians whose lives helped form ours; and to communicate these memories to my children. I wonder now if my need to write was born during those long nights in which my mother, like Scheherazade, kept back the harsh light of winter mornings and fought the oblivion of forgetfulness.

When I began to write, I returned to those long, magical storytelling nights in which my mother's memories became mine. And even before I understood what I was doing, why I was writing not only for myself but for my mother and her mother before that, and for all women who didn't have a voice, I wrote her stories. They had become my stories, the need to sing as powerful as hers had been in school.

Later, I learned that the holy fathers of almost every religion had taught, "Woman's voice is an abomination." I also learned how easy it is to deride, condemn, and ultimately silence a woman's voice, whether it is raised in song or speech, or written on paper. And how easy it is for women to collude in the silencing. And how difficult it is to find women's voices in literature. Where were my writing fore-mothers? Now I understand that my lifelong reading—voracious, indiscriminate, desperate—was the desire to find mentor-mothers like my own, to hear voices that came before me, to follow guides in the wilderness. As we all do, I searched for a reflection of myself in the books I read: a girl who, like me, dreamed of doing great things, traveling the world, solving mysteries, and connecting to people everywhere. Years passed before I realized that almost every woman in great literature who went after her desires either committed suicide or was punished: condemned as greedy, thrown under a train, murdered, dead of tuberculosis (after meeting her younger lover), kicked out of society, or forced to wear a great big letter that clashed with her clothes. It took me even longer to realize these women were all written by men. When I searched for women characters written by women writers, I found more suicides and madwomen, but also Colette's Lea, with the courage to turn away her younger lover, Cheri, and grow old alone; Isak Dinesen's storyteller, who insisted that women, "when they are old enough to have done with the business of being women and can let loose their strength, must be the most powerful creatures in the world"; Jane Eyre, who turned down security for love; Cathy, who turned down love for security; and Elizabeth Bennet, who got it all.

When I told my male professors that I wanted to write about the force and complexity of desire, they shook their heads and advised me: "If you want to be taken seriously, then write about things that matter, like war and politics." *But desire is at the heart of every-*

*thing that matters to me,* I thought. To write about desire is to sing, whether it's the blues, opera, or a jazzy riff. And it's an act of great courage—particularly for a woman. I think of my literary mothers: the Brontës, Austen, Woolf, George Eliot, Dinesen. And most of all Colette, whom I discovered at fourteen. Too earthy to take herself seriously, she was as sleek, sensual, and shameless as the cats she loved. Her dying words? "Astonish me. It's these last flashes of aston- ishment that I can't do without."

These were the women who, like my mother, gave me permission to dream big and to dive into the darkness despite my fear. In their novels the female imagination soars, unharnessed to patriarchal ex- pectations and demands. To me, the woman who writes freely and passionately about love, desire, and motherhood from a woman's point of view is a pioneer of sorts, one for whom love is a marvelous and terrifying adventure, the paradoxical core of life itself; love is a risky act without which there can be no self-realization. By visualiz- ing a society in which human beings need each other in order to live fully, the woman writer rewrites history, puncturing myths and strik- ing at the social order, compelling us to reevaluate our conditioned responses to women's passion. The happy ending is a particularly subversive act, quintessentially female: an ending in which no one loses, everyone gains, and the whole is much stronger than either of its parts.

I *crave* a woman's voice, not a faux-male voice that removes female sexuality from the equation. I need to read a woman who delights in being female. I need that in my soul. I need it for myself, and I need it for my daughter. And that leads me to the female romance.

Years ago, when we moved into a two-hundred-year-old house, I discovered that the previous owners had left behind a stack of paperback books, mostly Harlequin and Silhouette romances. You know the ones, with lurid covers of a muscular hunk in a clinch with a gorgeous woman. I quickly stuffed the books into a bag, determined to hide them from my daughter. Those books smoldered in the trunk of my car for weeks before I finally stopped at a local used-book store to donate them. Meanwhile, the bag had opened in the trunk, and the books had scattered. As I gathered them, one cover image caught my eye: a slender, strong-featured redhead wearing a bikini over which she'd draped a shirt. But it was the title that made me hesitate: *The Male Chauvinist,* by Alexandra Sellers. I'm still not sure why, but I slipped that one into my purse. I didn't know yet that Alexandra was one of the new breed of romance writers, or that she'd written a romance that is earthy and sensual, as well as an eloquent, dramatic insistence on women's ways of seeing. I never imagined that Alexandra, a scholar who lives in London, and I would become friends. The night I slipped into bed with my first romance, all I knew was that I'd found an intelligent, sexy book that gripped me. I read and savored it. And I was hooked.

A few stats:

• The average romance reader is thirty-nine years old.
• Of all romance readers, 45 percent are college-educated.
• More than 50 percent of romance readers work outside the home.

Literary writers, eat our hearts out: Romance novels account for 85 percent of published mass market fiction titles; their sales increased 212 percent in 1992, and they keep going up every year.

For many women, the romance is the only book in which a woman is the protagonist of her own life, the only book in which the fulfillment of her desires is crucial. And, contrary to popular belief, female romance is not pornography. Mary Bly, a.k.a Eloisa James, a college professor of Shakespeare, came out as a best-selling author of Regency romances as soon as she got tenure. In an op-ed piece in *The New York Times,* she wrote, "Intellectuals never seem to believe that a strong story and an interest in relationships could explain the popularity of romance. I've been repeatedly asked by academics whether romances are anything more than female porn—a question that to me seems linked to a fear of female sexuality. . . . "

And it's not just men who are asking these questions. Women who have never read a romance (or at least claim to have never read one) are among the genre's loudest denouncers, and usually on the grounds that it is nothing but cheap thrills. Actually, romance is the opposite of pornography. There is no such thing as Erica Jong's "zipless fuck" in a romance. Sex in pornography exists in a vacuum, an eternal present with no before or after. In a romance, sex scenes are never gratuitous; they come about as the result of both the hero's and the heroine's working through their differences and misconceptions until they see each other: two flawed but lovable individuals. A new, erotic subgenre of romance is gaining popularity; however, it still contains a story, slight as it may be, and more often than not, the lovers end up falling in love. The romance succeeds, I believe, because in its pages desire and love go hand in hand; one cannot exist and thrive without the other.

The archaeologist hero and the feminist scholar-heroine of *The Male Chauvinist* search for evidence of an ancient matriarchal society in Greece. Their discovery awakens in them both an enhanced awareness of how males and females—in particular, females—have been crippled by the distorted mirror male art has held up to them. The breasted ewers that Kate, the heroine, uncovers in Greece assuage a deep need in her to see "woman from the point of view of women . . . women who had a self-esteem so deep and so basic that as a product of today's culture she could barely relate to it. Yet she felt that if she looked at the pictures of the breasted ewers for long enough, she might be taught something; she might begin to learn a sense of her own value as a woman that had been denied her since birth."

Sound familiar? Years after I read this book, I spoke about romances at an academic conference in Toronto. My paper was as groping and tentative as I was, searching for answers about how I reconciled my feminism with my enjoyment of romances, and why I found them more gutsy, spirited, fun, sensual, and exciting than most works by female literary authors. I described the romances as fantasies by, for, and about women. When I finished my talk, a feminist scholar leaped to her feet and shook her fist at me: "If we want feminism to succeed, then women need to censor their fantasies!"

I refuse to believe that feminism inevitably leads to that Big Brother (Big Sister?) dead end, in which behaviors, dreams, fantasies, and, of course, desires are monitored. On the contrary, I believe that for feminism to survive as a viable force for women's power, it must encourage women's fantasies—sexual and otherwise. Let her fantasies roam wild and free. Allow her to tear off her veil and burqa and bare her face to the sun. To unlock the symbolic chastity belt that keeps her a virgin, holy in a man's eyes, and remind her that truly powerful minds are in constant evolution, fluid and receptive, uncensored, fearless.

Often when critics deride romances, they describe pre-1980 romances, most featuring a virginal, orphaned heroine struggling to survive in a world as threatening and incomprehensible as the hero. These novels, typified by the Harlequin romances of the 1950s to 1970s, reduced patriarchal society to the unreadable face of one man. The baffled heroine's attempts to decipher his face, gestures, and words reflected woman's desperation about being set adrift in a universe in which survival meant correctly interpreting the confusing, harsh directives bombarding her from all sides. The rules governing the heroine's behavior were written in a foreign language, one she was compelled to master at all costs. The stakes were high: Her identity and survival depended on it. The hero of the pre-1980 romances remained the only true judge of her worth, the final arbiter of her destiny as a woman. Both visible and invisible, the hero was an icon and a myth struggling to be human. The traditional romance moved from the heroine's personal identity to her public one, from her inner sphere to her external validation as a public human being and member of society with a verifiable, necessary role and function, even a title: Mrs. _____. When the heroine joined the "adult" world of married couples, her story was virtually over, her moment in the sun turned to shadow and ominous darkness. The final kiss, explanation of the hero's bewildering behavior toward her, and the marriage proposal reinforced and exposed the pattern for what it was: a continuation of the courtship/marriage/procreation cycle.

However, like every other literary genre, romance reflects its society and therefore is not static—a fact that is clear to everyone except those who have never picked up a romance novel. The genre has developed to include the changing realities of women's lives, post–feminist awareness, and the reader's growing desire for more sexual frankness. It is indeed on the battlefield of the body that the contemporary heterosexual romance wages its most subversive act: redefining sexuality on female terms. Liberating women from the conflicting pretenses that insist either that they have no sexual needs or, conversely, that they should enjoy indiscriminate sex, recent romances emphasize a mutual exchange of gifts between the woman and the man: Each teaches the other to trust. Once the heroine in the romance has deciphered the hero's enigmatic exterior, she has, in a sense, penetrated her own mystery: She has discovered her truest self, her potential, in his infinite, nonjudgmental, unlimiting acceptance of her. And her love for him has permitted him to discover himself as well. That is ultimately what the contemporary romance is all about: two hungry people searching for love in a dehumanized, fragmented world.

Freed from traditional limitations, the heroine can be divorced, a mother, handicapped, arthritic, homely, older, richer, and more educated than the hero. And the hero, released from many of the pressures of the traditional male role, can be blind, deaf, an ex-convict, overweight, myopic, poor, shy, illiterate, and impotent. Recent heroes have been Amish, Hispanic, Native American, everything from farmers to spiritually wounded Vietnam veterans. And when the reader ventures into paranormal romances, the hero can be anything from a gargoyle come to life to a robot to a bewildered medieval magician. I must note that the politically correct hero (as comfortable in a kitchen as in a corporate boardroom) is not as popular as he was in the '90s. He's still present and visible, but the dark, wounded male hero—ah, Mr. Rochester! Heathcliff!—lurks in the shadows. One could say he never left, but he is often camouflaged—not to offend feminist sensibilities!—as a vampire, werewolf, or visitor from another planet. The heroine, however, just keeps getting stronger; it is quite common for her to go after her man, seduce him, and save him from danger. All in a day's work.

Both the hero and the heroine come to each other, bruised veterans of the war between the sexes, simultaneously defensive and vulnerable. In many ways, they are emotionally indistinguishable: For both of them, accustomed to braving the world through their careers, love is the greatest hurdle they will ever confront. Recent romances feature successful heroines who have proven they can succeed on their own; now the great question is, can the heroine and the hero commit to each other and still stay whole, still stay loving and attuned to each other? The great romances are those in which two positive energies face each other and meet in the space between them, not out of weakness but out of love and life energy. Together, they become more than they could have been apart; together, they create a new language.

The language of romance is as richly coded and symbolic as the language of fairytales. Because it sings about desire in a woman's voice—so long suppressed—it is heightened, urgent, passionately female. And, like all writings about desire, it can be laughable and absurd. But, given linguistic, emotional, and physical freedom in the safe space of the romance, the writer creates a hero who does not attempt to squelch the heroine's independent spirit and unrestrained passion but rather encourages her, wishes her well, and accompanies her on her road to fulfillment.

"I know it's hard for women in marriage," Kate's archaeologist lover tells her, at the conclusion of *The Male Chauvinist*. "I know what can happen. I promise you, I'll never ask you to be what you don't want to be. I want you always the way you are—free and equal, the way I saw you the first night we had together—as proud as a priestess of the Mother Goddess." Thus, we come full circle in the romance—from a woman learning to see herself with new eyes to one teaching a man to see her with that same transfiguring sense of wonder and possibility; the true person within can be perceived only with the eyes of love.

Okay, so the romance is an imperfect female fantasy in a far-from-perfect world. Many feminists call it politically incorrect because of its emphasis on love between a man and a woman as the sole means of achieving human fulfillment. It's considered trashy women's literature by others who dismiss it solely on the basis of its lurid "bodice-ripper" covers. The utopia that romance offers, particularly in a world of bitter relationships between the sexes, degraded and abused women, and sexually transmittable, fatal diseases, is not to everyone's liking. And its overreliance on stock situations, formula plotting, and often sentimental, clichéd writing weakens its appeal to more discriminating readers.

However, in its abolishment of male and female stereotypes, its frank exploration of women's emotional needs and sexual desire, and its fearless examination of the complexities and implications of male-female relationships in a time of transition, the contemporary female romance is a beginning. It gives us the opportunity to hear a new language, a number of whose speakers are vibrant, articulate, often witty authors, many with PhDs behind their names. Provocatively feminist in their awareness, profoundly tolerant in their view of men, writers like Alexandra Sellers, Eloisa James, Julia Quinn, Jayne Ann Krentz, Nora Roberts, Jennifer Crusie, Laura Kinsale, Emma Holly, and Marjorie M. Liu delight in creating irreverent, alternative modes of relating between the sexes. Like the authors of groundbreaking science fiction and mysteries, they play with outworn conventions and false idols and hold up mirrors to our world. The way I see it, there is good writing and there is bad writing. A beautifully written story is magical, no matter what the cover looks like. I have never allowed my reading to be roped in by the so-called arbiters of taste. Similarly, I refuse to let my writing be roped in by the conventions of a literary novel that are, in their ways, as stultifying and suffocating as the conventions of a romance.

My first novel, *The Road to Fez*, explores immigrant awareness, Sephardic-Jewish identity, martyrdom, sexual politics, and life for Jews in Arab countries. Equally serious, however, is the theme of desire that underlies every word, gesture, and action in the novel. And no response to the book gives me greater pleasure than when a reader confesses, "Even though I knew it was wrong, I was dying for Gaby and Brit to kiss, and the wait was excruciating."

The wait *should* be excruciating. For me it was agonizing. *The Road to Fez* was a fifteen-year journey to fulfill my own seemingly conflicting desires: to live my life as a woman, wife, mother, daughter, and professor, and to live my life as a writer. Each morning, along with my alarm clocks—kids, husband, and dogs all tumbling onto the bed—I awoke with desire. I'm talking the real thing: a fever that left me breathless, mouth dry, heart pounding, entire body prickling with heat to the roots of my hair. I had to steal moments from my hectic life to follow the two main characters, Gaby and Brit, down their thorny, forbidden road to desire.

*Desire:* for a man or a woman or a god—or a room of one's own in which to dream, brood, write . . . what fascinates me most is that it is the one thing about ourselves that we cannot change. We can control desire, choose to not act upon it, sublimate or smother it, lie about it, but damned if we can change it. Life would certainly be easier if we could alter our desires, wouldn't it? If we could choose who or what we desperately need to touch?

But if we could, it would no longer be desire.

I can't recall when my characters began materializing in my world. I felt their presence as I cooked, changed diapers, studied for my PhD exams, and later taught in the university. As I wrote their story, I felt I had to become worthy of them, to share their courage and visions, to take risks the way they did. I found myself creating in a heightened state in which nearly every word was charged and electric. Each page introduced new dangers. I was writing about my people—Moroccan Jews—already a shameful subject for an immigrant girl who grew up in a cloud of secrecy and lies. But more, I was penetrating borders, one after another, to get to the forbidden core of desire: for a god, a woman, a man, a country.

And then one morning I tentatively crossed out one word and changed everything, for my characters as well as for myself as a writer. With a single stroke of the pen my protagonist fell in love—not with her adopted uncle, but with her honest-to-god blood-related mother's younger brother. Instantly the pen trembled in my hand, the paper burned beneath my fingers. (Why? Many writers write their first drafts, as I do, by hand. Also, I restored the above description of her uncle because otherwise what follows makes no sense.) I tasted the powerful lure of the forbidden. With each word I stripped away every disguise, every polite mask, as I penetrated to the pulsing heart of desire.

To me, desire hinges on the moment of recognition. The climax in a tale of desire—even more than the sexual fulfillment—is the moment when the lovers see each other and accept what they see. The moment is a shock of awareness, equal to the shock of the Prince recognizing Cinderella in her rags or Beauty recognizing the noble lover in her Beast. The miraculous moment when the lover sees you through a magic mirror: flawed and human, yet infinitely desirable. For that recognition, you will abandon your marriage, start a war, act like a fool, take risks you'd never have taken the day before. You're in the grip of a fever. You simultaneously yearn for and dread the cure. Desire is the piece of the puzzle of your life that never fits with all the other pieces. Jagged and sharp edged, it jams itself in, regardless of the other nice, neat pieces awaiting their turn. Desire may come in different colors, religions, genders, nationalities, appearances than you'd planned. Like the holy sparks of the Kabbalah, desire rarely comes gift wrapped or announced. Shards glitter in the dirt; they prick your fingers when you pick them up. They resist being captured. The harder you hold, the harder they squirm. And ahh, it hurts so good.

Why on earth would I write about anything else?

The moment when the spark stops fighting and you can loosen your hold, and you realize you're holding your desire—what you have always craved without knowing it—in your arms, and your desire is looking at you, eyes dark with passion, resentment, knowledge. And in these beautiful knowing eyes, you not only see the reflection of your desire, you see yourself in a way you've never seen yourself before. That moment is enough to make many people drop desire and run to the nearest exit, screaming, "Fire!" And never look back. Only in their dreams, and only with regret and loss that dim through the years until they've forgotten what they ever desired and why, and have covered up the empty space in the puzzle with a polite, well-behaved piece that says, "Yes, thank you."

But let's go back to the moment of recognition. You and the desired one stare at each other. Even if people surround you, you are both alone. This moment is simultaneously humbling and ecstatic.

How small you are, how helpless, swept by a tidal wave you can't comprehend, let alone control (at least for that moment). Yet how vast you are, part of a universe driven by desire—how fluid, formless, flexible, feral, feline—how ready to plunge into dangerous depths.

I stand in the room with my characters and whisper in Brit's ear: "Your mother just died and you're back in Morocco, and suddenly there he is: beautiful and terrifying and the closest link to your mother, with the same radiant gold-olive skin and warm smile. But he's also the town womanizer, sardine fisherman, ceramic artist, Jew in an Arab land, a man who lives on the border. You try to fight the desire that pushes you toward him, but you find yourself sneaking into his room to steal an item of his clothing, you put a love spell on him, you track him like a detective to the café near the sardine factory where you watch an older woman flirt with him, and wish you had the courage to bare yourself so openly, to grab him by the soul. When he smiles at the woman, the pain is so intense you can't watch anymore, so you lower your eyes."

I write: *I'm focused on my hands. The way the fingers branch out from the palm. The almost excruciating sensuality of our nearly webbed fingers. And toes. We're like ducks, birds, animals. Beasts, beneath the voices and clothes and masks . . . Gaby and Lydia at my side. Beasts, already gnawing at each other. A red clammy smell fills my nostrils. More than her Shalimar, the salt of the sea, the smoke of their cigarettes, the sardines . . . Words can't exit my mouth. Not yet. I'm undergoing a strange metamorphosis. More than the webbed animal hands. My teeth are sharpening, cutting through my cheeks. I want to bite. To devour. To slash and kill. Lydia? Or Gaby?*

I slip away from her and murmur in Gaby's ear: "Leave her alone. Go away, and don't look back. I know the last thing you want to do is hurt her. But her laugh is so bright and open that it dazzles like the sun. And each time you look at her, you feel yourself cracking like an egg. If you could put into words what you feel, you would say to her: 'Smear me over you. Glue me to you so I never have to leave, never come out of you, never . . .'"

I write: *I see my little cat, naked now without her hair, the hair I wanted to hide beneath. I saw you riding me like a wave, like a horse, laughing that beautiful laugh of yours, your hair falling over us like a tent. That's my vision. But what do you see? The toy you can't play with. The door you can't open. The forbidden man. Behind a veil. Like a woman. You can imagine anything you want. But I'm here, at your side. Look up from your writing. I'm here. Alive, breathing. A man, bella. Nothing more, nothing less.*

Now back up a little, behind my characters, in the shadows. Here I am. Winter wind blows outside my window, and the pipes have frozen, and my fingers tremble as they hold the pen, and in a minute the door will burst open and a voice will cry, "Mom, I'm home!" And I will wrench myself from Gaby and Brit, leave them straining to touch but unable to reach each other, at least not while I return to the other world—the family world—where I am Mom and I have children and they need to eat and we're out of milk and I have to do laundry.

*But.*

Let me linger in the heart of desire for a moment. Let me remember and relive—no! Let me *feel* desire each day of my life. Heart-crashing, eye-glazing, soul-aching. I can't survive without it. A detective of desire, I watch for signs in everyone I know, and even those I don't know. I eavesdrop on desire, I encourage desire, I am a desire mediator, a desire facilitator. I will never stop looking and *appreciating*. And I will never stop writing desire and, I hope, never stop reading it.

Once upon a time, we stood at the crossroads: between desire and loss, mystery and transformation, sensing truths about who we are, and why we are, and what we want, and how our hunger whispers and bleeds through the leaves. Today we know that if we want to move forward, we must first find our way back. The world of desire, seductive and elusive, glows in the woods like the enchanted cottage we dreamed of as children. The door is open, the oven red hot. We shed our skins and stoop to enter.

Gaby and Brit hurtle down the winding road to Fez. With me, sitting in the front seat between them, my arms around them. We have learned the dangerous truth, that the only way to get to ourselves is by first going through each other. Their desires meet and mingle with mine: to be heard, to be seen, to be whole. As we drive in the dark, the stars our only guides, I hear a voice in the night. A woman. Singing, keening, howling, shrieking, laughing, gasping, sighing. With a shock I recognize her voice as mine.

*Of the*

*Soul*

# After the Happily Ever After

Lisa Solod Warren

*"I was again alone in my bed, but not invisible as I had been to you. . . . "*

—Claudia Emerson, "The Spanish Lover," from *Late Wife*

*I* have long been a reader of fairytales, and I read the stories of Hans Christian Andersen and the Brothers Grimm over and over as a child. Those stories were gritty and real and often scary, but I liked them and felt their truth. When they were watered down by Disney and others, I felt sure—how, I don't know—that something essential had been left out. Real fairytales don't always have happy endings, while the palatable versions served up commercially always close with " . . . and they lived happily ever after." I suspected that wasn't the *real* end of the story. But what it was that should have come next, *after* the last line of the tale, wasn't clear either.

When I married the first time (and, I was sure, the only time), I felt that my eyes were open; I was pretty sure I knew what I was doing, and I assumed my motives were pure. And perhaps they were, but they were also tainted by my ignorance about myself and what I wanted—not to mention what I was getting into. Even if I knew that happily ever after wasn't as simple as it was in stories, and even though I had seen my own parents' marriage end in anger, disappointment, and recrimination, I was sure I could do better. I was convinced that I could manufacture my own happily ever after by sheer force of will.

I even ignored a very good clue: the fact that I wanted to run away, even as I took my final steps toward that moment when I took my then-fiancé's hand and said my vows.

I am not sure he didn't want to run, too, but for different reasons. He spent our first years as a married couple "kidding" me that I had forced him into marrying me. I spent that same time convincing myself that I didn't want out of the marriage. But, like many young brides, I tamped it all down and called it newlywed jitters.

We did the counseling thing early on, and the therapist recommended that my husband be more attentive, stop speaking *for* me and actually listen *to* me, and, perhaps most important, touch me more, show me more of the love he said he felt. But when the ink was dry on the divorce papers many years later, my ex told me that early advice had been "soul killing" for him. I don't think anything else he said ever creeped me out more than that statement did, because I suddenly knew that any intimacy I ever thought we had was false.

Twenty years into the marriage, I finally had the nerve to call it what it was: a bad marriage that shouldn't have lasted as long as it did. A marriage to finally give up on, a marriage too desiccated to resuscitate.

My ex-husband was a perfectly good man. He just wasn't good for me. That is a hard thing to realize, and an even harder thing to do something about.

When I married the first time, I probably knew myself about as well as we readers know those girls in the fairytales, which is to say, not at all. I had high expectations but little reality. My then-husband and I plunged into marriage despite our misgivings about the institution itself and, more than likely, about the suitability of each other. We did have some wonderful times, mostly when we were traveling or living abroad—which provided ample distraction from each other.

Yet whenever I allowed myself to think about my marriage, although I sensed something missing, something huge and untenable, it wasn't anything I could articulate. It was as if I had lost a limb and still had the phantom pain that accompanies it. But what had I lost? Or, perhaps more accurately, what had I never found? The absence of what I did not even understand—despite therapy—haunted me and was a source of deep anxiety. I knew, somehow, that what I had wasn't the kind of marriage I needed.

What I finally discovered I *needed* was intimacy, what I *wanted* was intimacy, *what I was not willing to live without again* was intimacy.

This realization was neither sudden nor profound and, until I met my second husband, not even entirely formulated.

I spent many sessions back in therapy, trying to sort out the reasons, muster the courage to leave a marriage that had left me desperately unhappy. As we talked and talked, I finally understood, at nearly fifty, that intimacy is won only through honesty, and that I had left far too much unsaid to my first husband. Out of fear, out of ignorance, out of the mistaken belief that he should have just known how I felt and what I wanted. It wasn't that I hadn't tried to talk to him—I had. I felt, for most of the marriage, that I was carrying the entire weight of it myself. Despite that, I hadn't been good at intimacy myself, mainly because I hadn't been aware of its true value. And, most important, I felt little deserving of love, no matter how fierce a face I put on it. And if one does not feel deserving of love, one can't fully love back, be intimate.

I could blame my parents, but at this point that's water under the bridge. Self-esteem issues don't even begin to cover it; the hole in my self-worth was big enough to drive a truck through. I disguised it far too long with humor, intelligence, bravado, a touch of narcissism, and tons of self-sacrifice.

So I made a certain transparency my goal as I put myself back on the market. I didn't flaunt it; I didn't even talk about it much. I just approached it in a take-no-prisoners kind of way. No more opacity: I said what I wanted, told every man I went out with who I really was (as far as I knew!), made no excuses, offered no explanations. I shed that very thin skin I had been wearing since childhood, only to find a thicker, tougher one that protected me like armor from the wannabes and led me right to the man who would become my mate. I made myself vulnerable, but by doing so I made myself stronger.

It wasn't that I had never been intimate with others, but the intimacy I had had as a child and later as an adult had been with women: good girlfriends and my sisters. I am not discounting that wonderful kind of intimacy that lets us reveal our warts and still know that we'll be loved. But the level of intimacy I desired with a man was something deeper: It was intimacy *about* intimacy itself. It was sexual intimacy tied in with emotional intimacy tied in with revelation, and all wrapped up in the ability to discuss things that might be painful or difficult or confounding.

I wanted so much to be able to parse it, to really examine it, all with my true mate. I wanted to be able to ask for things without embarrassment and reveal things without being frightened.

I believe that many women have learned to expect love from our sisters. Some of us even take it for granted, but we shouldn't; our women friends save our psyches daily and our lives more than once. We need to be grateful. But it's another matter entirely to be truly loved by someone who really gets you. And to be loved in middle age—with sagging breasts, soft tummy, errant mind, bag, and baggage—by someone with as much love damage as you have, well, quite frankly that's the most amazing, mind-boggling, and gobsmacking experience in the universe. Honest to god.

I found all of that.

And before anyone tries to pop my bubble or lay waste to my conclusions by reminding me that this is still a relatively new relationship, let me assure you: At fifty-one, I know full well the difference between okay and fantastic.

I learned about sex the hard way, but perhaps not an unusual way: through books that explained things far more complicated than I had ever imagined, and that revealed things to me far sooner than I would ever experience them. My parents, though liberal, were not forthcoming, to say the least, about sexual matters. There was no *Sex and the City* on television to turn to. When I finally engaged in sexual activity, I found it mysterious and thrilling. Being sexually desirable to men made me feel desirable in general. I had no idea then, and no idea really for much of my life, that most boys and men want sex in general, and that they generally desire any woman who will give it to them. She doesn't have to be pretty or smart or interesting, just willing. I was, as were many women in the '70s and early '80s, pretty willing. In fact, I was often as indiscriminate as my partners, even though I attributed to them far more discrimination than I admitted to. After all, they had picked me, right? So they must want *me* specifically, right?

Wrong.

But I was so busy not liking myself, because I didn't know myself or understand myself, that I gave others permission to make me feel like a good and beautiful and worthwhile woman.

And as far as I knew, intimacy and sex weren't even connected. I hadn't even a definition for intimacy. If love was connected to sex, or not, depending on how I (or the man) felt, what the hell was intimacy, anyway? And why would I bother going in search of it? Part of me didn't even believe it existed, not between men and women, anyway. Women were the only ones we women could tell our secrets to; men weren't interested, men would betray us, and they would use those confessions against us somehow.

I'm going to go out on a limb here and say that burgeoning feminism had a lot to do with this thinking. In some ways, feminism has betrayed us. We needed men like fish need bicycles, right? Men were okay to fuck, okay to have fun with, but seriously, now, men were clueless. They didn't get us. They didn't want to. We were better off not even trying to explain ourselves. What feminism did that was good was very good, but it never quite answered all the questions that women have about ourselves and our relationships, which is why revisionist theories are cropping up weekly and women are still searching for the perfect balance of love and work and children and life. Truth is, we won't ever get that perfect balance and we know it. Yet we continue struggling to juggle all our wants and desires, once we admit to them, and just hope that they won't crash into each other and send the whole act tumbling down.

My first wake-up call that there was something called "intimacy" in a marriage or long-term relationship was when, as a young bride, I began to hear my girlfriends' litanies of complaints about their men. At every book club meeting, every lunch, every playgroup session, most of the women would bitch and moan about how their husbands wouldn't talk to them, or wouldn't touch them, or wouldn't help them, or were lousy in bed, or oafish, or selfish. Men spent too much money or not enough, spent too much time at the office or were unambitious, were too fat or too self-absorbed. I felt uncomfortable listening to these complaints, but also completely unwilling to list my own husband's failings. I loved him. I had married him. That was that. It was disloyal somehow to reveal things about him that he had no control over my revealing. It was deceptive and just plain wrong to pull the covers off my married life—no matter how unhappy I was.

In fact, until the day my ex and I decided to separate, even my parents knew nothing of my unhappiness. Most of our friends thought we were fine. Only one of my sisters and my best friend knew any of the details, and even then, none of the really gory ones, and certainly nothing of the huge despair I felt, the crippling loneliness that I had trouble admitting even to myself.

I had spent so much energy raising my kids and trying to make the marriage work—somehow—that I didn't have a whole lot of time for soul-searching. Most of all, I feared divorce, saw it as a personal failure. Saw it as repeating my parents' inability to stay married. And I am a Capricorn. Steadfast. *I do not give up.*

Until I had to. Until I had to declare the marriage not only brain-dead but heart-dead too.

I vowed then and there to get what I wanted and never settle for less. Frankly, I assumed I would never marry again. I didn't really want to, so I thought I could just have lovers for fun. Then, sometime in late-late middle age or early old age, I might just give up and live alone, which didn't scare me at all. I had lived alone in my twenties; I had lived alone during the separation and for a year after the divorce (save for my daughter, of course, but without a man), and it suited me. Those nights when my daughter was with my ex, I actually began to relish my solo time at home. I couldn't remember having been alone in my own house before, and on those nights I could read for hours, eat yogurt for dinner, or write until after midnight, since I didn't have to get up to take anyone to school. I could meet friends for dinner and a movie. I could begin to think about my future with my daughter, and eventually solo. And I did. I began to make plans.

Enter Michael. The story of our meeting is cute but not necessary to the plot here. Suffice it to say that the first time we actually met face to face, I knew that I was either in deep trouble or in deep wonderful. True to my suspicious nature, I assumed the former. No one could actually be that right for me. He was my real-life doppelganger, my soul mate, my Vulcan mind meld. Except that he was a man, with his own quirks and weird habits that somehow made mine seem less . . . malignant.

For so long I had been so used to being criticized and dissected (first by my parents and then by my husband), had been made to feel that I was too needy, too complicated, too emotional, too passionate. The fact that someone accepted me for all my vagaries was too good to be true.

Yes, I am clumsy, and I tend toward hyperbole, and I have a quick temper, and I really like rap music, and I insist on the very Old Testament values of right and wrong, and I believe in God and evil, even though I consider myself an intellectual. I do not suffer fools gladly, and I am a bit of a snob. But I've got a lot of good stuff going on, too; only I never heard much about that from my ex.

Michael knows full well my flaws, but he does not dwell on them. He dwells instead on what is good and positive about me and about us. At first I reveled in it. It felt like suddenly staying in a first-class hotel after having only ever been able to afford a Super 8. But what I quickly learned was that turnabout was fair play. It was up to me to

(1) also accept Michael's flaws and foibles; (2) not assume that every time he mentioned something I did wrong, it spelled the end of the relationship; and (3) assume the best and just carry on. If he said he loved me, I should accept that as true; if he really was concerned about my pleasure over his, I should just lie back and enjoy it; if he asked, "What's on your mind?" I should tell him. And I should give him as much as he was giving me.

Sounds simple, right? But for someone who had gone through life both protecting herself and not revealing herself, it wasn't easy, no matter how many vows I had made and how many men I had auditioned with my experimental honesty.

True intimacy is scary as hell. It means that you're wide open in every way possible: mentally, emotionally, intellectually, physically. It means you reveal what you have to have and hope the other person is really listening. And it means doing some real hard, serious listening of your own. It means loving when one is tired or cross; it means doing things for the other just for the hell of it and expecting nothing in return; it means listening to the desires and wants of the other; and it means deciding what is more important: the imperfections or the virtues. It means not assuming that every disagreement is The End.

When I talk to Michael about intimacy, he is eager to help me understand what is different about us. Sometimes he says things that are so romantically sappy, they make me cringe. But he believes we are soul mates, star-crossed lovers who spent the first five decades of our lives on different planets, so to speak; he says that when he met me, he knew for certain that he was home. He shows me his writing, from years and years ago, that presages meeting me and what would happen. He tells me that the reason I assumed my ex was only criticizing me was that I did not feel loved enough to feel secure, to deflect the small critiques, which then built and built into large and insoluble ones. I accept my own culpability in that first marriage, but, as Michael also points out, had I been loved as he loves me now, I might have made the transition from wary to comfortable much sooner. What I have come to realize is that my ex was as insecure as I was, only he refused to confess that. He refused the intimacy that would have allowed us to guide each other to real intimacy.

Michael and I can talk about our pasts, and even joke when we reveal something about former lovers that makes the other a tiny bit jealous; we talk about our sex life, while it's happening, before and after; we talk about why our talking works and when it doesn't. We josh and jostle each other; we give in sometimes when we don't want to; we expose ourselves, knowing that the other will embrace that exposure and not use it against us. Most of all, we have a sense of humor about ourselves and the improbability of our getting together like this. And we delight in the sheer good luck of us.

For a very long time in my first marriage, I felt invisible. I was so lonely at times, I thought I could just vanish and no one would really notice. Michael sees me, hears me, gets me, and doesn't let me disappear even when I try to. His honesty makes me more honest; his intimacy makes me more intimate. I am not entirely there yet, though. I still hold some secrets close, still flinch when he touches me in certain places, still want to run and hide from his gaze sometimes. I still wonder what the hell I am doing married again, and part of me thinks it can't possibly last. But when I express these doubts, Michael just shakes his head and smiles: "You're the last woman I will ever be with. You are the last face I will ever see. You are my designated dirt-kicker, the woman who will bury me. Just go with it."

I am trying. I am. I am deeply committed to the happy *after* the happily ever after, to the true end of the story.

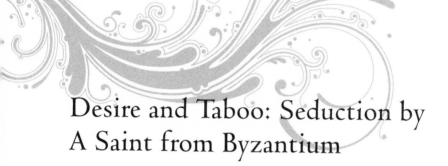

# Desire and Taboo: Seduction by
# A Saint from Byzantium

*Myrna Kostash*

$\mathcal{E}$dmonton, the 1950s: As a young child, I sat in the pews with my father, the great skeptic of our family, the reader of history books, and the thinker of "what ifs"—even though he was the son of pious immigrants and was himself a faithful servant of the Church, departing weekly on mysterious errands having to do with boards, consistories, and assemblies of the Ukrainian Greek Orthodox Church of Canada, Edmonton division. Dad often poked me in the ribs in response to something in the priest's sermon he found ridiculous or illogical, which I could only take his word for, as I did not understand what the priest was saying. We spoke only English at home.

At fifteen, I announced to my parents one Sunday morning, while we were all dressing for church, that I did not believe in God and would no longer accompany them to church services. My mother said, "You're too young to decide that," and that seems to have been that.

There were many more Sundays filled with church: the interminable, unintelligible liturgies (*Protestants* were in and out of church in an hour); the confessions in rote phrases of pidgin Ukrainian; the phrases of one or two of the venerable hymns of the Eastern Church—"Holy God, Holy Almighty, Holy Immortal, have mercy on us"—sung to the minor-key melodies of the Slavonic service that I always heard as dirges. (*Protestants* had cheerful tunes you could tap your toes to.) But it was more than just the length and seriousness of the services. My teenage years were when much of what had been pulling at my heartstrings—my lithe young spirit—were issues of what we now call social justice. I did not yet suspect that I might be called on to act in the world, but Lord, I believed.

I cheered Fidel Castro, I read George Orwell with deep conviction, Anne Frank's story crushed my heart, and Audrey Hepburn's self-sacrifice as a waifish nurse-nun alluring in her virginal vestments inspired the ideal of the unmarried, childless life. Hungarian refugees, tossed up in my elementary school, haunted me with images of their desperate flight from Russian tanks in the cobblestone streets of the Old Country behind the Iron Curtain, as did the display of black-and-white photographs, in the windows of the Hudson's Bay store on Jasper Avenue, of the wretched camps of the Palestinians dispossessed of their land. Stories of tormented animals left me distraught, and I mourned the untimely deaths of the UN Secretary-General Dag Hammarskjöld and American president John F. Kennedy as though I had lost members of my own family. As soon as I was able to conceptualize the meaning of what had happened at Hiroshima, of Jim Crow laws in the southern

United States, and of pass laws in South Africa, I knew that the world I wanted to live in was the world of impassioned reason, as delivered to me by arguments, texts, and exposés, all in the service of righting wrongs through the power of language out and about in the world.

One afternoon, I wandered out into the backyard, where my father was seated in the lawn chair reading—I myself had been reading Aldous Huxley—and asked him point blank if there was a God. He took the pipe out of his mouth: "Is there a God? If there is, He's a principle of energy, of the eternal cycles of nature, and of the cosmos. . . . " There was more, I think—the "I am" of God as a mathematical theorem. Was this an answer? I promised myself I would take his word for it.

Later, as a part-time hippie in the 1960s, living among people who sat in the lotus position during solemn rituals of getting stoned, and who I thought were immeasurably more *evolved* than I, I became interested in the books they kept in their Afghan tote bags. I remember Alan Watts's *Nature, Man and Woman*, Hermann Hesse's *Siddhartha*—and the *I Ching*, around which we gathered to throw Chinese coins, over and over and over again, until we decoded something that made sense.

I am impressed now by how many more hours I devoted to the cryptic runes of an exotic Asian sage—"He who crosses the great water knows good fortune"—than I was ever prepared to give to the sages of my own tradition. St. John Chrysostom, the "Golden Mouth," for instance. Or Bishop of Constantinople, who wrote in the 5th century: "When you discover the door of your heart, you discover the gate of heaven"—which I now have written on a Post-it note at my desk, as it seems immeasurably more helpful.

Decades later, traveling through east, central, and southeastern Europe on political and intellectual errands, I surprised myself by entering churches. Not just any churches, but Orthodox churches, the ones with the squat domes on stout brick walls, which gave no hint from the outside of the beauty within. In the shadowy corners lit by oil lamps, I took a kind of rest in them, unquestioning of the sense of homely peace that settled over me as I sniffed remnants of incense and beeswax, gazed at the icons who gazed back at me, and mumbled the few lines of text I did know from the hymns and prayers of the liturgy. Whether this was in Ukraine, Romania, Serbia, Macedonia, Bulgaria, or Greece, I knew that it was all one church, Orthodox, Byzantine, Eastern, and I had a right to be there, even if I didn't quite understand the details. Although I had spent an entire childhood and youth inside an Orthodox church, I had not paid much conscious attention to the liturgical proceedings, but, by sheer osmosis, the atmosphere, sounds, smells, and colors had somehow permeated me at the cellular level.

I had been baptized Orthodox and all these churches were open to me, as were their prayers, their feast days, and their saints.

Then, seven years ago in northern Greece, I sat for the first time in the Basilica of St. Demetrius in Thessaloniki, inside the burnished gold–shedding light from the domes and the thick stumps of candles dying in front of the mother of God and the atonal chant of the priest as he censed us, a handful of women in late afternoon, heads bowed as the smoke of the incense made its way to heaven, and with it our spirits, while the city roared outside. And I prayed, the only prayer I knew—*Otche nash, shcho iese na nebi,* Our Father, who art in heaven—because, I felt instinctively, all other texts were burdensome here.

"Home," wrote poet Don McKay, "is the action of the inner life finding outer form." For me the process has been exactly the reverse: My outer life—my life as a student, a citizen, and a writer—has been struggling to find its way home to an interior form.

I looked around me in that great 7th-century basilica, surrounded by images of the city's patron, Demetrius. Had I found a form in the icon of a Byzantine saint? I was startled by the possibility.

I was in Thessaloniki only to research a book about Byzantium. This was a culture and a history that fascinated me, and I had come to one of its sources. The book would be a literary nonfiction, I hoped, such as I had already written; and as a nonfiction writer I had always insisted on the primacy of the world "out there," even when I wrote in a voice all my own. It was a passionate voice, saturated with cultural identity, history, and politics, a voice honed over thirty years in the nonfiction trenches, with a reputation as a leftist, a feminist, a cultural nationalist, a multiculturalist, a regionalist, what have you. My inner life was not the point, I felt. To draw on it—its "unending series of emotional experiments" (to quote another correspondent about the value of women's diaries)—for its own sake was self-indulgent and had little to do with the matters at hand—with Byzantium, for instance.

"The illusory importance and autonomy of private life," wrote German philosopher Theodor Adorno, "conceals the fact that private life drags on only as an appendage of the social process."[1] All through the decades of my intellectual maturation and beyond, even as the idealized models collapsed—the Left into a dustbin of history, feminism into postfeminism, the "peace dividend" into perpetual war—I believed passionately in the possibility of human solidarity.

But as I stood in the Basilica of St. Demetrius, surrounded by and venerating images of his ineffable beauty, I can see now that I was struggling for a "self" that was neither reducible to some private psychodrama nor dismissible with an ironic, despairing flourish of postmodernism. I was admitting to myself, icon by icon, that my "self" was embedded in the matrix of spirit, as well as in history, politics, and culture. And even as I began to thresh about for a spiritual vocabulary for my desires, I knew that "salvation" was not personal but would still somehow be a communal struggle, as "liberation" and "revolution" had been. That it might take on the form of the Ukrainian Orthodox Church of my childhood was not yet an issue; the struggle was.

I have spent most of my conscious life as a secular humanist, receptive to movements that followed upon my adolescence: the New Left, the counterculture, feminism, Canadian cultural nationalism, environmentalism, Soviet and east European dissidence. I was overwhelmed by wave upon wave of distress and outrage at the iniquities of the powerful and ruthless around the world, and I found solace not in spiritual practices but mainly in political texts (and the songs of

Bob Dylan). I pored over Marx and Lenin in Sunday morning reading circles, Germaine Greer and Kate Millett in feminist reading groups, and Malcolm X, Régis Debray, and eventually the entire library of New Left Canadian critiques of the world order in the books I was piling in my own library. If that's what we mean by "modernity," there was a very good reason why I spent most of my life inside it, namely my conviction that the enlightened mind is a capacious enough organ to enable me to live life as a good and just person.

And I suspected that faith in the transcendent was some kind of luxury for the lucky few who know how to pray.

Then I met my saint.

He is Demetrius, young, pretty faced, beardless, with thick hair tucked behind his ears. He wears the green tunic and red cloak of a Byzantine army officer and holds a round shield and long-armed cross. He died young, speared through his right breast, in the basement of the Roman baths in the Macedonian city of Thessaloniki, for the crime of preaching the gospel of Jesus Christ. The year was 304, and he was going to become a saint, one of the most powerful in all of Christendom.

I found him in a book. I was reading books about Byzantium, trying to find a subject for my own book, a focus, or at least a passageway into the history of the civilization that radiated for a thousand years around the eastern Mediterranean world from its home in Constantinople, the city of Roman emperor Constantine, founded in 324. Both my Canadian and European stories begin in this place: the triumph of Byzantine civilization in the eastern Mediterranean, and the Balkans after the fall of Rome in the west. It was this civilization that my Slavic ancestors entered, when they accepted Christianity and an alphabet from the Eastern Church, and it was a version of this experience that my Ukrainian grandparents bore with them on their immigrant trek to an Alberta homestead.

I read that Demetrius, a nobleman, had been martyred and hastily buried in the red earth of the Roman baths. Then the little shrine marking the spot fell into ruin, the relics disappeared, and, after a time, the details of his life and death vanished from living memory. But several hundred years later, during the period of Thessaloniki and Byzantium's greatest peril, when the fate of European civilization hung in the balance, Demetrius reappeared.

In the early 7th century, Greece and the Balkans were overrun by wave upon wave of barbarians who didn't stop until they got all the way through to the Peloponnese. But there was one prize they never did take, though they tried over and over again, besieging and assaulting its walls and gates to no avail: the city then called Thessalonica, second only to Constantinople, the jewel of the northern Aegean, fabulously wealthy and infinitely desirable. But the city was impregnable. For the Great Martyr and Holy Warrior Demetrius had come back, riding his red horse on the ramparts, performing the miracle of the defense of the city.

So goes the hagiography, the life of the saint. Intrigued, I looked more closely at the iconography: his slender figure astride his horse, his red cloak billowing in a heavenly breeze, posed triumphantly on the battlements of Thessalonica while the squat little figures of the bedeviled barbarians mill about uselessly at the gates and bury their dead. I look more closely still: The barbarians are Slavs.

I was hooked.

I had found my subject. What I didn't realize was that he had been waiting for me, too.

A few months ago, away from home, I picked up the copy of the Gideon's Bible shelved discreetly in a hotel drawer and let it fall open. The passage I read there was from James 3:6: "And the tongue is a fire, the very world of iniquity; the tongue is set among our members as that which defiles the entire body, and sets on fire the course of our life, and is set on fire by hell."

It's still a shock, that harsh biblical language of judgment, yet it's so vivid and stirring. I had "left the church" precisely in order to go out into the world of ideas and argument, *my tongue on fire:* How could I agree that such fiery speech could ever "defile" the entire body of the community? If I had to choose between the iniquity of the spiritual "tongue" and the clamour of the social "body," I knew which I would pick.

Then, one hot July afternoon in Saskatchewan's Qu'Appelle Valley, the air so stilled by heat that even the flies could not be bothered to lift themselves off the windowpanes, I sat with a friend, also a writer, who had bought this land we were sitting on, a sere and undulating landscape shaped by the meandering ribbon of water in the valley bottom. We talked about ambivalence and anxiety, that peculiar state of people who have experienced themselves all their lives as rational beings (we two, for example), only to be sabotaged, blindsided, shaken, upended by what my friend called "a longing for the holy," which arrives seemingly out of the clear blue heaven but which also, if you think about it, makes perfect sense. I was listening to him with mounting agitation, for I guessed where this was heading.

My friend, an environmentalist and amateur ornithologist, is a practicing Roman Catholic (after a long lapse) who is unafraid, to judge from his books, to speak publicly as a man of faith, and to interrogate that faith. The "sense" to be made of this was that not everything could be known by the exercise of logic and judgment (a modesty lost to us since the Enlightenment). Considering all the materials I had gathered in my "Demetrius project," did I not feel, he asked, the urge to go beyond the narrative and intellectual limits of history, ethnology, and what I was calling my deep, personal cultural grammar? Did I not want to push the boundaries of what I already knew from intellectual experience, a push from my religious heritage, not to mention from a certain saint of Byzantium? Saints are our intercessors with God, and here was one who was tapping me on the shoulder. God may or may not be out there (or in here), but we certainly aren't going to find out one way or another by the application of our reasoning alone. We are likelier to find Him through the slippages offered by uncertainty and ambivalence, what my friend called the "anxious threshold experience" of traveling between rationality and faith, doubt and spiritual longing.

When political scientist Peter C. Emberley investigated the phenomenon of so many members of the '60s generation searching for "spiritual" meaning in their middle age, he made this observation: Our youthful commitment to social and political change, and to the communities we lived in, had been, in part, tools of consciousness— love and solidarity, hope and compassion—through which "the divine" could now speak. Like secular ideals of revolutionary change, Christian morality has always expressed faith in the possibility of change, renewal, and amelioration of the human condition.[2]

Decades after our engagement with the great movements for liberation and justice, we return to churches and temples, or at least to spiritual rites and rituals, not to gesture our private despair about the collapse of political and social projects but to acknowledge the "return of the repressed" desire for some kind of collective hope for transcendent ideals in a sickened world.

And so I went to visit a new friend of mine, an Episcopal priest in Edmonton. "What is the 'self' beyond its private life?" I asked. "Is it fully encompassed by the historical, the political, the sociological? If not, what are the 'documentations' of this larger self?"

Father Don fairly jumped out of his chair and went straight to his Bible and read from Romans 8:26. That St. Paul might be a source of wisdom and consolation was rather a shock to me, who had thought of him only as a misogynist who believed that women should be silent in church (this turns out not to have been his writing). But I listened. "Likewise the Spirit also helps in our weaknesses. For we do not know what we should pray for as we ought, but the Spirit Himself makes intercession for us with groanings which cannot be uttered." I confessed, feeling stupid and unlettered in this Christian language, that I didn't really get it.

"Self-understanding is seeing ourselves as God sees us," Father Don interpreted, with considerable patience. "Part of our fallingness as humans is to see ourselves only as self-created"—I was all ears— "and not in His image. The self is in fact embedded in God's knowledge. This is the source of our internal coherence." The "fallingness" made me squirm (it seemed the sort of thing a Protestant would say), but I felt a little leap of my spirit. Something was expanding within me at the idea that my "self" might be the creation of some transcendent energy beyond economic, historical, cultural, and gendered necessity.

This would have to be, in some sense, a "secret self," as Emberley has written, for the news that I was seriously interested in the tradition of worship in a church that prided itself on its roots in Christian antiquity would, I feared, shock friends and family. Wouldn't they wonder how I could reconcile my social and political values with the doctrines of a patriarchal institution dead set against, for instance, same-sex marriage, abortion, and premarital sex (although it tends to not make a fuss)? Would I really submit to the discipline of Orthodox spiritual practices? Great Lent, for instance, forty days before Easter of not eating meat, for heaven's sake, but prostrating myself before icons? Isn't there some more "reasonable" cult I could join, mother-goddess worshippers, for instance? Could I not be accused of seeking just another, but more exoticized, version of postpolitical self-fulfillment?

As I rose to leave, Father Don detained me: "Christian truth develops along a progressive line between the self at one end and God at the other, with Christ halfway between. Where would you put yourself on this line?" I experienced a couple of seconds of familiar anxiety: Just as I had always wanted to give the "right" answer to political questions put by political activists, I wanted now to give the "right" answer to this man of God so that he wouldn't think I was wasting his time. But I answered truthfully: I could see myself moving to the idea of the Divine, with the help of saints and the church fathers, but Jesus, well, I could not truthfully say I was moving to *Him*. I felt apologetic about this, but for the moment I felt only a kind of giddiness, thrown off-balance by something "unutterable."

Father Don asked me if I'd like him to say a prayer, adding, "No pressure!" Embarrassed, I hesitated, but then agreed (no one would know about this except him and me). It was a longish prayer, thanking God for His presence as we struggled with these issues, and asking Him to protect me as I tried to find my way.

Soon I took to clipping and posting wise or lyrical quotations from other writers who seemed to have anticipated my quandary: whether a spiritual seeker must abandon her intellectual capacities in order to look for God. I recognized the challenge from earlier in my life, back among the hippies and the politicos, the counterculture versus the revolution, or, among the feminists, smashing patriarchy versus swooning with the moon goddess: Choose one or the other. The paths cannot be straddled. But now I was reading of Richard E. Byrd, a polar explorer who was spending the winter at the South Pole in a tiny cabin on the ice and who believed, even in that desperate circumstance, that his despair ("man's despair") was groundless, once he allowed his feeling that a "beneficent intelligence pervaded the whole" of creation to "transcend" his rational thoughts and enter his heart. It was that "transcend" that hooked me, as I wasn't sure about the "beneficent intelligence." Yet an orthodox priest-scientist I spoke with, and to whom I admitted my stumbling efforts, as a rational writer, to accept the Christian "reality" of mystery, grace, and revelation, retorted that, as a scholar of quantum mechanics, he had never had difficulty with the idea of energy endlessly forming and reforming in clusters of matter, deforming and forming again. *Resurrection? Transfiguration?*

"Are spirit and mind really at such cross purposes?" I asked Father Don on a second visit, thinking of what happens in the act of creativity, that mysterious arrival out of nowhere of a thought or image you did not know you were thinking or seeing. I asked him, may we not discern here, in the creative moment, the collaboration of the spirit and the mind? He whipped out St. Paul again: Romans 12:1–2.

"And do not be conformed to this world, but be transformed by the renewing of your mind, that you may prove what is that good and acceptable and perfect will of God."

Mind, yes, but mind *renewed*, transformed into the highest faculty of human nature—the eyes of the heart, "the eyes of your understanding" (Paul to the Ephesians), as though we could turn our gaze inward straight to our knowing the will of God. "Jesus cannot conceive of a mind and spirit that are not in relationship," Father Don said animatedly. And not for the last time will I be both bemused by and envious of his apparent intimacy with the Word, not to mention the Living God.

"Illumine our hearts," Orthodox Christians pray before the reading of the gospel begins. It is not Christianity that needs to be "rationalized," writes Orthodox theologian Vladimir Lossky, but reason that is to be "Christianized." "I believe," we begin, and perhaps from the believing proceeds a new understanding of who and where we are, and not the other way around, as my lonely rational self has always assumed.

November first, the Saturday before the Feast of St. Demetrius, "Soul Saturday," one of the handfuls celebrated during the Orthodox liturgical year in memory of all the dead. I looked for a mass this morning—and found it at my childhood church, St. John's. There were about ten of us, including two priests in purple vestments, for we were in mourning. As snow fell outside, a soft light filtered through the stained-glass windows, while inside the candles flickered blue, green, red in their votive cups.

Two cantors have also joined us. One, a janitor by trade, is tall and bony, with a pitch-perfect baritone with a glasslike clarity; the other, a retired priest, small, pink faced, and white haired, sings in a youthful, unquavering tenor. Together, their voices take up the Trisagion hymn "Holy God, Holy Almighty, Holy Immortal, have mercy on us," in the simple melody I learned as a child, and I am so grateful for their gift of this (no artsy-fartsy fiddling around) that I weep.

This liturgy is so intimate. We few have gathered as though on behalf of everybody else, and we create a little space of prayer and reflection inside a day—Saturday—usually spent rushing around. We have dropped out of it, as though from another planet, to land here, repeating ancient gestures from another civilization.

As for St. Demetrius, he is here as patron of the dead. Today the first name of everyone who died this year in the parish is read aloud. We sing: *Vichnaia pamiat'*, eternal memory, even though I have no idea who these people were. It doesn't matter—we've all agreed to be the community that remembers in this service. And so the dead linger on for a little while longer because we stand here, holding candles and hearing their names: Paraska, Anna, Dmytro, Steven, Sophie, Nestor, Jason . . .

Finally, we are silent. We blow out our candles. The priests withdraw behind the icon screen and close the royal doors.

I linger in the silence, loitering in this new space of sanctuary. "Speech is the organ of the present world," wrote St. Isaac the Syrian. "Silence is a mystery of the world to come."

## Footnotes:

1. Cited by Jacqueline Rose. *London Review of Books,* 20 April 2006.

2. Peter C. Emberley. *Divine Hunger: Canadians on Spiritual Walkabout* (Scarborough, Ontario: HarperCollins, 2001).

# Hitting Back

*Debra Magpie Earling*

## *1.* Confrontation

I  grew up believing some grievances are best settled with fists, not words. While I'd enjoyed myself in public school and had many friends, when I changed schools in the third grade to attend Catholic school, I was bombshelled by my mean-spirited classmates. St. Paschal's was a surly world of penance, forced prayer, and earboxing nuns; and all of the skirt-measuring and ruler-slapping had made the kids hard. But I was under their radar until the day I brought in my great-grandfather's buckskin beaded vest for show-and-tell.

"My grandfather was the chief of our tribe," I told the class, ready to launch into a story my mother had told me about my grandfather. The teacher interrupted me.

"So," Sister Victor Mary said, leaning forward on her desk and tapping the pencil holder with her finger as if she was trying to figure me out, "what you are telling us is that you are an Indian princess."

The students smirked at me as I stood behind the shield of my grandfather's vest. Still, I felt suddenly transformed. I was now an Indian princess. I embraced the idea immediately.

"Yes," I said, standing taller. "That's what I am," I declared, even though I had never heard of an Indian princess.

"Let me get this straight," the nun said. "Aren't you bragging a little?" I realized that my smile had become uncomfortably tight. I lowered my chin to my chest. "Please sit down," she said, as she rose from her desk.

When I returned to my seat, Sister Victor Mary did not release me from her chastisement. "Debbie Earling," she continued, and the students craned in their seats to relish my reddened face—grateful, I suppose, that I was now the new victim in the class. "You will spend recess in chapel praying for forgiveness," she said, adding, "as penance for your boastfulness."

The next day on the playground, two girls shoved me to the blacktop. "Indian princess," they jeered at me. My big brother came to my rescue but then gave me an earful, too. "Why'd you go and tell them you're an Indian princess, you idiot? Don't ever say we're Indians again," my dark brother said, believing he was passing. Then he turned his back on me and ran off to play with his friends.

I found myself avoiding the other kids and their taunts by hiding in the lilac bushes at the edge of the playground. Sometimes the playground monitor would force me out of the bushes and I would stand beside her, hoping she would protect me from the other girls who took every opportunity to remind me that I was different from them.

My brother began keeping his distance from me, too, as if this tactic would provide him immunity from his Indianness. I'd become a weirdo, a freak. I felt pitiful and weak peering out from the lilac bushes at the Red Rover lines, all the kids laughing, shouting, and playing without care. "Quit acting like a dummy," my brother would tell me once we got home.

My mother began offering me words of advice: "Stand up for yourself," she would say when I'd come home sniveling. "Don't let those kids push you around." She gave me her permission to fight. "Beat 'em up," she said, "and they'll never bother you again."

My father was a champion boxer, and he taught me how to crack a good punch, showed me how to marry the freight of my third-grade muscles to forward momentum, the merciless weight of me power-jumped and thrust into my bull-charged but puny fist.

"You've got to make the first punch count," he said. "You've only got one chance."

But I never threw that good punch, not even when Martha McIntyre called me a "dirty Indian" to my face, or when, a year later, Daniel Millsap threw my skirt over my head, right in front of a bunch of goggle-eyed boys.

I guess I just didn't possess the lightning wit I needed to jack the quick jab, my rage following my slow heart like thunder—ten minutes too late.

I have never been sly enough to see the sucker punches. I never see the jab coming. I have no triumphant put-downs, no crunching blows that will bulldoze cruelty or end confrontation. But if I consider myself lucky to be so dim-witted in a heated situation, every so often I've wondered why I *don't* act when a damning moment shoves me, or when there's a mean, spitting son of a bitch charging me with insults. Sometimes, too often, I desire most to be the person who throws the power punch.

# 2. Punch Line

I'm teaching a graduate-level comedy class in the art of stand-up comedy.

In the class is a man with little feet, a porkpie face. His smile is grimacing, his eyes tight. He is self-satisfied for now. All attention is focused on him.

"My wife is the star. I'm just the trophy husband," he says. *Bada bing, bada bang.* He says this without flinching; his is a comedy act without humor. No one laughs. No one sees him as a trophy of any sort, and this is in itself hilarious because the undertone of his voice suggests all seriousness. He is joking on the square. He sees himself as his partner's prize, stunning arm candy for a successful wife. When no one cajoles him, he crosses his arms over his chest and stretches out his short legs. His froggy, huffy countenance distracts the students. I've already warned the students that not every line will get a laugh. We try to ignore him. I suggest we move on to the next stand-up act.

When the class is ending for the day, he makes an attempt to re-deem himself. "I'm an actor," he whines, and, being an *actor* means he can't perform for the class. He turns to his colleagues with a know-it-all voice. "I know about acting. This is not an acting class," he complains. "We haven't done skits. We haven't done character sketches. We've been given nothing in the class," he says. The students file out around him. One woman's lips quiver. "I can't do stand-up. We should just quit the stand-up." She's clearly frightened by the class venue, a downtown theater, before a live audience.

"See," he says, "we've all been talking."

"Come to my office later," I say, hoping he won't.

When he shows up, he takes a seat without an invitation. "I've been taking acting lessons," he says. "I'm taking this brilliant class. We're learning something in there." I let him go on. "It's a beginning-level acting class." I can't help smiling. I think about him telling the class he's an actor, as if he has appeared on many stages, auditioned for choice parts, and had supreme authority in all things performance. I'm embarrassed for him, but I do not shift my eyes from his twitching face, my eyebrows raised. He knows I'm onto him.

"I don't respect you," he says, dropping the comment casually, as if he is saying he doesn't like succotash or the color of my shoes.

I look into his oily eyes. "You should drop the class," I tell him. If I were a man he wouldn't speak to me like this. If I were a man, we would settle this outside.

The next class meeting, there he is, sitting in the front row, a squirmy grin on his face.

I place my books down beside the podium before I address the class. I take a deep breath. I remind the students that the stand-up act is not a requirement to pass, that they may turn in a story for the final if they don't wish to take the stage. I try to look beyond the smug little man but cannot. He's rallied half the class and he has a somewhat disgruntled following. The class is half for, half against the final theater stand-up act. One of the "for" students shrugs his shoulders. "I make an ass out of myself for at least twenty minutes every day," he says. "What's five minutes here?"

There is a stirring in the class. The actor pleads with the students: "I don't want to be in a program where my colleagues make fools of themselves." He's become the dog in the manger. If he can't perform a stand-up act, he doesn't want his colleagues to perform one, either. He glares at me.

*In a flash I imagine myself grabbing a book from my table, feeling the heft of it before I swat his face—a loud smack to his forehead. I feel the quivering heat transfer to my hands, relish the sting. Actor is goggle-eyed, and before he can regain his senses, I grab him by the collar and yank him to standing. I've got one hand at the nape of his neck, the other on the back of his pants, and I hoist him out of the room with a ferocity I haven't felt since childhood; his legs are flailing in their run, he is snuffling and whimpering. I bang his head on the door a few times, until a student sheepishly steps forward to open it. "Thank you," I say. I take a little run with him so I can throw Actor down the hall, to where we won't be subjected to his sniveling. I take a deep breath once again.* Calm down. *I sit down at the table in the front of the room and survey the bleating-eyed students.*

*"Anyone else have a problem?" I say. I light a cigarette, drag hard until I feel the hazy sweetness swirl in my chest. I raise the lit cigarette to the class. "Well," I say, staring them down, "are you fur me or agin' me?"*

## *3.* Two Brief Asides

Another long department meeting where we are discussing hires. "This is just reverse discrimination," a male colleague complains. "I mean, we've hired too many women already."

One day, a colleague steps into my office. "I was just wondering what you thought about our university," he says. "You *are* our affirmative action hire."

"Huh?" I say. "Who, me?"

## *4.* A Slew of Slights

I'm out with my colleagues following an afternoon department meeting. We're relaxing over a cup of coffee, and the talk is easy. It's a pleasant day. It feels good to be in the company of smart people, talking about ideas and projects informally. One of my colleagues puts his hands down on the table to say, "This was a good idea. We should get together more often."

I feel good and I speak up. "Hey," I say, "I've been thinking about throwing a wine-tasting party."

"Now, there's a good idea," a male colleague says. "Count me in."

Another one of my colleagues, who prides herself on political correctness—a hippie with kissy-kisses and huggy-hugs for her colleagues, laughs like a horse and says, "What would we be trying, Thunderbird?" Ha ha ha, they all laugh. *Ha ha.*

# 5. Don't Take This Wrong

I've just returned from Paris, and I'm back at school and feeling logy. I'm heading back to my office when a colleague gestures to me. "May I have a word with you?" she asks. She asks me to close the door. I'm not expecting a confrontation; maybe I'm too tired to recognize one coming.

"Oh," she says, feigning concern, "you look tired." I *am* tired but thought I was looking pretty chipper.

"Yes," I say, "I'm pooped."

"Will you be traveling again soon?" she asks.

"I'm heading out this weekend," I say. "I have a reading in Utah."

"Well," she says, clucking her tongue. Her eyes look sympathetic, but her smile seems false to me, rehearsed. "You know," she says, "well," then "well" again, "the other writers aren't being asked to travel to other universities. And maybe, well, you know, you should be turning these offers down."

In the dark room, I shift in my chair and rub my eyes, blinking and bleary in the hazy light that remains luminous but contained in her small window.

"I'm not sure I understand," I say, and I don't. I think about my messy bed, the explosion of clothes sprawling from my yawning suitcase, wonder when I will find a moment to repack.

She nods her head to me in unlikely deference and looks away for a moment, as if what she is about to tell me is something I've never heard before, something that might come as a revelation to me. She pats my leg. "And you must know," she says, and chuckles a little to break the news to me, "you're only being invited because you're Indian."

I find a note in my office mailbox from Helena High School. "The senior class of Helena High School," it reads, "would be honored if you would be our commencement speaker." I read the note again and again. I dropped out of high school. I feel humbled and proud, excited. I step out into the hallway and rattle the invitation in my raised hand. "Hey," I announce, so happy that I'm sure my colleagues can recognize the lilt in my voice. They peer out from their offices with smiles on their faces.

"Good news, I hope," one colleague says.

"Guess what Helena High School wants me to be?"

One colleague sauntering by quips over her shoulder, "Their mascot?"

Ha ha, again. *Ha ha ha.*

# 6. I'll Give You Something To Cry About

I've been offered a job, a big job, a wonderful job, and I'm out to celebrate with my fiancé. We've come to a local bar and restaurant for a drink, perhaps a light meal. The bar is crowded, and the only place to sit is at a table right next to one of my colleagues, who is seated with some of the graduate students. I'm having a second glass of wine when my colleague taps my shoulder. I turn to her and smile.

"So," she says, "are you taking the job?"

"It's a lot to think about," I say.

"I'll tell you something," she says, her lips shining with alcohol. "You'd better take it."

I haven't caught on yet. I'm not sure how to respond, so I smile, nod my head.

"No," she tells me, because clearly I am not getting her drift. "If you think for one moment that you are going to get more money than the rest of us here, then think again."

I'm dumbfounded by the meanness throbbing in her voice, her sudden sullen eyes. I look at her to see if she is drunk, but she appears sober. My fiancé is chatting with a friend, enjoying himself. It's supposed to be a night of celebration, a night of new hope for both of us. I want to get up from my chair, but I feel stuck. I have a hard time believing she is saying what she is saying.

"You've been traveling too much," she says.

"Yes, I know. I'm tired," I agree.

"You don't care about your students," she says. "I get plenty of offers to travel but I don't. You want to know why I don't? Because, unlike you, *I care* about my students."

"I care about my students," I retort, but my answer sounds lame in the face of my colleague's wrath. I shouldn't be defending myself. "I have to travel," I say. "It's part of my contract." She ignores this statement.

"You don't even know what's going on in the department, about Tom having an affair with a graduate student."

I keep my mouth closed but am gape-mouthed in thought. The student she refers to is graduated and gone. My response is edged now, and like a dupe I'm in her trap. "I don't care," I say.

"Yes," she says, leering now. "You don't care." Her face becomes slack, I imagine because she doesn't want to draw full attention to her meanness. But she has raised her voice.

"I don't care to gossip," I tell her, smug, more than a little self-righteous. "I might not like the guy, but I don't believe he would have an affair with a student."

I glance toward my fiancé and he is listening to our conversation. "What?" he's mouthing. He looks puzzled, his head cocked, listening. I shrug my shoulders. I don't know how our good evening took this sudden plunge. Later he will tell me that if he hadn't heard what she was saying, he would have had a difficult time believing she had said it. "She looked so calm, so serene," he told me. "It looked like you were both having a pleasant conversation."

"Look," I say, trying to extricate myself from trouble and goad her at the same time with my choices. "I think I'll be going over to Native American studies, anyway. I haven't exactly had the best time in the English department. I've had some problems." I'm blabbing now, talking like a rube. Where's my stunning comeback? My wit and charm? This is precisely the moment where I should rise up on my hoity-toity graduate sheepskin and calmly, but with a razor-sharp dazzle of words, redeem myself. But I don't. I don't even have a dazzle of words.

I pull the race card. I do. "People here, well, they don't like Indians," I say. And even though I'm speaking the partial truth, it feels wrong.

"Give it up," she says. "If you had any real grievance, you'd have a lawsuit. As a woman, I've been more mistreated than you've ever dreamed."

I'm baffled by this comment and thinking, *What? I'm not a woman?*

"You have nothing to complain about," she says, and with this she laughs as if she's huffing. "Just go back to Native American studies," she tells me, swiping the air as if she is dismissing me, or maybe as if she has told me a good joke.

*First I toss a glass of wine in her face, and while she is spluttering and gulping, I grab the beer bottle and smash it over her head. The whole crowd is watching me. Men open their arms to protect their women; they face me, their eyes wide. I grab the wine bottle and break it on the edge of the table. The crowd roars and steps back against the wall. Everyone is scrambling from their places, heading for the exit. The red wine reeks. I hold the jagged bottle up over my downed colleague. When the police arrive, they try to humor me, motioning for the patrons to step away. "Drop the bottle," one officer commands. "Drop the bottle."*

*"All right, all right already," I say. I will come of my own volition—a free agent in this world. They do not handcuff me. One of the graduate students stands up and slaps me on the back. "You didn't take any shit," she says. "You're a role model."*

*The crowd parts and I leave to the sound of applause. Applause, applause, and I turn to see my wobbly-eyed colleague attempting to stand. "Don't ever talk down to me again," I say. "I'm not your whippin' Indian."*

"*What happened here?*" *the officer says.*

"*She was saying mean and despicable things to this woman. She's a racist,*" *the graduate student says.* "*The Indian had no choice.*"

*The owner steps from the crowd, stands over my felled colleague.* "*Is this true?*" *he says.* "*My gawd, is this true?*"

*She glances up from her wine-matted hair, her lips rubbery.* "*It is true, blobble, blobble.*"

"*Ma'am,*" *the owner says,* "*this bar is a hate-free zone.*"

*The officer lifts his voice to the crowd.* "*Hate hurts,*" *he says.* "*People, when are you going to learn that hate hurts?*"

# 7. The Comeback

I'm out on the town with a man I admire. I've dressed up for the occasion. I want to look good; I want the night to go well. We're seated at the bar, waiting for a table, when I excuse myself and head to the bathroom. A man leans over to my friend but speaks toward the group at the bar. "There must be a shortage of white women," the man says, winking at my friend.

"That may be, that may be. . . ." My friend pauses for a moment, long enough to get the attention of the man and the rest of the group at the bar. "There may be a shortage of white women," he repeats back to the grinning bigot, "but there's sure an abundance of assholes."

I hear this story later from the female bartender. "Boy," she says, "I wish I could quip a comeback like that."

"Don't we all," I say. "Don't we all."

# *8.* The Final Word

My mother and I are in Santa Fe for the Mountain and Plains Bookseller Association Awards. I have told her about Santa Fe for years and I've wanted to show her the small town, but she hasn't come here to see the sights, or even the miracle of the stairs at the chapel of Laredo I have spoken about so often. She has come to see me receive the award for Best Novel. We spend an afternoon strolling the streets, but she is not well. She has difficulty walking and her asthma is fierce.

"Let's go somewhere and relax," my mother tells me. I've told her about a haunted hotel, and she wants to go there. The streets curve around, and we get lost several times before we find the place. I'm worried about my mother, but she keeps her sense of humor. "We just keep driving around and around," she says, "but we're not lost. Look, we've been past that store three times."

We finally find the hotel and are seated in a bar lit with chandeliers and sunlight. "I don't care if it's early afternoon," my mother says. "I'm going to have a glass of wine. This is a celebration," she says. The bartender eyes my mother and it occurs to me that his look is derisive, that he does not want to serve an Indian a drink in his fancy bar. I'm sure my mother is aware of his attitude, too, but she ignores him. We are having a good day, and my mother is happier than I have seen her in a long time.

"This is a beautiful town," my mother tells the bartender, "but we had a hard time finding this place." He grins at her. "Yes," he says, springing at the opportunity to speak his mind, "the joke in Santa Fe is," and he leans forward with his punch line, "the town was designed by a drunken Indian."

He stops laughing when my mother straightens her back, places a sizable tip on the table, and pushes it toward him. His grin is hard now but his eyes look pinched. She stands to leave and the man appears dumbfounded, even a little chagrined. She has left her full glass of wine on the table. The bartender calls out to my mother as we slowly walk out of the bar. "Ma'am," he says, and his voice squeaks. My mother is dignified, regal in her stance. "Thank you," he says, and my mother nods to him. I look at the bartender as we leave, and he appears unmistakably humbled. He has placed his hand over his eyes.

When we get outside, she smiles at me and pats my hand. I recognize then that her action carried more weight than wit and stinging words, more power than any punch. "I've learned it's better," she said, "to kill them with kindness." I loop my arm through my mother's arm, and the sun is so dazzling, my eyes water.

# Is Time on My Side?

*Zoë Fairbairns*

*It's rubbish, of course. I don't believe a word of it.*
*I don't even know why I bothered to look.*
*I only stumbled upon it by chance. I was messing around*
*on the Internet late at night, as you do, and, without really*
*thinking about it, happened to type something into Google.*
*I clicked, ticked a few boxes, and there it was.*

*M*y mother had no time. "I haven't got time," she would wail, as she hurtled around the house from domestic chore to domestic chore, listing all the things she would prefer to be doing, if only she had time.

"I wish I went to the theater more often, but I haven't got time."

"I used to love tennis—wasn't bad at it, either—but these days, where would I find the time?"

"Even if I'd stayed on and got my nursing qualification, I wouldn't be able to use it—I have no time."

Signing cards to old friends at Christmas, she would scribble at the bottom, "We must get together in the new year!" No matter how many times she underlined "must," it never seemed to happen. "Where does all the time go?"

For her, it went to housework. In the England of the 1940s and early '50s, domestic conveniences were in short supply. She had neither a washing machine nor a dishwasher nor a fridge nor use of a car. What she did have was a book on how to run a house. I found it when I was about six. While other little girls were making secret forays into their mothers' bookshelves to uncover forbidden information about sex and childbirth, I got stuck on domestic time management.

The book—which I no longer have, and whose name I have forgotten, but whose sickly-yellow cloth cover I can see with my mind's eye, and whose grim message to womankind is etched on my memory—was aimed at the 1940s woman managing a household "on her own." At first when I saw this phrase, I thought it was a re-proach to me and my sister and our father; it seemed to echo what our mother was always saying about being expected to do every-thing on her own. Only later did it dawn on me that "on her own" meant "without servants."

The book chopped the housewife's day into hour-long and half-hour-long chunks. Each chunk was devoted to some dreary, backbreaking task. Reconstructed from memory, it went something like this:

| | |
|---|---|
| 7:00 AM | Rise; put on fresh housecoat and light makeup. Serve husband tea in bed. Draw his bath. Prepare and serve breakfast, the table having been laid the night before. |
| 8:00 AM | When your husband has left for work, wash breakfast dishes, dry, and put away. Scrub scullery surfaces. |
| 8:30 AM | Open all windows to ventilate house thoroughly. Strip all beds. |
| 9:00 AM | Clean bathroom; put towel, face flannels, and mats in laundry and replace with fresh ones. Scrub and disinfect WC. |
| 9:30 AM | Make beds and tidy bedrooms. Sweep out hearths, refill coal buckets, plan meals for the day, and prepare shopping list. |
| 10:00 AM | Dress smartly, apply light makeup, go shopping. |
| 10:30 AM | Return with shopping and put away. |
| 11:00 AM | Vacuum hall and stairs. |

And so on, and so on. I searched down the list for a moment of peace for the poor housewife but found only this:

| | |
|---|---|
| 2:30 PM | Free time for sewing (unless there are children to see to). |

I didn't know which was worse: the idea that the nearest you got to having free time was being expected to sew, or the realization that even that grudging little respite might be withheld if there were children. Children and free time did not mix. It was our fault, mine and my sister's, that our mother never played tennis; our fault that she had abandoned her nursing career and had lost touch with her old friends. It was our fault that she didn't earn any money and consequently got bossed around by our father, who did.

I asked my mother whether she actually did all those jobs every day. She wept and said, "No, but I ought to. Other women manage; why can't I? Whatever you do, Zoë, don't grow up to be like me."

*I've been told my death date. I Googled "When am I going to die?", ticked a few boxes about my health, heredity, and lifestyle, and now I have the answer. I want to be in control of my time. I've always wanted that.*

The nuns at my school had no time—they had handed it all over to God—and so they urged us not to waste ours. If we had a spare moment, it was probably a sign that whatever we had been doing before, we had not done properly, so we should do it again. Or we should get out our atlases and learn the names of mountains. Or go to the chapel and pray. Stack up those indulgences against the awful day of judgment, when time would become a never-ending *now* of bliss or torment, depending on our behavior in the meantime.

I found a remedy in writing: Writing didn't make time stop, but it took my mind off how fast it was rushing by. And it gave me something to show for all those vanished minutes and hours and weeks and years. In my early teens I read *The Young Writer* by Geoffrey Trease and, following its advice, scoured newspapers, magazines, and the *Writers' and Artists' Yearbook* for opportunities, which I followed up on during my school holidays. From the start I always met deadlines. I took pride in it. If my work wasn't accepted or I didn't win the competition, at least I had met the deadline. If there wasn't a deadline, I set my own, imagining an editor in a green eyeshade, fierce but kind, pacing up and down, waiting for my copy to come in. Behind him (it was always a *him*) on the wall, a big clock ticked.

Deadlines put distance between me and my time-less mother, clattering around downstairs in the kitchen. By now she had a modern cooker, a car, a washing machine, and a fridge; sleek, clean radiators had replaced our dusty, fuel-hungry open fires; but she still had no time. Housework, she explained gloomily, expands to fill the time available. I wondered how she could know that and not do anything about it. I raced back to my room, to my deadlines. *Change typewriter ribbon. Write poem on "Forgetfulness" for* Elizabethan *magazine. Two carbons. Send in by 30th. Write advertising slogans for Kattomeat (5th) and Pure Gold cigarettes (25th). Work on novel.*

When reading, I always seemed to end up with stories of women trapped by domesticity: Andrea Newman's *The Cage,* Radclyffe Hall's *The Unlit Lamp,* and Henry James's *Portrait of a Lady* all made me shiver. I identified strongly with Esther Greenwood, protagonist of Sylvia Plath's novel *The Bell Jar,* who, when her mother suggests in midafternoon that her frantically typing daughter might like to get dressed, replies, "I'm writing a novel. I haven't got time to change into this and out of that."[1] I shared Esther's sense of urgency. It was only later that I found out that her creator had committed suicide.

*You have to take these websites with a pinch of salt. They're a bit of a cynical exercise, put there by people who have a vested interest in depressing us with thoughts of mortality. They then sell us products to help us cope: funeral plans, gym memberships, eternal salvation, home equity release plans. They have to be bogus: Even if they do know your death date, it stands to reason that they're not going to tell you. The profitability of their enterprises depends on that uncertainty.*

*But since you ask—it's April 3, 2033.*

*Not bad, eh? Twenty-six years to go.*

*On the day I die, I will be eighty-five and one-quarter years old.*

In the late 1960s and early '70s, women's liberation burst into my consciousness, telling me that I was not alone in my perception that women didn't have time because they were required to give it to other people. In *The Feminine Mystique,* Betty Friedan noted that many modern American housewives were spending more time on housework than their mothers had. So-called "labor-saving" appliances were not lightening their burdens but adding to them.

The home freezer, simply by existing, takes up time: Beans, raised in the garden, must be prepared for freezing. If you have an electric mixer, you have to use it: Those elaborate recipes with the puréed chestnuts, watercress, and almonds take longer to prepare than broiling lamb chops.[2]

Was that the answer, then? Don't have an electric mixer and don't grow your own beans? That might have been okay for Friedan's American housewives, but on my side of the Atlantic, women were calling for revolution. Wages for Housework campaigner Silvia Federici theorized that capital had created the housewife for specific purposes of its own, i.e., to keep the male worker physically and emotionally healthy so that he could better endure the work and social relations that capital had reserved for him. . . . Despite these circumstances, women had always found ways of fighting back, but often in an isolated and privatized manner. The problem, then, became how to bring this struggle out of the bedroom and the kitchen, and into the streets.[3]

I wasn't sure about taking to the streets. I didn't have time to take to the streets. What was the point of following Virginia Woolf's advice to women writers to claim a room of our own if we were never allowed to go there? Accusations of bourgeois individualism were muttered when I snuck off early from meetings or missed demonstrations, but I thought novels, short stories, and poems could revolutionize the world just as effectively as taking to the streets could.

There was a war on, and the spoils of the war were women's time. Men wanted to take it from us and turn it into wealth and freedom— their wealth and freedom. It was up to us to hang on to it.

*Twenty-six years to go. Not bad, not bad at all. Twenty-six years is a lifetime for some. A life sentence for others. A judge sentencing a violent criminal to a long term once said, "Your parole officer isn't even born yet." As a remark intended to bring home to the culprit the seriousness of his situation, it could hardly have been bettered. But I get quite a buzz from the idea that the clerk who is going to issue my death certificate has not only to be born, but to go through all the business of infancy and childhood, education and career choices, before he or she gets to me.*

I mean, I would get a buzz if I believed it, which I don't.

Writing. Political activism. Looking at websites. Disbelieving what they say. These are just some of the strategies I have employed to try to keep control of my time. Another has been to not have children. If people ask me why I haven't got any—and I don't mind their asking, as long as they don't mind my asking why they have so many, or so few—I just say, "I've never wanted to."

I don't say, "I haven't had time to have children." Perhaps I should. I'm always running into people who could write a book but have never had the time. They mean, *I'd like the fun part of being an author, but there's no way I'm going to take on all that work and worry and heartache, all those demands on my time. I wouldn't dare.* That's how it's been with motherhood and me.

I resented my children, and I didn't even have any. I thought they would steal my time. I tried to disguise the pity I felt when my women friends had their first babies, and my mixture of exasperation and amazement when they had their second. Could they have forgotten so soon what a ghastly ordeal it had been for them looking after the first, the restrictions having a tiny baby placed on their time? I hadn't forgotten; I had heard all about it *from them:* the impossible juggling acts needed to keep a career going, the glass ceiling, the fact that they couldn't even go to the loo or have a bath in peace, let alone read a book or write one. These things used to make them cry and rage, yet here they were, volunteering for a repeat performance. There were times when I wondered whether my role in the life of some of my friends who were mothers was to act as a repository for their resentment, looking after it for them (and writing about it—there are an awful lot of furious mothers in my fiction) so that they could forget about it and have another baby.

Glad to have been of service. But these days, like the aspiring author who fancies going straight from the blank page to the Booker Prize without the messy bit in between, I start to regret the fact that I will not spend my twilight years, all twenty-six of them, surrounded by grandchildren. I rerun the mental video of my life to see if I could perhaps have squeezed in a pregnancy or two and, if so, when? My twenties, when my partner and I were probably super-fertile (not that we ever put it to the test)? Impossible; we lived in a tiny rented flat and had no money.

In my thirties, when my first big international paperback deal brought me hitherto-unimagined wealth? No, because it also brought with it a stream of commissions, travel opportunities, speaking engagements, fellowships, courses to teach, projects to get involved with—all of which were much more satisfying ways to fill my time than dragging some baby around. My forties, when the razzmatazz died down and left me with writer's block? No, I was much too depressed, and I had to look for other ways of making a living. Other ways to sell my time.

I get up at 6:30 AM and make a ninety-minute journey to a trading estate on the outskirts of London, where I sit at a workstation for ten hours and fifteen minutes (including one hour off for lunch, unpaid), watching TV. I watch films and documentaries, game shows and makeovers, election broadcasts, soap operas, *Jerry Springer*, whatever I am given. I listen through headphones to dialogue and sound effects, and write everything I hear into a computer. I then edit the words into captions, for the benefit of deaf people who want to watch the program.

I'm a subtitler. It's the perfect geeky job for a writer who needs a second income, and for someone who likes to keep an eye on time. Time matters in subtitling. You think about it constantly. You have to. The average deaf adult reads at a speed of 900 characters per minute. For children's programs, it's 690. If the people in the program talk faster than that (and on *Jerry Springer* they talk faster than you would believe, and they all talk at once—you have to unravel it), you'll end up with too much text on the screen. A red light flashes, warning you to edit. Meanwhile, a spreadsheet is keeping track of whether you are achieving your required productivity total. If not, you'd better speed up. There are fluent English–speaking graduates in call centers in India who would be only too happy to replace you at one-third the wage. Just when you are building up a head of steam, *ping!* The machine disables itself. It's a health and safety break, during which you're supposed to perform a series of exercises, as demonstrated by a character on the screen. If you don't, a message pops up: "Think how much you value the use of healthy hands. Are you sure you want to skip your break?" Shamefaced, you go back to wiggling your fingers, as instructed by the software, but by now you are falling behind on your productivity figures again, figures that are checked every month by management and drawn to your attention at your annual appraisal.

And so the person who once shuddered at the drudgery of housework, who dreamed of taking control of her own time, the person who thinks she knows her own death date, is at the mercy of a machine that numbers her seconds, sets them against her keystrokes, flashes red lights at her when it thinks her sentences are too long, and even tells her when she ought to be feeling tired.

So do I hate it? Actually, no. It's worthwhile work. Some of the programs are well made and enjoyable to work on. It's a privilege to be able to contribute to making them accessible to people with hearing impairments. And even when the programs are terrible, an important access issue is at stake: Why shouldn't deaf people watch bad TV if they want to, just like everybody else? The wages are okay—three shifts per week cover my basic needs—and the rest of the time I can write. My coworkers come from interesting backgrounds: We've got a stained-glass-window maker, a film critic, a neurolinguistic programming consultant, a suicide-prevention counselor, and any number of writers. The pressures of the workday can be stressful, but they can be soothing, too, if only in contrast with the unstructured blank of the freelance day. (Many writers dread the blank page; I have a much stronger fear of the unproductive hour.) I can't write full-time anymore; I can't afford to, and anyway I don't have enough material. As a subtitler, I work with someone else's material, and someone else pays me for my time.

In a recent article in the London *Observer* on the subject of cryogenics—postponing death by freezing cadavers to await resurrection—Peter Conrad wrote: "The Greeks saw human beings as creatures defined by their mortality, which is why they invented tragedy. Gods do not need to die, and animals do so without knowing about it in advance; it is the special prerogative and the demoralizing curse of our species to spend life in anticipation of an end."[4]

I don't know anyone who's planning to have their body frozen, but I do know people who are taking this "anticipation of an end" very seriously indeed. They're easing themselves out of their jobs by way of part-time hours; they're setting up retirement communities; they're adapting their homes to accommodate disabilities they don't suffer from. They're signing over their homes to their children to avoid nursing-home fees; they're marrying or entering into civil partnerships to avoid death duties. On the other hand, I've got other friends of the same age who are still wondering what they're going to be when they grow up.

I'm in the middle. The knowledge that I've got twenty-six years to go, according to some life-assurance table of averages, is not, I must finally admit, much help. What use are averages when your life has become like a version of that movie in which a couple on a diving holiday suddenly find themselves marooned in the middle of the sea? In my version, it's more like I'm going swimming with a group of my friends and it's all very nice and sunny and the sea is blue and the swimming is easy enough and we chat and have fun, only every so often, one of my friends disappears. Sometimes they struggle a bit, sometimes they just go, but the result is the same: I've got one fewer friend. The shark got them, and the shark is circling. We can't see it, but we know it's there. There are still plenty of us left to enjoy the water, the sky, the swooping seagulls, but whoops, there goes another one.

And then what? Well, your guess is as good as mine. All we have are guesses—religion is a guess, as is atheism. I am more convinced by the secular argument that, since this material world is the only one of which we can have knowledge, the only worthwhile morality is one that makes the world a better place for the people living in it. And the only important judgment is: Did we, in however small a way, do that? Which doesn't make the idea of eternal damnation—or eternal anything, for that matter—any less frightening. I have no more wish to contemplate the beatific vision for all eternity than I have to be cast into the fiery furnace.

At least in the fiery furnace you can rebel. Whoever built it is clearly a sadistic bully, but sadistic bullies can sometimes be outwitted and usually end up being overthrown. I have confidence that we the human race will, if necessary, do that. It may take a while, but it will give us something to aim for, something to occupy our time.

But what if there is nothing? What if it's just eternal consciousness, with no time, no deadlines, no performance targets, no beginnings or ends, nothing to suffer from, nothing to enjoy? That's what worries me. I mean, what could be worse for a person who always wanted to keep control of her time—a person who wouldn't even perform a simple basic animal function like reproduction for fear of losing that control—than to find herself plunged into unlimited quantities of the stuff?

Yet I've got a few plans. There's a cottage by the sea that I always meant to live in. I might spend a couple of million years there, waiting for the cliff to crumble. And I'm prepared to take a bet that as long as there are human beings living on Earth, there will be a city of some kind in the place we now call London. I've lived here for most of my life, but I haven't begun to explore it properly. How about one street every thousand years? I can drift into every house, examine its structure, learn its history, listen to the story of everyone who ever lived there, then move on. If mortality is unmanageable, eternity is worse. We'll have to find a solution. We'll have to start practicing. I'm starting now, while I still have time.

## Footnotes:

1. Sylvia Plath. *The Bell Jar* (London: Faber & Faber, 1963), 127.

2. Betty Friedan. *The Feminine Mystique* (London: Gollancz, 1965), 241.

3. Silvia Federici. "Wages Against Housework." In *The Politics of Housework,* ed. Ellen Malos (London: Allison & Busby, 1980), 256.

4. Peter Conrad. "Wake Me Up in a Hundred Years," the *Observer,* Review section, 21 January 2007, 23.

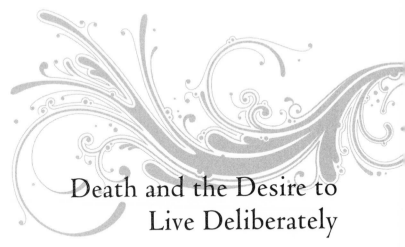

# Death and the Desire to Live Deliberately

*Maggie Bucholt*

*M*y friend Annie and I sat in a darkened movie theater, eating the last of the chocolate Ferrero Rochers and watching the closing credits of *Lantana*, an award-winning Australian film. Annie and I loved a night out at the movies, especially seeing independent films that depicted richly developed characters, as a novel would. Slumped in our seats, our heads resting on the backs, we talked about the film as the lights flickered on.

Annie gazed over at me with a satisfied expression. "You know what I liked about all the characters?" she asked. "They were complex."

I nodded. The film was billed as a sophisticated thriller, but it was actually about the inexplicable actions of people who are faced with stressful challenges and hard choices in love and life.

A few months later, at age fifty, Annie, a soft-spoken woman who collected Green Man motifs and was a fan of strawberry-rhubarb pie and Dunkin' Donuts coffee, was faced with just such a challenge when she was diagnosed with Stage 4 colon cancer; the disease had spread to some of her lymph nodes. She underwent immediate surgery and, miraculously, did not need a colostomy. I wept when I heard the news, knowing the survival rate for colon cancer, the second leading cause of cancer deaths, is one of the lowest. Annie was diagnosed long before Katie Couric lost her husband to the disease within a few short months and began her campaign to make "colonoscopy" a household word.

In the five years that followed, Annie endured two more major surgeries (a complete hysterectomy and removal of portions of the large and small intestines); three rounds of debilitating chemotherapy that caused hair loss, violent diarrhea, and fatigue, as well as numb hands that forced her to wear gloves in the middle of summer; and innumerable trips to the emergency room for serious blood clots, once on her lung, another time on her liver. I remember her bravery and determination, but I also recall her moments of despair, and the dangerous game of denial that she played. Finally, though, I remember her tranquility on the day she died, after having fought the good fight.

What happens the moment you die? Is there an afterlife? Annie and I had talked about it, prior to her illness. We'd discussed the twenty-one-grams conundrum, that miniscule amount of weight that the human body supposedly loses at the moment of death. Was it your soul escaping from your body, or your body's energy being discharged? How would we ever know? It seemed destined to remain one of life's great mysteries.

Another of those mysteries is how we, as individuals, will approach our own deaths. Can we predict with any certainty whether life's complexities will affect the way we react and the decisions we make in this regard? Because I was witnessing my friend's struggle with that very question, I found Annie's long end-of-life journey very compelling. Disturbing, yes, because she was my friend and I adored her. But it was about more than just my emotional attachment to her; by necessity, her struggle made me wonder how I would handle myself in the same situation.

Throughout the five years of her illness, Annie's quiet courage was intriguing and inspiring. Her illness and subsequent death filled me with sadness, of course, yet they fascinated me, too. I'd never had intimate conversations about living and dying with someone who hovered between the two, and I needed to make sense of what had happened, and what was happening, while it happened: the mystery and misery of death and this wondrous thing we call life.

I was hopeful after Annie's first round of chemo and, at times, fiercely defensive when anyone said Annie would die, or that she might last only a few years. Complete remission was not unheard of, I argued. And Annie was a fighter. In truth, I was stunned by Annie's diagnosis, and by the fact that the illness had hit someone so seemingly healthy, someone I knew and loved. I felt vulnerable, too, especially when the cancer returned; I was haunted by those insensitive comments from friends that Annie was dying. I knew that if Annie could be afflicted by cancer, it could happen to me, and the thought was sobering. Although I've been fortunate to enjoy good health thus far, I kept wondering, *How would I react if I were in Annie's shoes?* Often, I fell into "what if" mode and stopped during a particularly hectic workday to do something enjoyable and to take stock of myself, my life, all the while thinking about Annie, how she was coping so admirably. I began acknowledging the pleasures in my own life—my husband, my children, my work—on a regular basis. If I were given Annie's prognosis, I knew somehow that I wouldn't take to my bed and ruminate over my spoiled, too-short existence, but would I have the courage to push back and squeeze every drop of living out of the days that remained, the way Annie was doing? I realized not only that I admired Annie, but that I too wanted her inner strength, which allowed her to continue living a fulfilling life.

From the beginning, Annie spoke freely about treatments, about the antidepressant pills and sessions with a psychologist that helped her cope. Although she wasn't self-righteous or saintly, thankfully, the occasional bouts of snappishness that erupted in the early years of her illness were brief. Frankly, they made me uncomfortable; they seemed so unlike Annie. At the same time, I could understand what triggered the outbursts, and how difficult it must have been for her to confront her feelings of helplessness, the sense that she had lost control over her life.

She wasn't always forthcoming when I asked how she was, and I understood that, too. I wasn't her closest friend, and in the middle of her illness, my husband and I moved an hour and a half away; but whenever I was in Boston, I accepted her invitation to visit, although it was only during her "off" weeks of chemo, when she was feeling better.

It wasn't until after the second unexpected surgery that Annie's attitude changed remarkably. Prior to the surgery, the cancer had been in remission. Seeing her strangely swollen stomach, I realized the illness had returned and she was in denial about it. During dinner at our house, I experienced moments of horror and helplessness when she insisted calmly that it couldn't be cancer again; she was cancer-*free*—the doctors had said so. A few days later, Annie's husband, John, called to say that Annie had been admitted to the hospital for emergency surgery to have two large tumors removed. I went to see her, bringing her a book, *Embers,* by Sándor Márai, a forgotten Hungarian novelist, that I knew she'd enjoy.

Annie was awake when I got to her room; I kissed her dry cheek and hugged her, mindful of the IV tube connected to a port just below her collar bone. She smelled of fragrant shampoo and soap, not the usual hospital standard, and her cropped auburn hair—she hadn't lost it yet—was freshly washed and blown dry. She didn't look ill; she looked refreshed and was in excellent spirits—serene, I realized later.

I pulled a floral print–upholstered chair closer to the side of the bed and gave her the thin volume I'd brought. She smiled and expressed her pleasure as she placed the book on the pile by her bed. She told me that I could order room service if I was hungry. Room service! We laughed; she showed me the menu, which included an entrée of fettuccini pesto with vegetables. "Too bad I can't have solid food yet," she said. She talked about how much she liked her surgeon, a woman with three children, whom Annie affectionately referred to as "Wonder Woman" for having removed the two tumors—one as big as a grapefruit, the other a cantaloupe—along with her uterus and ovaries. She paused. "She says they think they got everything."

Annie also explained how aggressive her type of colon cancer was, how she'd have to have a different, stronger kind of chemotherapy.

She folded back the cuffs on her pajama sleeves one at a time, slowly. "You know, right, that I'll be on the chemo indefinitely?"

I knew, and I tried to keep my eyes from welling up.

But her smile was radiant. "I know it sounds dismal. But everyone has to die sometime." She gazed out the picture window, above the sprays of pink, purple, and white bouquets on the sill. "Today, though, is a good day. You know me, how I hate getting out of bed in the morning." She turned to me, her eyebrows knitting in a thoughtful way. "Well, yesterday I was up at dawn. Right from here"—she patted the white bedding—"I could see the sky out that window. Pink and gray. Beautiful, just beautiful."

And then Annie, being Annie, swung her legs over the side of the bed, her IV tubes hanging from the port in her neck, her feet searching for her slippers. She walked several times a day, she said—doctor's orders. She took my arm.

"How far do you go?" I asked as we walked and I pulled her IV stand. The hall made a complete circle around the elevators.

"All the way around."

Thoreau encouraged us "to live deliberately," and after that second surgery, when she finally accepted that the illness might not be conquerable, Annie did just that. Compelled by her strong ideals, she took back control of her life and began volunteering with hospice.

Although her husband expressed his misgivings, Annie's will prevailed. My admiration for her increased. Twice a week she drove to the local hospice to prepare breakfast for those who were ill and dying and had no one else to care for them; she accompanied patients who were well enough on errands, or just sat with the ones who weren't and held their hands. After undergoing training, she went to individual homes to relieve round-the-clock caregivers, one of whom was a grateful fifty-year-old woman who'd quit her job to stay with her dying mother, a woman who spoke only Portuguese. The language barrier didn't deter Annie, who stopped volunteering only when she was too ill to continue.

I knew Annie chose hospice work as a way to nourish her spirituality, her soul, and perhaps in a way to prepare herself for her own death. She shared how she'd discussed her need to do good with her family's Zen master. The spiritual counselor had married Annie and John in a Buddhist ceremony, a fact I hadn't known before her illness. During our conversations, she told me many things I hadn't known about her, but the one thing she didn't say was how she felt the illness was compressing her life.

About five months before Annie died, we had lunch in Harvard Square. Distressed by her paleness and by how impossibly thin she looked, I asked Annie how she was feeling. It had been a year since she'd had her third surgery, which removed more tumors and more of her bowel. Since that time, she'd been taking bevacizumab, a promising anti-angiogenic agent (a cancer drug that cuts off the blood supply to tumors), along with her latest rounds of chemotherapy. It was an abnormally warm spring day, and we sat on white plastic chairs at a small table at the crowded restaurant, where we split an enormous sandwich. Annie's half sat untouched on her paper plate.

"There's nothing more they can do for me," she said in her matter-of-fact way. She stirred her iced tea with a straw. The cancer, she said, had metastasized to her liver and one lung. Then she talked about her doctors, how grateful she was for the surgeries and the cancer-fighting drugs that had prolonged her life.

I saw Annie four more times after that; twice Annie and John visited us together, the second time for a dinner party my husband and I had for our anniversary. Her body was emaciated but her eyes were bright. The third time, about a month before she passed away, I had a business meeting in Boston and stopped by to see her.

That day in September, shafts of sunlight filled the living room where we sat; we talked about books, films we wanted to see, and the state of the war in Iraq, which she vehemently opposed. She showed me a new sweater and vest she'd bought. Then Annie made us coffee. The painkillers, she explained, made her sleepy, and she was no longer able to stay awake in the afternoons—or to drive safely. A neighbor was on call in case of emergency while John was at work. She had decided to enter a clinical trial for a promising cancer drug, not only to extend her life, but with the hope that the drug might be of help to others. Still, she spoke of traveling to Glasgow; Annie prided herself on her Scottish roots. I had misgivings about such a long trip, given her condition, but I didn't share them with her after seeing the determination in her eyes. She said her current goals were to travel to Scotland with her son and husband to visit their daughter, who was participating in a Glasgow exchange program, and then, back in Boston, to see her son graduate from college. She made it overseas but died shortly after returning from Glasgow.

On a Sunday in mid-October, my husband and I visited Annie, knowing that it would be for the last time. I went into the bedroom, where a few weeks earlier she'd shown me the sweater and vest she'd bought, to say goodbye. I was unprepared—shocked, really—to see how her body had diminished in less than a month. The pain medication was no longer doing its job, and she moaned softly. I held her thin, cold hand in my own, and told her I loved her. Another friend, sitting on a bedside chair, gave her an eyedropper full of water, and we exchanged stricken glances. "I love you," I said again, my voice tremulous, and the corners of Annie's mouth turned up for the briefest instant.

I've spent a long time thinking about the choices Annie made in my own attempts to sort through my still-raw grief. Sometimes I wake in the middle of the night and remember the long, at times painful, process Annie had to endure, and I'm saddened by her too-short life. She was not one of the so-called "lucky ones" who succumbed instantly, to a heart attack or an accident. For five years, she knew what would eventually claim her life, and at times she undoubtedly suffered not only physically but emotionally as well, knowing she'd never see her children married or be a grandmother. She could have reacted differently to her plight, become an angry, embittered woman, and let those feelings tarnish the few years she had left. She didn't. She never let her illness dictate the quality of her life or her outlook. In the end, she died in her own home and, with the help of hospice, on her own terms.

I have always had a "living will," also known as a healthcare proxy, a notarized document stipulating that when I can no longer make medical decisions about my own future, I do not want to be kept alive by artificial means. My husband and I have had many conversations about the way we want to die, and seeing Annie that last day, surrounded by her family and close friends, reaffirmed our convictions that she had chosen the best way. Compassionate and caring, they took turns by Annie's bedside. In the two days prior, many others came to say goodbye; a mutual friend described those visits as a "lovefest." The strong painkillers had made Annie's words barely decipherable, but she was delighted with her friends' presence and insisted on moving from her bedroom into the larger living room, where she was encircled by those who loved her.

When I remember Annie, I think about her composure and courage and the way she embraced death. She didn't dwell on her limited future. She marched into each day with an inner fortitude that I can only aspire to emulate. I think of her resolve, which allowed her to master the art of dying with grace, and to compress the physical act of leaving this earth into only a few days. Annie didn't take five years to die; during that time she was deeply committed to living, and to living her life to the fullest, up until the end, when she was unable to do so. As Thoreau said in the days before he died, "One world at a time."

Throughout the indignities of surgery, hospitalization, and treatment, Annie never lost her compassion, her humility, her joie de vivre, her love for her husband, her children, her friends. She shined a bright light on a meaningful path, and died with the strength and courage that I desire for my own end-of-life journey.

# No Other Medicine but Hope

*Myra Goldberg*

# 1.

I lived on or off desire until I was thirty-seven. The desire to explore the world, to know myself, to understand other people, to write a book like *Pride and Prejudice*, to be someone like me but without my faults, to be someone entirely different, to love and be loved. To have all the sex I wanted. To be worldly (also unflappable and not constantly surprised by life), to have patience, to be someone people could count on, to be able to count on myself. To know how to make decisions. To be honest, even wise. To have better hair. And, alas, undermining all the rest, to be right all the time.

By middle age, I had acquired some versions of the items on my desire list. The trade-off for acquiring these items was that I had to give up being right all the time, which was not as hard as it might have been—being right all the time makes you wrong a lot, which is embarrassing.

Without the energy and ambition of desire, I would not have found love. Without love, I wouldn't have had a path to travel or a reason to practice hope and its larger cousin, faith. Faith, hope, charity (sometimes translated as love) were not strangers to everyone else in the world, but they were new to me.

I stopped living off desire when I was thirty-seven, because the man I lived with and loved had open-heart surgery and came out of the hospital determined to live exactly as before. This meant living on a sailboat and eating and sleeping irregularly, drinking too much, and doing any drugs offered by his rock'n' roll friends. If he acted too young to die, maybe he'd *be* too young too die.

My desire for Louie to take up the burden of his mortality, swallow his medicines, and change his lifestyle didn't help. Finding more communicative doctors and a therapist he liked didn't help much, either, but they were a start.

Those things were doable, which is one prerequisite for hope or hopefulness.

We moved so that we could live on land, as Louie put it, which was a little healthier than life on the boat, since there were food stores and we had heat and hot water. Still, I would get calls from Louie's job, where he hadn't showed up, from the tax collectors about the boat. There was a night with no calls; Louie was in jail. He crashed the car twice. He missed doctor and therapy appointments. My desire for him to stay healthy could not substitute for his desire to not notice that he was sick.

I felt hopeless. I got the flu. It rained in Oakland every day, all day. Our shower grew mold. My brother, Louie's best friend, had recently had a baby and didn't want to hear about our troubles. My cousin told me I sounded suicidal over the phone, which gave me an excuse to give up and go back to New York, where, still worried, I checked with my internist about Louie's condition. The internist gave him five years, more or less, if he kept drinking. I thought about taking him to Greece (based on Keats's idea, in "Ode to a Nightingale," of tragic death in a "beaker full of the warm South"). Instead, I checked in with my sense of responsibility. Louie had a doctor, a therapist, and an apartment, due in no small part to my efforts. He had friends and a job, due to his own charm, wit, intelligence, and lovability.

Years after he was told to stop drinking, my brother, Louie's new girlfriend, and Louie's other friends told him they would stop seeing him if he didn't get sober. Louie began attending the Oakland lesbian bikers' chapter of AA, where they know something about despair, and offered hope as a series of small acts. Maybe his own desire to live had checked in by then. Maybe the threat of losing his whole world moved him as my leaving him had not. Now, twenty-six years and a few AA chapters later, Louie lives in California, a sober, responsible, loving, and funny grandfather, who, even after a second heart surgery, takes good care of himself. I'm in New York, the occasionally demoralized single mother of a teen, who learned at thirty-seven that desire for something is a way to get started, but that it can't itself make things better. Had Louie not loved his life and his friends—or had his friends not loved him—he would not still be living.

While desire often burns brighter for being frustrated, hope can be *practiced*. Wash the dishes or make a call when you're feeling hopeless, and you'll start to feel a little more buoyant. Being hopeless, or acknowledging your powerlessness to bring your desire to bear on the world, can be the beginning of learning how to practice hope.

These days, my teenage daughter requires not just the daily practice of doing what is doable (which I call hope), but faith, too, meaning long-term hope, often in things unseen. I have faith that my daughter's gifts and good sense will bring her a life she loves, although at times her daily life can cause me to despair.

And neither faith nor hope is possible without love, because who would go to the trouble of practicing either for someone, or something, they don't love? The road is made by walking, says the African proverb, but the trip through the woods is based on love.

# 2.

At Space for Grace, first people eat. Canned soup and white bread. Most of the eating gets done by people who are really hungry, because the food is only okay. Someone always sings a gospel song after the food; the singer, usually female, is always breathtaking. Then we all sing a few hymns and listen to a list of things to do that week—meetings, services, food pantries, clothes to sort. And this is followed by a very short sermon. It is Wednesday. Midway through the work week. People have been fed, moved by the human voice, handed a few things to do. They have sung and they have listened to a little wisdom.

Now we reach the heart of the evening. People stand and talk. Some raise their hand to catch the spirit. They talk about sick mothers, sons in prison, their search for a job, a big exam they're preparing for. There is a prayer team to pray for these folks, and the rest of us, who pray less professionally. We are black, white, from the neighborhood, from out of town, well heeled, doing okay, poor. Most of the people speaking are African American, because this is essentially an African American Baptist prayer meeting and they know the ropes. But it matters that we're a mixed bunch, because we are reaching toward the root of what's human.

The end of this invariant Wednesday evening is an invariant song: "I feel like going on. I feel like going on. Though trials comes on every hand, I feel like going on."

I believe in religion like this, the process we've followed and the path it puts us on. I believe in its wisdom about fellowship and trouble and hope, although I don't believe in God and I am too Jewish to feel comfortable with Jesus.

This service, repeated every week, leads you to hope, and repeated, week after week, to faith, the safety net of hope, the sense that you are held in a web that will hold even as you stumble.

## *3.*

Hope can come from acting. And action can come from hope.

Hope, said someone about the administration's approach to Iraq, is not a plan.

True enough, our president seems more like head cheerleader than leader. But hope might lead you to planning. And you might have a plan that could lead you to hope.

# 4.

My mother, resilient by nature, is prone to hopelessness. Once, under the influence of a cortizone shot, she spoke of sitting in the car with the motor on and the garage door shut. I was eleven or so. After that, I got nauseated in the garage—as well as in the car. I learned to drive with great difficulty, late in life, although I grew to like it. I was offended by my mother's hopelessness when I was young because it scared me, and I still react badly to people who carry on about what seem like pebbles in their path. But I have also noticed that an absence of hopelessness, grief, or despair can lead to getting stuck. A cheerful stuckness permeates our public dialogue these days.

"Back to you, John," says the news anchor, after reporting on seventy-three people blown up by a car bomb in Baghdad. Our public discussions tend toward the factual or technical. Were there or were there not weapons of mass destruction? Can we get a resolution from the UN that will legitimize our invasion? How many troops do we need? Are our interests at stake? What we don't do publicly is ask whether we have the right to kill people just because they have a leader nobody likes. It takes a long time, in this climate, to ask aloud if we should come home or settle into dying and killing because we've come such a long way at such cost, and it's embarrassing to have been wrong.

Something about our public dialogue isn't simple enough.

In 1964, according to *The New York Times,* Lyndon Johnson said on tape that he knew the war in Vietnam was pointless, but that he was afraid he'd be impeached if he withdrew.

Impeachment is not a death sentence, although it is a gigantic embarrassment. Still, the war ended in 1975, many, many lives later.

The wish to be right all the time, removed, lets in the knowledge that you are wrong, which lets in despair. Still, without despair, you can't stop doing the same thing over and over. And you can't be hopeful doing the same thing over and over.

We are, as a people (in public matters, anyway), cheerful, rather than hopeful, foolishly optimistic on the one hand, and foolishly pessimistic on the other. We see the world—ourselves and our enemies—as existing in a fixed state, rather than a fluid one. Hope asks you to try things, then to see where you've landed. It doesn't assume that anything is necessarily the end of the story. And though many things are unendurable, most *aren't.* Our public discussions, for example, consider defeat worse than murder. But defeat, met on a road with other travelers, can be endured, and if one can feel like going on, win, lose, or draw, at prayer meetings, we can go on from our debacle in Iraq. The content of the faith that hope offers is that victory is not the only prize. The prize is the practice of making things better, and the hopeful feelings that arise from that practice. So I wash dishes instead of leaving them in the sink, send money to Amnesty International, apologize to someone, meet my elusive teen for tea. Wear a button: STILL AGAINST WAR.

# *5.*

So if hope has little or nothing to do with outcomes, we are not hopeful as a way to make something desirable happen. What happens in this world is only a little about our hopes and desires, our strategies, tactics, or processes. We hope because hope is a way to carry ourselves through a life that holds many possible outcomes and many people, their desires, tactics, hopes. As the *Bhagavad Gita* says, do the next right thing, regardless of outcome. That means speaking in a clear, rather than cutting, way to your teen who has signed your name on her absence slip. Or giving a good tip. Or smiling, as my friend says, at the thought of your troubles, then letting your smile lead you to another state of feeling. Hope is not an answer, a question, a solution, or a way to victory. But it makes you a good companion for yourself and for others (hopefully) to travel with. It keeps you traveling, rather than dug in.

This is my life, my friend said after her daughter fell ill. She told me that, for a while, she waited for her real life to return to her: when her daughter would be well again. Now she saw that everything that happened to her was her life. Her daughter was on her own schedule, not my friend's.

Hope rests on the idea that the bad things that happen to you (or your lover or your country) are as real and need to be dealt with as much as the good things. Hope assumes that your trouble can be dealt with, if not conquered, but not without seeing where you went wrong.

Work with it, said the barrista at Starbucks about my bum knee.

My mother, at ninety-five, has had enough life, she says. I think she's right. She's exhausted. Sleeps most of the day. Still, if you tell her a funny story and you talk loud enough for her to catch your drift, she laughs.

If you Google "faith, hope, charity," you can find Corinthian ringtones for your cell phone or order meaningful Christian tees. You can also learn about a rhythm and blues group called *Faith, Hope, and Charity*, formed in 1969 in Tampa, then disbanded in 1979 with their last hit: "Don't Pity Me." Charity, notes the note, can be translated as love.

# Desirelessness:
# The Greatest Desire

*Melissa Pritchard*

*T*hree hundred million children under age eighteen suffer from hunger worldwide. Three hundred million is the entire population of the United States.

Every five seconds, a child dies of hunger on our planet. Hundreds have died while I've written this essay.

There are 15 million orphans in sub-Saharan Africa, their fathers and mothers dead of HIV/AIDS.

The U.S. estimated budget for the war in Iraq, in 2007, is $110 billion.

The suffering of millions of children would be alleviated by just $3 billion in food aid.

Another sixty children, our brothers and sisters, have just died, unfed.

Life goes by quickly, much of it spent in service to desire or to the consequence of desire. Wanting seems endless, fulfillment elusive. All great religions, all paths of spirituality, all great myths, folktales, stories teach this, yet we resist. I resist. I desire. I want. I ache for the mercurial, miragelike nature of the thing, person, or ideal pursued.

The first thing I remember desiring obsessively was a bicycle for Christmas. I was nine or ten and for weeks had asked and asked, begged piteously, for a bicycle. On Christmas morning, there it was: an elegant, cream-colored bicycle, with navy pinstriping, under the tree. But it was for my sister.

I was a middle-class child of the suburbs; the next thing I remember desiring passionately was a horse. For several Christmases in a row, from ages eleven to thirteen, I pleaded, cajoled, wept for a horse. And, sure enough, one Christmas morning, there was a horse under the tree. A horse made of ceramic. A toy equine, my parents' way of telling me they could not, would not, afford the real thing.

Those were my earliest remembered lessons in the uneven equation between desire and fulfillment. Cruel to discover that the intensity of my longing, the aggressiveness of my pursuit, the stubbornness of my asking did not guarantee attainment. The world, it seemed, was not in service to my desires.

By thirteen, I had entered the sorrow of desiring persons. My desires went forth, weak but stubborn bolts of fire, toward a certain girl, or a certain boy, a form of wanting that was to last decades. I desire someone now, even as I write this, and not much differently from the neighborhood boy I desired and dreamed of at thirteen. The lesson of eros is vulnerability, the potential for rejection, for humiliation, for one's desire sitting heavily upon the heart, unlived, unmet, unwanted by the other.

The French poet, philosopher, and activist Simone Weil, a contemporary and friend of writer and French Resistance fighter Albert Camus, once said that the great human question was "Why am I being harmed?" Albert Einstein said the single great question to ask is if the universe is friendly. Benign. Wishing no harm. Desire's relation to harmfulness is complex, combustive, riddlesome.

So desire can move from a child's simple wish for a bicycle or a horse to an adolescent's yearning for love and symbiosis with another to an adult's wish for a spouse or heart's companion, for a child, a family, a career, achievement, measurable success. And even beyond these are the universal human desires for freedom, creation, beauty, pleasure, and ease, for dignified work and a sense of purpose.

Yet the greatest spiritual teachers, faithed or uncreeded, point to a blissful state of being beyond these innocent, even biologically inspired desires. . . . They point to a state of desirelessness supported by the practice of surrender to something greater than oneself, call it Creator, Great Mystery, Divine Being, God.

As a child, I found learning to swim frightening. I resisted the first lesson—floating. When at last, with paralyzing terror, I surrendered myself to the power of water, hoping it would bear me up, support my little weight, I was amazed. I think of surrendering to God as a similar sensation, more psychical than physical.

Yet there is often a residual resistance, a sense that I know what is best for myself, a suggestion that my multiple desires might form an essential map leading to authentic self-realization. I stumble on paradox, contradiction. Do I trust my desires from moment to moment, accepting that if they are not met, I was not intended to have them? The Western mind is said to be more aggressive in the pursuit of desire, the Eastern mind more accepting of "flow." Which is best? How are we to live within the condition of fluctuating desires, from the most basic to the noblest? And in the pantheon of infinite desires, from a bicycle to a soul mate, to a community of family and friends, to success in realizing one's talents and gifts, to the purchase of a particular pair of shoes or a coveted book, which are best to focus on? When is desire greed and desirelessness martyrdom?

The great sages, gods, and goddesses, the myth-tellers, speak in lofty abstractions, in conundrums, parables, and riddles, because each of us must determine these things within the very specific context of our own lives, as experience teaches us and as our actions unfold and shape our destinies.

When I turned twenty-eight, I transitioned from the desire to write poetry, which resulted in the occasional mediocre, mood-inspired poem, to a more passionate, fierce desire to write fiction, to learn the craft. From the urgency of that desire, I determined a practical schedule. As a housewife and mother of small children, I would manage to write one to two hours per day, every day, a minimum of two pages. Discipline, by supporting and focusing my desire, resulted in a first book of short stories, published and prize-winning. I had learned a great secret. To match desire's urgency with self-discipline and patient work would encourage healthy ambition and potential achievement.

Seven published books and numerous literary prizes later, as a full professor teaching creative writing, I could be seen as proof of the pragmatic success of focused desire. And yet Desire is a child of Eros, and so her voice changes. Just as we are tempted into complacency, she points us in another direction.

*You say you can't create anything original?*
*Don't worry about it.*
*Create a cup from which your brother, or sister,*
*can drink.*

—Rumi, 14th century poet and mystic

For two years now, desire has whispered unrelentingly of another path, not the outer one, secure, salaried, laureled with academic and literary achievement. Desire whispers to me to step away from my easeful life and attend to the suffering of the children of the world, to the suffering of the planet. It is as passionate and urgent as the desire I once felt to write stories and novels. Desire now asks me to risk newness, to collaborate on creative projects, to use the power of education, the magic of poetry and story, to help give strength and new identity to marginalized adolescents. The path is not laid out, there is no map, and this was and still is an exhilarating/terrifying journey, but when I took my first steps, I found wonderful others ahead of me as guides and mentors, many of them younger than I by decades.

I am learning that when one's desire is to be of service, when one's ego is willing to surrender for the greater good, the external world moves rapidly to help and to make manifest. If I simply desire a romantic love to make me happy, to publish books and win literary awards so I feel I am worthy of existence, if my desires are mainly to enhance myself, they move slowly, meet with obstacles, are often thwarted. Even in their attainment or achievement, they are shadowed by guilt, envy, a sense of temporality, any number of things to demonstrate that the success of the self, the vaunting of the self, an individual's fame, is short lived.

When I won the Flannery O'Connor Award for my first book of short stories, *Spirit Seizures,* my dream of being a writer, my desire, was glitteringly realized. And so a new desire emerged: to write *more,* to become an even more recognized or "famous" writer, and my ego, through this new desire, became for years chronically irritated. I had both the gift and the disease of ambition. Yet even in the first flush of literary success, I was aware of friends still struggling to publish, aware of the imminent collapse of my marriage, aware, too, of my nonliterary friends not really understanding who I felt I was. Even in the excitement of winning, I sensed the essential emptiness and shadow nature of triumph. After all, another person had won the year before, another would win the year after, and so on. My ego took to inflating and deflating, almost at will. I felt insecure, giddy; it took months and the solitary habit of writing to become balanced again.

I am grateful for recognition I have received, I do not minimize its effect and ability to give visible support to my own or anyone else's work, but I have seen the other side of what we call success as well. To this day, I cultivate an equally grateful detachment from the invisible work, work unrecognized or unpublished or unread, necessary work erroneously called failure. I am even tolerant of my not writing, a state I have been in for a year now, because I sense it is a state of dormancy that will yield fresh eloquence.

The word "desire" is often associated with eros in its sexualized definition. A male friend of mine, a military officer, recently answered without hesitation when I asked him what he associated the word "desire" with: "Power." Power! I associate it with longing, with the thing longed for, distance an essential part of desire's equation. Unattainability feeds desire, dreams feed desire; desire ceases when the thing is achieved, attained, consumed, and another desire rises up to take its place. By "power," did he mean the power to pursue, to realize? I wonder.

In January 2006, I followed an intuitive, expensive, impractical desire to go to Calcutta, India, and meet the people involved in Kalam, an innovative arts and education project in the marginalized areas of the city, in red-light districts and railway stations. Desire gave me the power to travel into the unknown, and my visit was transformative. It became the first outward manifestation of my desire to move into artist/activist work. One year later, I am returning, taking five graduate students with me to begin to build a collaborative international outreach with Kalam and the Daywalka Foundation. Desire's whisper has led to action, action to manifestation, and perhaps that is what my friend meant by "power." Desire as fuel for manifestation. As transformative energy. Desire as a calorie.

Perhaps desire's most humbling lesson is that personal desires, even with disciplined effort, are sometimes successful, sometimes not. The romance fails, the story is rejected, the dream house, dream child, or dream project becomes a challenge, new troubles arise and the gift is part poison. But when desire is linked to service, to the good of another or others, the world steps in quickly, often with seemingly miraculous speed, to usher in the reality, a reality distinguished by near-magical qualities and often by a dazzling independence from what one initially envisioned. Desire based on serving others, as well as a healthy caring for oneself, desire based on the compassionate loving-kindness all great spiritual teachers describe, exceeds and surpasses all of one's dreams. The greatest of desires, desirelessness, is recognizable by its companion, joy.

Desire exists in us as love, as life's longing for itself. And when we learn to surrender to that divine desire, when our personal desire is willingly fed into that fire, when we are swept up and consumed in a power and grace, a joyfulness and a miraculous reality of manifestation that could be called desirelessness, in truth we have entered the most sublime of *desires*.

On November 17, 1944, a twenty-two-year-old Jewish poet and wartime parachutist, Hannah Senesh, was captured, tortured, and executed by Nazi forces. This poem, this prayer, is hers:

> *Blessed is the match consumed*
> *in kindling flame.*
> *Blessed is the flame that burns*
> *in the secret fastness of the heart.*
> *Blessed is the heart with strength to stop*
> *its beating for honor's sake.*
> *Blessed is the match consumed*
> *in kindling flame.*

For the

Real

# My Desire

*Joyce Maynard*

*I*t's not a man, though I have loved my share of them. No hunger ever gnawed at my belly, from the inside out, like the longing for a baby. It was true when I was twenty, and though I gave birth to three of them in the end—all in their twenties now, long gone from home—it's not all that different for me now, at fifty-three.

Some women (the lucky ones, maybe) outgrow the yearning. A few never suffer it in the first place. The sensible part of me, the brain that can assess my life and recognize what I've had in abundance, and what I've missed, would say here that the time has come (a little late in the game, even) to shower the kind of tender care I gave to my children on my own self now, or the larger world, and give to other projects the kind of passionate, probably obsessed concentration and focus I gave, so long, to child-raising.

Now I can devote myself to work, undistracted by the noisy appearance of little boys slamming doors and looking for snacks, as they show up off the school bus. I don't stay up late in tearful battles with my daughter, or drive hundreds of miles to take my younger son to a tennis tournament, or his sister to check out a college, or his brother to a Michael Jackson concert, or to the emergency room to get his appendix out. More than the physical demands of all that—not to mention the financial ones—what I'm released from now is the emotional preoccupation: the worry that someone was unkind to one of my children, that one of their hearts might get broken, that one of them has a dream in need of nurturing. Whatever issues they suffer over now, they take care of, by and large, without me.

I am free (good news). I am free (bad news). So now what?

Except, of course, being a parent never ends. The children grow older, grow up, cease to be children at all eventually, and still, you remain their parent always. It is a state of being that endures—like religious faith, or shrapnel embedded in flesh, like fear of heights, an incurable illness, like the need to breathe and eat, like love. Terrible and wonderful, source of the deepest potential for pain and the greatest potential for joy, it's as much a part of my daily life, as much a part of who I am as breathing. A person doesn't graduate from parenthood, or leave it behind.

What does leave is that fleeting stage—seemingly endless while you're inhabiting it, that you look back on later like a moment in a dream—when your child was a baby, and the whole world lay in your hands. A baby touches down in your life for only a little while, creating this strange, otherworldly state of being where time barely exists, night and day merge, and all there is in your universe, practically, is this one fact: *baby*. And all that matters to you is making sure she's happy and safe.

That's the part that disappears, and though what replaces it may be richer, deeper, more complex, and ultimately more satisfying, there will never be anything like it again.

Twenty-three years have passed since I last gave birth. At the time, I didn't know he'd be my last child; I was just thirty, and though this was my third baby, placing me above the national average already, I believed another one or two remained in my future.

Over the years that followed, I kept my eye out for the moment when the opportunity for another baby might arise. (Oh, I did way more than keep my eye out for this. Divorced at thirty-five, I assessed future suitors, for years to come, with an eye toward their fatherhood potential.) I held on to the prospect of some future baby like an un-opened present. There were all those eggs inside my body still, waiting for their release into the womb, their chance at fertilization. Never mind that I was short on money, short on time, short on patience, not to mention short on a partner. I had a case of baby love the size of a minivan.

I loved everything about babies, even the parts people make a fuss about. I didn't mind the messiness. I didn't mind diapers particularly, or the way a baby keeps wanting to be picked up all the time. I loved the feeling of a baby in my arms, a baby on my lap, a baby pressed up against my chest, not to mention nursing her. Those first few months were exhausting all right—a time when my whole life was occupied with virtually nothing but baby care. But the other part was this: I maintained an utter assurance that whatever my child needed, I could provide. Whatever was wrong in her world, I had the power to fix. Maybe this wasn't really true, even then, but that's what it felt like, and the sense of contentment and assurance, the clarity about my role in life at that point was more than I had ever known before, or ever would again.

Parents of babies often complain about having to get up in the night for them, but I never did, because I kept them in the bed with me. They were always within reach of my arms, my breasts. The connection we had in those days was so primal, I didn't even fully wake when one of them needed me; I just reached out and held whatever baby it was against my body. There was no feeling better than the warm, faintly damp little package, making soft snuffling sounds and fitting itself into the curve of me. My babies' father was there, too, but really (and maybe this is telling), the love affair at that moment was between the baby and me.

From the moment a baby's born, though, she begins to leave you. First she leaves your body. Then your arms. Then she leaves the breast, departs from the bed, sets out on her own two feet (even before then, she sets out crawling). If a mother does her job right, the direction her babies move in is away, out into the world, where they will find new loves: baseball, or dinosaurs, or fashion design, friends, a bass guitar, a beat-up Toyota, a political cause, a boy, a girl. Grown-up babies still love their mothers, and if we're lucky they even come home to visit now and then, but our role diminishes, as it should, and what remains is no longer as simple as food, clothing, warmth, love. When problems arise—as problems invariably do—they aren't the kind that can be solved by holding your child, feeding her, putting her in dry clothes, singing a song.

So, even as I have grown in my appreciation for all the stages of parenthood that followed that first one, I carry this nostalgia for the one that began it all. Looking, now, at a photograph of my young self holding my infant daughter, or one of my infant sons, I can hardly keep from sighing out loud. Those babies didn't die. We are lucky people; nothing tragic occurred. Still, the people in the photographs might as well have emigrated to Australia, they are that far away now. I mourn them. Miss them. Want them back.

It's almost a physical ache, this longing to hold a baby. It comes to me at odd moments, watching a young mother in a restaurant, struggling to eat her meal and feed her baby at the same time. And I—with my hands free to cut my own chicken and lift my fork without danger of dropping a piece of spinach on an infant's downy head—would rather get up from my table, abandon my plate, if she would let me take her baby while she had her meal. What do I care about a gourmet meal if I can hold a baby?

Sometimes I even offer. Now and then, the young mother accepts. (This happens on airplanes too, on occasion, especially if there's a young mother traveling alone, and looking overwhelmed, and the flight is long, and the baby's fussy, and at some point the mother— whom I will have been studying, though I try not to be too obvious about it—will look as if she's at a loss for what to do now, or maybe she just needs to go to the bathroom, and I ask, with more of a tone of casualness than I actually possess: "Would you like me to hold your baby for you?")

The first thing I do, when I get a baby in my arms, is walk off someplace with him. When I get a chance to spend a little time with a baby, I like to get him away from the distraction of his parents, number one. I want him to myself. I want to lay him out on the rug, study his toes, whisper in his ears, sniff his head, stroke his soft pink palm, feel his fingers curling around mine. Maybe I dance around the room with him (no chance we won't be perfectly in step). I may sing, and if so he doesn't look fazed when it's off key.

Maybe what I appreciate most about this baby love of mine is how uncomplicated it all feels. (I doubt I even need to point out how different this is from love of a man. Or love of a grown child, or an adolescent one, or even a three-year-old.)

With a baby, there is no need to talk about anything. No need to analyze. I don't have to discuss with a therapist what's going on between us, or read a book to know what to do, or check in with an expert. When a baby comes into range, I become an animal woman. A woman in love.

I have this belief that I can make any baby stop crying, no matter how upset she may be. There is some basis of reality in this conviction, though there have been some rare exceptions to my record. I don't think it's that I have some magic power, but I think babies sense in me (babies being all about sensing things, because feelings are all that exist in their world so far) that they are in the hands of someone who feels, with them, the way Pinkas Zuckerman might, picking up a violin. Familiarity. Supreme confidence (mastery, even). And love. Babies know when a person is nervous, or scared, or ambivalent, and when she is not. So they tend to recognize me as someone who won't be thrown if they spit up or cry or do any of the other things babies like to do, that I don't mind, because they're all part of babies. A baby, passed into my arms, is likely to sense how happy I am to be with him. Which is a nice feeling for a baby to have.

Over the years, I have tried to tone down this baby thing of mine. I thought maybe if I hung out more with other people's babies, I'd remember all the bad things about babies that I'd forgotten, and stop wanting one all the time. But increased exposure to other people's babies—like increased exposure to crack cocaine, maybe, not that I know this personally—just made me want the object of my own particular addiction that much more.

I was getting older, meanwhile. The eggs kept dropping into the uterus, regular as clockwork, but their quality had to be declining sharply. Still, it was never pregnancy that interested me most, or the notion of passing down my own genes, or looking down into my arms to see a face, looking up, that resembled mine. So my obsession, focused originally on the notion that I might one day conceive and bear another child, simply shifted to adoption, where I encountered a vast number of women, my age or close enough (though not so likely to have had children in their twenties, as I did), who were embarking on motherhood in their forties—in their fifties, even. The way some people might track the adventures of teen idols or sports heroes, I read stories about these aging mothers and their babies, imagining whether I could ever be such a person myself.

Around this time—for reasons having nothing to do with my feeling about babies, though, it could be said, there may be no place on earth where the babies are more irresistible—I bought a house in

Guatemala and started traveling regularly there. Invariably on these trips, one sight that would occupy me would be the adoptive parents at the Guatemala City airport, heading home with their new children, usually around six months old. Mostly these were married couples, where I remained single, and mostly they were younger than I. Still, I would find myself standing in some line at the airport, so utterly lost in the act of watching these couples with their babies that the person in line behind me would have to poke me and say (maybe in English, maybe in Spanish), "It's your turn."

They were talking about checking my bags, of course. Though for me, the words seemed like an invitation.

I was carrying on with my life during these years, mind you. I don't mean to suggest that the yearning for a baby in my arms so utterly distracted me that I didn't pay attention to the three very real and present offspring I had already raised. In all kinds of ways, they are the ones in my life who offer the tangible gratifications of parenthood, whether they're home visiting (a rare event) or checking in long-distance.

My daughter is twenty-nine now, my sons twenty-five and twenty-three. It is not so far-fetched to suppose that sometime within the next few years, one or more of them may become a parent, making me a grandparent, of course. At which point, if I am lucky, I may once again have access on a semi-regular or at least occasional basis to a baby or two. I resist the impulse to raise this possibility with my children, though they know me and my feeling about babies enough to know, without my doing so, how I will feel about that. And I will know, too, the danger of being too overbearing in my thrill over their babies. *Their* babies, not mine.

I don't want to suggest that I am one of those desperate, baby-crazed types who steal infants from maternity wards and head out on the lam with them. When my children have children, I will keep a lid on my besottedness, and behave. I hope.

But in truth, there is nothing moderate or measured in my feeling about this baby love of mine. I am a greedy woman when it comes to babies. I am a crazy woman, about babies. Drunk with desire. And for a rare, brief time, nothing else matters but the feel of that baby, wrapped up in my arms, as the whole rest of the world disappears.

# Babyquest

*K. W. Oxnard*

## *F*oreplay

I didn't always desire a baby. I wasn't one of those naturally maternal girls who dreamed of being a mother as soon as she acquired the language to express it. I didn't crave baby dolls, didn't practice feeding the ones I did have, and when my sisters and I played house, I was just as happy being the child or the dad as the mom. My 1960s and '70s childhood fantasies veered in two divergent directions: becoming a stewardess in a jaunty Yves Saint Laurent or Pucci uniform, flying around the world in posh supersonic jets, visiting exotic locales, meeting handsome men, and being taken out to restaurants with overpriced wine and gorgeous views of the sea or mountains (or preferably both); or being president of the United States and making history with my brilliant and progressive policies. Yes, I was a weird kid.

None of these dreams, you will note, involved children.

My mother's love/hate relationship with us went a long way toward souring me on having kids of my own. Mama's mantra, "Don't get married and have children; it'll ruin your life," erupted from her almost daily, and I not only heard and ingested this misanthropic motto but took it intensely to heart. In my mother's defense, I saw how exhausting raising a family could be. She struggled to keep my sisters and me fed, clothed, educated, and entertained, at first in a tough marriage with my father, later as a single mother, and finally in a stable but eventually unhappy marriage with our stepfather.

She had been a baby herself when I was born, twenty years old, naive and needy, still longing to make her way in the world as an architect, designer, engineer, anything other than the mother of children. As the eldest of her "Irish triplets," I was roped into caring for my sisters in small and large ways: *Help your sisters get their clothes on or you'll all be late for school; don't cry if your sister hits you, you're the mature one, you should be able to handle it better; let your sister go to acting camp, she wants it more than you.* Children, in my mom's view, drained everything out of life. Although a mere eighteen months old when my sister Robbie was born, I heard the great sucking sound of lost attention and connection to my mother, as first one, then two, other beings absorbed her energy and focus. Have children? What idiot would want that?

Yet, like most girls, I was inevitably drawn into the orbit of young babies whenever they came into view. Most of my mother's friends who were her age had waited longer to have families, and we spent a lot of time having brunch or dinner in the homes of couples with infants and toddlers. Soft little creatures they were, making adorable cooing noises and, mostly, letting me pick them up without wailing for their mothers. Unlike with everyone else in my world, especially my parents and sisters, I did not have to try hard to gain babies' attention by being clever in front of their friends, by doing homework without being asked, by taking out the garbage, or by playing Chutes and Ladders one more time. No, like beef jerky or gummi bears, babies were pure instant gratification in a squishy, moist package.

I had a knack for soothing little ones. I held them close, breathed in the wet oatmeal smell at the nape of their little necks, played peekaboo and the bouncy game, and marveled at the way they looked deeply into my eyes and smiled their toothless old-man grins. They were delicious, sensual little beings who could absorb me with a giggle, break my heart with a whimper. No plastic baby or porcelain Madame Alexander doll could hold a candle to the wonderful heft of a well-fed six-month-old, with tiny toes so smooth and plump, wisps of hair that bloomed into curls around their ears, bellies as fat and shiny as potpies. I loved their bubble suits, their onesies, even their stinky diapers. While they wriggled and cried when their parents changed them, I was a new player and thus pleasantly distracting, so I volunteered even for this, the most reviled of all baby duties, because the look on the baby's face when it was suddenly clean and dry was worth any amount of smelly poop. I carried babies around on my back, playing Indian squaw with my little budding brave in a papoose. And best of all, when I was tired of a particular bundle of joy, I could hand it over to the parents and go home, warm with the memory of having been an excellent au pair for an hour or two.

Familiarity breeding not contempt but boredom, I could never have been as enthralled with my sisters. They were too close in age, for starters. Mama eventually married my stepdad, Michael, and moved us to Puerto Rico, far away from our extended family, so we girls spent days, weeks, and months in the Caribbean sun, playing tennis, riding horses, swimming in the pool or the turquoise sea, fighting over Play-Doh and the backgammon board.

But clearly something was missing. Whenever I saw an ad for bottles or baby food, or when we went to the grocery store and there were young mothers pushing wide-eyed babies in carts, I sensed it. And at some point I realized that Mama and Daddy Michael could deliver me my very own little squishy playmate. Finding any appropriate opening, I began to pester my parents for a new sibling, specifically a baby brother.

"Wouldn't it be fun to take a baby to the beach, Mama?" I asked, using budding feminine wiles and long eyelashes to advance my case. "I can help take care of him. I'm good at that!" When Daddy Michael drove us to school, I helpfully pointed out that a baby brother would look just as handsome as he, and that we tomboyish girls could help teach him how to throw a ball and other athletic stuff. While I'm sure my parents had many wonderful reasons for wanting a child—Mama might see it as a way to cement the new marriage, or perhaps finally make child-rearing a conscious choice instead of a surprise; Michael could have a biological child of his own—I didn't think much about those rationales. All I knew is that when they announced they were pregnant, I was ecstatic.

Little Michael, or Miguelito, as we dubbed him in honor of the Hispanic island of his birth, became my very own live baby doll. I loved everything about him: dark curls, long skinny torso, sparkly brown eyes, gurgles I pretended were a language only he and I could understand. I was ten and so proud of him I could hardly stand it. After school I waited until Mama had fed him; then I took Miguelito for long walks, protecting his delicate head with a hat and pulling the stroller's sunshade down low. Despite those efforts, he developed a wicked little tan, never complaining about the heat or the wind, just gazing in curiosity at the tropical sun bouncing off the Caribbean, and at the tourists as they strolled by and said, "*¡Que niño bonito!*" Each time, I nurtured the silly fantasy that little Michael was *my* baby, that they were congratulating *me* for his beauty, his precociousness, his dazzling smile.

As he grew, so did my affection for him. Our favorite game was "airplane." I lay on the straw rug on our living room floor, stood him up on his amazingly long legs, then hoisted him by his belly onto the soles of my feet. "Fly, fly!" I commanded, and he squealed with pleasure as I rocked him back and forth, pretending he was soaring over the earth. To be responsible for the joy and protection of such a wonderful little creature—it was better than ice cream, Nancy Drew books, better even than my favorite pastime, riding horses on the beach. Miguelito remained my baby for a very long time, a willing participant in my own little game of "house." I changed his diapers, fed him, bathed him, and let him curl up next to me when he was scared of storms or eerie TV shows. Eventually he grew too old for that sort of mother-hen routine—and after all, he had Mama, me, *and* two other sisters, plus Daddy Michael: four nannies and a man-servant, as our family only half joked.

As I moved into my teens, I babysat for other families, but for various reasons those with babies grew sparser, and I was reduced to hanging out with preteens, watching bad television. When I left for college Mike was eight years old, deep into Atari and other boyish games, and he no longer followed me to the door with his lunchbox, proclaiming, "I want to go to school with my geeerls!" I had raised him, in a sense, and though I missed him terribly, I had a world to conquer, after all.

## Conception

I spent my college years at Brown, a campus famous for its liberal conscience and a strong social engagement with Providence and the world at large. I became engrossed in a host of pursuits: taking classes on arcane ancient texts and Italian renaissance literature; founding an alternative house focused on holistic health; reporting for WBRU, Brown's commercial radio station. I launched myself into a brave new world of intellectual challenges, though I was still drawn to nostalgic childlike experiences of my own, such as watching art films at the wonderful Cable Car Cinema, where we sat on old couches, entertained before the feature by a mustachioed man making shadow puppets on the screen. Babies were the furthest thing from my mind.

In my college years, the thought of birthing, much less raising, a child was anathema to every cell in my body. I was emotionally fragile, having just emerged from a semester-long depression related to my mother's divorce from my stepfather. The nest, as my sisters and brother and I lamented, had left us, and I felt untethered, loose in a tough, lonely world. As a family we had moved every six months to two years, so my time at Brown was fast becoming my longest stretch in one place.

My siblings and I had suffered through my biological father's alcoholism, my mother's constant unhappiness, and now two divorces. With my gaze resolutely on my own truncated childhood, I couldn't imagine ever making room for the idea of being responsible for someone else's. If my thoughts strayed at all toward a future family, they brought nightmarish images of myself as an angry, embittered woman, forever blaming her "mistakes" for the loss of her freedom, her power, her potential, and the ensuing grief and dysfunction in those "mistakes'" lives. Since I had already lived it from a child's perspective, it was simply unthinkable to visit this wrath and disappointment upon another generation. So I chose not to think about it at all.

Soon it was graduation time, and with it came an extraordinary opportunity to travel the world with my sister Robbie. We saved money that summer, every penny matched by my stepfather, and set off for Asia in the fall of 1987. It wasn't a stewardess gig, but something even more glamorous and intrepid: I was now an international backpacker armed with notebooks, a tape recorder, and an ostensible study project on perceptions of the United States via the foreign media. No classes to attend, no boss to answer to, no schedules or itineraries imposed by anyone other than me. After a life of being what my sisters and I referred to as "upscale baggage," toted around by various parental units to cocktail parties, resort openings, court-enforced custodial vacations, family reunions, and relocations, I got to carry the luggage myself. I was in grown-up-girl heaven. Every day I awoke to my own agenda. I went where I wanted to go, stayed put when a place and the spirit moved me. I felt as free and in control of my destiny as anyone possibly could.

Inevitably, my return to the United States was abrupt and anticlimactic. The intensity of traveling in close quarters with strangers gave way to ambitious peers in New York, whose passion for a late-1980s pursuit of the almighty dollar I did not share. The depression that had visited me in college reared its persistent head again, and, like so many New Yorkers before and after me, I wound up on the couch.

Thank god for my shrink, Sarah. She scraped me off the asphalt and led me into my next adventure, an excavation of my past and my soul that literally saved my life. We spent four years wading through all of the usual early-childhood swamps, with Sarah urging me to thrust my feet into the emotional mud in order to finally release myself from its soupy hold. Sarah asked me often about my future dreams, which involved writing a novel, getting a tenure-track position at a good university, and traveling to exotic locales, with a soul mate to share the journey. Her questions about children always ended with my protestation that I was not ready, might never be ready. Indeed, I would be a bad mother, I feared, because I would not know how to love a child in just the right way. I was twenty-seven and had begun to write fiction, an activity involving its own conception, gestation, birth, and postnatal care. I was deeply satisfied with my newfound calling.

When I was about twenty-eight, though, I began to notice babies again. Not just the cute ones bundled up on the subways against the Northeastern winter, their mothers tugging on stringed mittens and parkas, their noses and cheeks shiny as they left the steamy subway cars of the IRT. *All* babies. I had always been partial to the six- to eighteen-month-old crowd, with their camera-ready pudginess, their preverbal goo-goo communications, their high "squishy" factor. Now I found myself staring openly at infants who could barely make eye contact, neonatal vision too rudimentary to focus on anything for more than five seconds. Cute, interesting looking, or ugly, it didn't matter; even newborns called my name. I flirted with them all shamelessly while waiting in line at H&H Bagels, played silent peekaboo on crosstown buses, blew them kisses as their parents bustled them into cabs. Some New York women find men with babies irresistible, making time with the little ones at Zabar's or Tower Records in order to suss out whether their dads are single and looking for a new mother figure for Junior. As for me, I didn't give a hoot about the dads. I was all about the tykes. Give me a crowded waiting room with three little ones, and I found a way to entertain all of them, one by one, a baby dazzler nonpareil.

I shared this new craving with no one. Me, one of those horrible obsessed women who contracted such a bad case of baby fever, they made bad marriages? Me, the definition of independence, a retrograde suburban-mom wannabe? Me, the staunch feminist, a (gasp!) nurturer? One winter afternoon, at a meeting to organize an upcoming conference on gender politics, a lesbian graduate student at NYU took umbrage at some idea of mine and spat the word "breeder" at me—clearly the worst insult she could muster. I mulled this over for days. What gave me away? Was there some glaring aspect of my clothing, my posture, my facial expressions, that acted as the ultimate tip-off? Here I was, trying so hard to be a writer, spending hours, days, revising my stories, working on not one but two novel manuscripts, only to enter a conversation with a group of heady New York intellectuals and be exposed not as who I wanted to be—Susan Sontag in a black turtleneck—but for who I really was, Donna Reed in a pinafore.

As always, I took my dilemma to Sarah, who laid it on the line. "If you really *don't* want children, why did the comment hurt so much?" I hemmed and hawed, pointing out that I had fought hard to enter the MFA program, to be taken seriously, to make a name for myself as someone who considered the written word sacrosanct. Again, Sarah moved past this obfuscation and got to the pith.

"Why do you think you'd be a bad mother, Katherine?"

Staring at a painting of two vague figures floating in a sea of red (a Rorschach version of the Madonna and child?), I thought hard about it, trying to divine the source of my hesitation.

"Because I'm afraid I'll be like my mother, I guess. Constantly feeling torn away from my work and my life. Um, resentful, you know? Self-absorbed. Children need a mother who's available—someone who can really focus on them and not feel as if she's always missing something better when she's caring for them."

"So," she persisted, "do you think you won't be able to balance those things better than your mother did?" She paused long enough for me to take this in. "You are very different from her. And don't forget: You would be *choosing* to have a family."

I was silent for a while, and then out came the question that had plagued me for years, though I'd never actually formed it into a sentence. "Do you think I'll be a good mother?"

I heard Sarah shift forward in her chair behind me. "I think you'll be very intentional and caring, and that you'll work very hard at it. I think you'll be a very proud and committed mother."

I was stunned. I felt as though I'd been carrying around an anvil strapped to my head for nigh on three decades, and someone had just pointed out that it might be easier to take it off and move around without that extra weight. I was *not* my mother! I would make mistakes—but they would be *my own!* It was the simplest of revelations, but as profound to me as any religious epiphany.

In the midst of discovering myself as a writer, I also began to look at babies differently. No longer were they illicit pleasures to be hidden from my ambitious literary friends. Now they were to be celebrated and discussed openly, with fervor. What I'd pushed away from all my adult life now drew me urgently. I was exhilarated, electrified, free to express the true me, a woman who wanted it all: family, work, love, the whole kit and caboodle. I had conceived the idea of conception, and I was as heady with emotion as any newly pregnant woman in the throes of a hormonal roller coaster. I couldn't wait to get started.

Unfortunately, the men in my life did not feel the same way.

## First Trimester

I spent most of my twenties dating several men who were ready for marriage and, ostensibly, children, while I, of course, was not. So I sent them off into other marriages and heard through the grapevine about their marital and familial exploits. One got his wife pregnant right away, within six months of the wedding, then moved them all to

London and Milan, only to divorce after ten years. Another married the socialite he'd wanted me to be, had two kids, and then proceeded to divorce her and make a new family with his second wife. A third told me he wanted to get engaged because interest rates were low. None of this made me wistful for these guys, and I suspect they did not propose to me in the end because they knew in their hearts that I would say no.

So imagine my surprise when, at the perfect childbearing age, after having the huge revelation that I did, actually, want a family—that in fact it was my *destiny* to be a terrific wife and mother—I could find not one man who agreed with me. It was the classic scenario: Boy meets girl, boy chases girl, girl runs away, boy is even more interested in girl, boy proposes, and they live happily ever after. Except it played out in reverse: Girl meets boy who says he wants children, girl chases boy, boy says he's ready to make that commitment but never pops the question, until girl gets freaked out about her eggs disappearing and breaks up with boy, only to have boy knock up his next girlfriend and marry her instead.

This happened again and again, starting when I was about thirty and becoming increasingly intense and frustrating into my early forties. I guess you could say it was a form of perpetual morning sickness. I'd wake up every day thinking this would be the day when the nausea and malaise would dissipate, when the guy in whom I'd already invested time, energy, and love would suddenly motivate and get the cojones to move forward with me.

I could have pulled the sneak attack, but I didn't. I was so up front with these jokers about my intentions that my own friends actually suggested a little subterfuge just to get the deal done. Not my style, alas. I could no more lie about my goals in life than I could claim to enjoy fast food and NASCAR races. I knew some women who had implied that they were on the pill, then accidentally "missed" a dose, or claimed to have an IUD when they really meant a DUI. These were not options for me.

No, for me the dilemma exists in the fact that I am a terrible liar. To hold on to more than one version of a story, to memorize the elaborate details involved in such dissembling, is beyond my limited capabilities, despite my skill at Texas Hold'em. So I blurt out my wants and needs (a solid relationship, marriage sooner rather than later, and kids, not necessarily in that order) early on, making it clear that if the fellow needs to walk, he should do so now before our lust becomes an entanglement or a missed period.

Trouble is, there are an awful lot of men out there who, when faced with a woman plainly stating her needs, somehow envision themselves as that kind of guy—the kind who can actually do what she asks, even when they are completely incapable of such action. These guys aren't evil, just clueless about what they truly want. They meet me, become smitten, assume that I'm excited about continuing my itinerant lifestyle indefinitely, and then figure I'll somehow "forget" about kids. Or maybe they hope that the urgency around my aging eggs isn't as pressing as I make it out to be. Or they just think with their pricks. My favorite Yiddish expression, loosely translated, goes like this: "When your dick stands up, your head is up your ass." Or in my case, up mine, as many men have tried to smooth-talk me into waiting just a little longer, they are almost there, they are on the verge of proposing, they just need a little more time. You get the picture.

That is the kind of guy I have attracted in spades.

Other women have a gift either for finding men who actually want a family, or for meeting men at the most vulnerable point in their lives, so that they'll agree to anything to keep her. I, on the other hand, meet man after guy after dude after bloke who likes me—yes, he likes me very much—but he doesn't have a clue what to do with me. *Aren't kids expensive?* they ask. *Kids take up all your time, don't they? Can we still travel after we have kids? I don't want to be stuck in one place or at a job I hate just because we have to raise our kids. Can you go surfing in Costa Rica with children?*

You'd think all this demurring by the opposite sex might deter me. Perhaps I'd consider going lesbian. Which I did, if only intellectually. I knew deep down I could never pull it off, and when I saw *Kissing Jessica Stein*, I realized that I, too, relished the political ramifications of a same-sex relationship, but was totally unequipped for the reality of life with another woman. It was a sign of my true desperation that I quizzed my girlfriends about it from time to time. But I really do want the whole shebang: a life partner, a mate, a husband with whom to laugh and cry about the ridiculous and wonderful adventures of raising a family. So girls were out.

Why did I seek out such cads in the first place? The answer to that is complicated, indeed, but the simplest answer is this: I didn't seek them out. They sought *me* out. I learned at Brown that men might talk a good game about getting asked out, but in truth they hate it. The very act of calling a man somehow emasculates him, robbing him of some crucial impetus he needs to get the ball, ahem, rolling. It's as if by making that first move, I threw the first bowling ball, and he refused to toss in the second ball for fear of looking foolish or fey. No matter that we would both score, regardless of whose fingers had touched the ball. It had to be his idea. Or, at the very least, seem like his idea.

Which brings me back to that pesky honest streak of mine. I have never been skilled at subterfuge, and I just couldn't, in good conscience, sidle up to some prospect, get him all hot and bothered, lure him into life with me, and then spring my baby lust on him six months or a year in. I wasn't a pest about it, but whenever it seemed like we were heading into The Conversation, I was straightforward and open about what I wanted. I usually received one of two responses:

Asshole #1: "That's beautiful. I can't wait to start my life with you. What color eyes do you think our children will have?" This usually erupted from the mouth of the guy who was wild about having sex with me, and indeed, these guys were often quite careless about birth control. I reminded them often that if I got pregnant, I would keep the baby, and they seemed perfectly okay with that. Yet when it came to giving me any kind of promise for the future, their language became suddenly vague and noncommittal: "I can see that happening in a couple of years, when we know each other better." This after we'd lived together for months, had spent every holiday with his family or mine, and had traveled together cross-country for months in a VW van with his standard poodle.

Asshole #2: "I hear what you're saying, but I'm just not quite there yet. I'm trying to get on your page. I've never felt this way before about a woman, and you're the first person I've ever considered having children with. I can't believe I'm even talking this way!" These types tended to be slightly better about birth control, and they made scary comments about children in the grocery store or on television, such as "See, kids can be such little shits!" or "Twins! Their life is over."

Needless to say, hearing such reactions was extremely discouraging. Yet, like a horse on a long trail ride, I still knew where home was, and I was heading straight for the barn. My craving for babies grew even fiercer, more powerful, as my thirties became my forties. It was in full flower at this point, maturing into a new, more secure form of yearning, like a raptor pining for its nest. Or something.

## Second Trimester

I guess I was closing in on forty when the idea of having a baby on my own began to seem more and more appealing. The men who breezed in and out of my life had many charming qualities, but fatherly tendencies were not among them. My sister Robbie was the first one to suggest going it alone. "You may not find the right guy before it's too late. What if you just go for it?"

I don't know about most women, but that phrase conjures up all kinds of things: trying out for a spot at a comedy club's open-mic night, say, or entering one's blueberry pie into a state fair contest. Starting a family on my own, however, seemed at least a slightly more serious pursuit, and one requiring a lot more thought, planning, and chutzpah. At the time I was living in Maine, working for a nice company that actually paid me a salary and wonderful benefits.

I hated that job.

Not that I have anything against a regular paycheck and great health insurance. God knows it was a relief to be earning real money for the first time in my life, and to be digging myself out of artistically driven credit card debt. But, despite its enlightened attitude about its products, this company exhibited all of the dysfunction of the family that owned it, and I frequently found myself arguing with various management types about implementing the marketing efforts we in the communications department had slaved over. Anyone who knows me personally will tell you that I am no shrinking violet in the workplace. I am much more of a raging gladiolus, poking my nose sky-high, opening loud blossoms up and down my stem, and generally lording it over the garden during my passionate but short corporate life span—"short" being the operative word.

Despite the awkward fit, I knew I had a good thing going. Writers don't come by lucrative nine-to-five jobs with bennies very often. As long as I kept my mouth shut and focused on writing my little copy, everything was hunky dory. The question was, could I suck it up long enough to take advantage of the company's very generous maternity package? More pointedly, could I stay in Maine, land of the icy sidewalk and no family nearby, while raising a baby on my own?

As my fortieth birthday approached, I tunneled into my little five-hundred-square-foot apartment in Portland's West End and pondered. I felt like Pooh in his tree, holing up for the winter, taking stock of my empty honey jars, and wondering if I would ever be able to plow through the snow to get more. Maine is a beautiful place, rife with some of the most stunning landscapes the East Coast has to offer. I fell in love with it, despite my Southern blood, and ended up doing crazy things like surfing in the middle of winter off Higgins Beach. I was no stranger to harsh weather, lonely nights, and long winters. But with a baby? All I could think about was what would happen if my infant were sick at 3:00 AM and then I got sick, too: Who would take us to the emergency room? How would I navigate the shoals of daycare versus nannies, snowsuits versus blankets in the stroller, midnight feedings and snow removal, all as a single mother with no family around to spell me?

My friends encouraged me, like Robbie had, to "go for it," but the deeper I delved into this vision, the sadder I felt. As much as I wanted a baby, the idea of raising it all by my lonesome, not just without a man, but without any other familial witnesses to the baby's growth and progress, struck me as tragic and very wrong. My friend Bob, a doctor who, like me, still hoped for the love of his life and a family, urged me to reconsider. "You have to do this, or you'll regret it for the rest of your life."

"Yeah, but I may also regret raising my kid in the tundra as well. What if it turns out to be a timber wolf instead of a baby?"

I just couldn't wrap my head around it. So I made plans to leave Maine, to travel and explore new places, and to see where I might re-configure my life to be closer to my family. Maybe it would lead me to the right man. Maybe it would help me find a different job that would enable me to make a baby on my own. If not, well, I had to try anyway. Maine was a cold place for me, not just geologically but also emotion-ally. I had tried every which way to work myself into a family-building scenario, and it simply had not worked out. It was time to move on.

## Third Trimester

So here I find myself, in Savannah, Georgia, my hometown, surrounded by family, working as a realtor, making good though unpredictable money, and still pondering the baby question. I have bought a house, found a fertility specialist ob-gyn, made good female friends, and already chosen the public magnet schools where my children would be happy. And yet. Several relationships have come and gone, most of them due to the Baby Issue. When men look at me, they must see everything *but* a matriarch. I have never figured out why they don't consider me the marrying, mothering kind. I am a fabulous cook. I am reasonably jolly. I tell entertaining jokes at parties. Babies and kids flock to me. I don't look like the dog's dinner. And I really enjoy sex, stupid movies, throwing a football around, and listening to my man's stories. And yet.

So here I sit, pregnant with desire, debating my choices. Move forward with the man who is as eager for children as I, but who lives in the Rockies (ah, Match.com) and may not be as compatible with me as we hoped a month ago? Or spend time with the wonderful man of my dreams, who told me on our third date that he'd had a vasectomy? Let all potential beaux go until I have a child on my own, *then* look for a soul mate? Or allow my body to slowly lose its fertility until it makes the decision for me?

I have never really cottoned to the idea of single parenthood, largely because of Mama's experiences, which bore into my skull from age three. For all my gallivanting and fierce independence, I am rather old-fashioned when it comes to children. I think they are far better off with two parents (of any gender) than with one. As attractive as I find the idea of being able to make decisions about a child's upbringing with no potential dissent from a pesky husband, in truth, I would relish that give-and-take. Part of the reason I want children so badly is that very opportunity to work as a team, a family. To learn how to negotiate the various needs and wants of a group, instead of just blindly following my own whims. I have been a solo act for so long that the sound of my own voice gets on my nerves.

Yes, I am fat with this urge to procreate, bursting at the seams, praying for an inducement, yet none arrives. The OB of life has deemed it best to let nature take its course. So I wait. I caress my belly. I wonder if and when the new life will emerge, or if I will have to reach in and take matters into my own hands.

# Wanting My Daughter's Children

*Sharon Leiter*

*I* stood by my daughter's hospital bed and watched her encircle herself with children: the five-year-old, Jacob, slender and dark eyed; three-year-old Andrew, chubby and blue eyed; the sleeping baby— a third son—in her arms. My own mother had birthed three daughters, and there had ever been something shameful, laughable, in that. The men on the block, rowdy and voluble in the prejudices of the times, had derided my father as a "buttonhole-maker." But my daughter's production of sons was something else: an incitement to awe, tempered with sympathy, to be sure, for the woman who would have no daughter to dress up or to sit by her companionably, who would fight to survive among wild boys. Yet the birth of three boys was still a triumph. Appalling how little has changed. We love our daughters; we worship our boys.

My daughter's smile was tired but true. She had been an only child, and this gathering was her undoing of the spell that had isolated her. What my husband and I had not done for her, she had done for herself. And kindly, so kindly, she had invited us into it, offering us the bounty we had unthinkingly denied her. I stood at the foot of the high bed while my son-in-law took the picture.

Later that day, when my husband, Darryl, and son-in-law, Sean, took the two elder boys to the park, I sat in the armchair at the foot of my daughter's bed and cradled my new grandson while she slept. My daughter had joked that the baby looked like a little Yoda, with his round face and pointed chin, his old man's eyes, his wispy hair and outstretched seashell ears. Sure, his nose was wide, but I knew he would grow into it; he would be beautiful, just like the other two. *I'll just stay here,* I thought, meaning not the quiet hospital room, but the bitter place within, where I had blundered without warning. The knife-sharp remorse I had lived with through my forties, the grief I believed I had outlived, was suddenly back, in all its unforgiving fury. *You thought you'd escaped,* it insisted, *but you haven't, you won't. You'll never stop regretting your sin of omission.*

In my forties I wrote a poem for my "omitted" second child:

*When were you to be*
*and where was I?*
*You owned no place in me*
*until the time for you was gone.*

*Now seeds of that oversight*
*startle me awake.*
*Gardens of absence*
*grow around your face*

*and what you never were*
*becomes the image of a dream*
*when all our love*
*was spent on living things.*

But writing down those words proved no turning point, not then, not now. The healing power of transforming pain into poetry was a myth, it seemed, along with so many other things I had believed. The writing had produced a poem, a chant I could murmur to myself, a flimsy ladder of words I could cling to as I swung above an emotional abyss. But it couldn't fill the house with the voices of my unconceived children.

Nothing could change the reality that, while there was still time, neither my husband nor I had managed to want another child more than we wanted to make it in academia. Darryl took one temporary job after another, commuting back to Robin and me on weekends. I chugged along on my tenure track, publishing my "tenure book" with a prestigious university press, but I got no tenure; instead, I was ejected from my dreams in a two-line note placed strategically on my desk by the cowardly department chairman. The shrink who tried to put me back together had no doubts that I had made this happen, worked against myself by alienating tenured faculty, because I didn't *really* want this career after all. I hated the pressure to excel that had dogged me all my life, and *really* wanted to be free of it. Perhaps. But I had certainly *acted* as if I wanted tenure during all those years of dedicated teaching, doing committee work, writing articles, attending conferences, slaving away on the book.

Yet who can extract the fish of true desire from the teeming river of the psyche? Maybe the shrink was right. Or maybe it was just my bad luck that those five individuals who slapped my life off its course were a bunch of turds—small-minded, mediocre, envious. None of *them* had published a book. One was hostile, obese, and stuck in a crappy marriage; one an alcoholic; one a thief; one asexual, insomniac, and voyeuristic; one a panderer for student popularity by telling dirty jokes. Over the years I've met others who either knew of my former department's depravity or were personally screwed by it, so I tend to feel I was not to blame for the disaster from which I've never fully recovered: the sacrifice of my second child for a career that was unjustly snatched from me.

That night, Darryl and I stayed with Jacob and Andrew in their home, allowing Sean to spend the night in the hospital room with Robin and the baby. Both boys had fallen asleep in the minivan on the way home, had let themselves be transferred to their beds without protest. My husband removed their shoes while I cleared a space for Andrew in the midst of the stuffed bears and dinosaur figurines populating his bed.

Sometime in the early morning hours, Jacob and Andrew appeared in the bedroom where we slept and climbed into bed with us. Jacob, in perpetual vibrant motion in his waking life, slept peacefully, while the sweet-natured, resilient Andrew thrashed and kicked, wrestling with the bears of his dreams. I tried to enfold him, but my powers held no sway in the place where he strove.

I moved to the edge of the bed to shield myself from his flailing limbs. In the intervals of sleep, I dreamed a litany of those blood-linked dreams that visited repeatedly, intrusive relatives who would not be denied: the taxi ride to the hospital with inflated abdomen and empty womb, the family party for the absent guest, the fabulous city I had not managed to explore, living only along its perimeters. Then the lost-purse dream—the agony of putting this essential part of myself down for an instant, finding it nowhere. In its latest version I'm on a car journey with my daughter, and when I lose my purse she reassures me, "Don't worry, Mother. My purse is big enough for both of us." The first time I dreamed this dream, I had welcomed a new era in my life. But now I disbelieved the dream and would have refuted it, had there been a court of the unconscious where such matters were argued.

I awakened in my daughter's large bedroom to find husband and boys gone from the bed. Across from me stood the long French antique dresser, with its ornate mirrors, that had stood in my mother's bedroom for thirty years. I could not have lived with my mother's furniture any more than I could have lived my mother's life. But Robin viewed the furniture as an heirloom, endowing the family line and its possessions with a solidity and continuity they had never had.

My family had been immigrants who left most of themselves behind in Russia. In the early days of their marriage, my parents had papered the walls of their tiny Brooklyn apartment with brash patterns, crowded its rooms with overstuffed satiny sofas and love seats, chunky mahogany tables topped with nymph-encircled lamps. Instead of paintings, the walls had been hung with a series of black lacquered boxes, backed with mirrors and filled with clay figurines: ladies and gentlemen of another century, domestic and farm animals. My mother had plucked them all from the cheap, bewildering array of neighborhood shops. In time, her taste had grown more sophisticated—witness the French antique bedroom set—but she had continued to paper the walls with what seemed more suitable for gift wrapping. For her last decades she had chosen a shiny silver, reminiscent of aluminum foil, a Reynolds Wrap sea shot through with black, white, and orange islands.

The neighborhood where Robin and Sean live with their children, with its wide, gently sloping, manicured lawns, is generally serene, silent. The houses, while not ostentatious, are large and solid, set well back from the road, made of brick and wood painted in pale, genteel tones, and fringed with tasteful plantings. When they moved in, neighbors appeared at the door, bearing flowers from their gardens, home-baked breads, good wines. It was a club, despite the absence of pool or clubhouse, and the arrival of new members was an occasion. With the force of the obvious, it struck me that this was what Robin had always wanted, what she had envied as a child, living in a garden apartment, who watched as her schoolmates were dropped off in their single-dwelling Edens. She wanted a doctors' and lawyers' neighborhood, with its houses of many windows, two parents, and, perhaps most important, its brothers and sisters ensconced in the many bedrooms.

In the hospital on the day after the new baby's birth, I run into my daughter's doctor, a man I know all too well, on the elevator. That serene, brown-skinned man, who never seems to age, beams at me the same way he first did a quarter of a century ago, sealing my daughter's fate as an only child, when he removed my womb. He is much beloved, a specialist in difficult births, with a gleam of celebration in his eyes that has always intrigued me. He is in green scrubs, a white shower cap covering his dark hair.

"Beautiful baby," he says by way of greeting.

"Thank you, Doctor. Thank you for bringing him to us."

This is becoming our tradition, the second time we have engaged in such an exchange. The doctor beams. He never tires of bringing babies into the world. He is of medium height, with a lithe, youthful figure. It is still a matter of amazement to me that the doctor who removed my womb twenty-five years ago has now delivered two of my daughter's sons.

He removed it vaginally, piece by piece, my hopelessly injured womb, a tumor attached to it like a barnacle to a ship. Others had said this could not be done, that the tumorous womb was too large, but this doctor had known better. I congratulated him, for my emptiness was proof of his talents. He had spared me an incision and I recovered rapidly. The biopsy showed uterine cells dividing with growing alacrity, the doctor explained, so I had been wise to act when I did. I was forty; I would not have had another child in any case. *Yes, good, right decision,* I boomed from the new emptiness where my womb had been. But I had been contemplating another child for so long now—at least a decade—that I could hardly be expected to give up the habit of yearning for another. I still felt that, if and when I at last made up my mind to do it, this doctor, with his extraordinary skills and serenity, would be able to help me.

For years afterward, I considered a foreign adoption and collected articles and announcements of meetings without ever attending one. For even then, I could not bring myself to take another child into my life. How can I explain myself? I still hoped to succeed at *something,* and wouldn't another child get in the way? When I was young, I had been "programmed" to not reproduce too extravagantly, for my mother, while insisting that having children was the greatest thrill of her life, had warned me, in no uncertain terms, not to become a housewife like her.

Neither of my two sisters had more than one child, apparently having received the same mixed message. At first, when my daughter was young, I couldn't bear to put a second child between us. As the typical middle child, I had longed for an exclusive love. And I wasn't determined enough to counter my husband's anxieties about the extra responsibility of another, or confident enough to believe I could raise a second child myself while he commuted. There are theories—all equally valid and invalid. And there is the buried, unconscious decision that proclaims itself and can never be fully translated.

Shortly after my fiftieth birthday I was diagnosed with scleroderma, a painful, deforming autoimmune disease that hardens the connective tissue of both the skin and internal organs. Some people die of it; others are mildly impaired. I was lucky. All I lost were partial use of my hands and a government career I was succeeding at despite myself. The gains compensated. During my long recovery, my fierce, outdated longings for both child and career receded, making room for the infinitely rich immediacy of living. My elderly parents entered their final days, and I took care of them. They both died within the same year. Just as they vanished, my first grandson entered my life.

Robin brought him to me on a night of the full moon, after driving cross-country from Los Angeles to Charlottesville. It was Halloween 2001, and flying from Los Angeles in those post-9/11 weeks seemed out of the question. Jacob was six weeks old, spotted with infant acne, losing his birth hair; his eyes, which had opened so knowingly on the day of his birth, were closed. Darryl and I made the young family comfortable in the bedroom/nursery we had prepared, white-furnitured, as my daughter's nursery had been, with her rocker newly painted. When they were all asleep, I held the moon-faced baby on the couch, beneath the moon shining down from the skylight, and sang to him.

For the next three months, as Robin and Sean searched for a home of their own, I woke every morning with a single joyful thought: *Jacob is downstairs.* I would race to the bedroom and knock on the door. Robin always welcomed me. As I changed the baby, we kvelled at the miraculous changes that had taken place in him overnight. He was growing fat as a little sumo wrestler, dark eyed, ever more beautiful. While Robin showered or slept, I took him on his morning tour of the house, pointing out lights, windows, pictures. When Robin and I ate breakfast, we admired Jacob's ever more vigorous kicking beneath the colored loops and lights of the infant gym. Then we'd bundle him into his carriage and take long walks with him, singing him all the old songs. Robin nursed him; I fed him his relief bottle. I carried him to my bed and let him listen to my old Chinese music box, dangled bright objects above his head. I put his high chair in my kitchen and talked to him as I prepared dinner, as I had done with Robin as a baby. Nothing—no sober leavening of "reality"—intervened to dim the euphoria of those days. The past had been returned to me; I was a young mother again.

I knew, of course, that Robin and Sean would move into their own house sometime soon. I looked for houses with them, subtle as I knew how to be, praising anything within a fifteen-minute radius of us. But Sean wanted to buy a house close to his office, on the northern edge of town. "Move there, go ahead. I'll see you maybe once a week," I said. Robin was torn between what Sean wanted and what I needed. She loved sharing the baby with me, but she wanted her own life. What could I do but summon the mature, maternal, accommodating part of myself, deny my heart's desire, and tell her to do what was good for her and Sean? *Of course I'll visit. Yes, often. You know I will.*

I did. I helped set up the new house, and I visited several times a week. I scooped up Jacob at every opportunity, held him, sang to him, played with him tirelessly, made myself a favorite. I knew we had a special thing. No one knew him, made him as happy, as I did. I thought about Jacob obsessively, in alternating waves of bliss and longing, summoning his beautiful face, reviewing every wondrous gesture and expression. I carried him within, through all the lesser moments of my days. I was in love.

On the days when I didn't see him, I felt something unnatural was happening—that he should live and breathe and experience his life without me there was wrong. I felt both grief and guilt. Surely he felt my absence as abandonment.

Only time, with its stern, merciful persuasion, showed me otherwise. As my daughter's family settled into its own grooves, my "baby-
sitting" schedule accommodated itself to their needs. I now had
two lives: one in my daughter's house, as a "young mother," making
cream-cheese eggs for Jacob and then Andrew, changing and dressing
them, wheeling them through the woods, singing them to sleep; the
other in my own lovely, silent house, as an aging woman, burdened as
ever with the empty, aching places of my soul. The common wisdom
is that grandparents have it all: the joy of being with the kids, and the
freedom to leave them to their parents at day's end. I can't deny that
I'm grateful to collapse after a love- and adrenaline-fueled day with
the boys, but my life is in two pieces, and I don't know how to reconcile them.

"How's the Yoda baby?" I asked, entering my daughter's room,
but she didn't laugh this time. The joke was hers, after all, and she
seemed worn out. The baby was sleeping and my daughter wanted to
sleep, too. There was nothing she needed from me just now.

"I could stay," I offered, "in case he wakes up and you want to go
on sleeping."

"I'll try to nurse him when he wakes up. Why don't you go home,
get some rest?"

Sean was with Jacob and Andrew. He'd taken off two weeks to
help his wife.

"I could use some rest," I lied. What I really wanted was to spend
myself, to exhaust myself with my daughter's family, as if they were
my own. But Robin had dismissed me and would summon me when
she needed me again.

"Won't it be great to sleep in our own bed?" Darryl asked, as we pulled into the garage. He turned off the ignition and removed our overnight cases from the trunk.

"What an old woman you've become!" I said.

He was silent. My comment was transparent enough. *Old woman. You've ruined my life. I'll never forgive you.* To release the tiger pacing in my chest would have been pure indulgence, the unleashing of a beast I had long ago defanged but continued, in some part of myself, to feed.

"Why do you talk to me that way?" he beseeched. "I guess you're just tired," he said, dismissing me, exempting me from fairness, from kindness, from decency itself.

"Robin with her three boys," I managed to say.

"They're your grandkids."

"It's not the same."

He carried our overnight cases up the stairway to our bedroom, leaving me to my own devices. *I can't be here,* I thought, and then it occurred to me that I needn't be. There were phone calls to be made, and in each annunciation, the birth, the baby, would be mine alone.

Who I wanted to call first was my mother. This was the essential call, and without it some part of me would forever reach into a void, unrecognized, unreceived, calling out my news to the one who most needed to hear it, who would rejoice with me as no one else could. The newly awakened sense of that deprivation, to which I had not yet grown accustomed but had learned how to bear, reminded me that certain losses—the deepest ones—are irrevocable. The tiger yawned and retired. I was sixty-three again, not half-unhappy with my life.

I will not see my parents again. I am not a young mother. I have not been given a second chance to do what I didn't do. I have three beautiful grandsons. Between gratitude and self-forgiveness I make my way.

# Writing My Way Back Home

*Erica Jong*

**W**hen I was a little girl and couldn't imagine life without my family, I used to think that when I grew up I would travel the countryside with all of them—my parents, my grandparents, my sisters—in a round vehicle on wheels, with an ever-replenished refrigerator in the middle and a top open to the sun and stars. In my mind I called it the "Roundling" (I never shared this fantasy with anyone—as if I knew it was somehow incestuous or forbidden), and in my imagination we were all together forever, traveling in lazy circles through beautiful landscapes, always safe, always fed, always united.

Now my beloved grandparents are dead, my athletic, musical father is astonishingly dead, and my unforgettably fierce mother is fading away. My sisters have their own lives, partners, children, and troubles, and so do I. They sometimes act like my worst enemies. This dream of eternal togetherness is outlandish. But if I take myself back to the child I was then, I understand the fantasy of the Roundling as safety, stasis, freedom from sorrow. Nothing changes. Nobody dies. Nobody grows up—or old. Why did I suddenly remember this long-buried fantasy while writing *Seducing the Demon*? I haven't thought about it since I was a child.

Because writing is an attempt to preserve the past, to keep it safe and hermetically sealed in a sort of time capsule. Writing is the ultimate Roundling, keeping us all young and together forever.

Nobody can write without wanting to bring the past into the present, or without wanting to show how the past informs what happens today. The deepest struggle we experience, the struggle that makes us the unhappiest, is the attempt to stop time and keep all our attachments intact. Attachments cause pain. We must learn to detach, and writing is the opposite of detachment. Or is it?

I've been fencing with attachment and detachment, particularly in the last few months since my father died. I want to write about him, but I don't want to freeze—or murder—him in the pages of a book. For years I thought I understood him, but it was only in the last phase of his life, when he was ill, that I suddenly saw him as a tough little Jewish boy from Brownsville, fighting for his life with his fists, his wit, his tenacity. I understood why he was often so stubborn and so hostile under all his humor. Stubbornness probably saved his life when he was young.

He wasn't the tallest or the strongest boy, but he was the most determined. He could shoot baskets as accurately as the tall guys. He could flatten anyone who called him "kike." He loved the piano, but he was a drummer in his bones. Sometimes you can't know people till they are almost dead.

What a fighter my father was! During his last hospitalization, he tried to escape from the emergency room, from the ICU, and from his hospital suite on the fancy private floor of Mount Sinai. He was right. It was the pneumonia he caught in the hospital that would finally do him in at ninety-two, not any of the three types of cancer he got and conquered. He seemed to have foreknowledge of his demise, and he struggled like mad to get away from those resistant germs he knew were awaiting him. He pulled out breathing tubes, peeing tubes, IVs. He did not go quietly.

More than once I kept him from getting out of bed. How could I have done that? Once someone is in the hospital, he is bound by the iron rules of the institution. I have always hated institutions and so did my father. In his frenetic exercising twice a day, in his attempt to control his money, his daughters, his sons-in-law, his wife, he was expressing his need for absolute freedom from the rules of others. He lost that freedom at the end.

Sadly, I played my own part in his loss of control. I didn't mean to. He was failing, but now I wish I had let him escape the hospital that killed him.

He never would have had a fantasy of a Roundling. His greatest fantasy was escape. He escaped at the piano, the drums, the basketball hoop. He escaped by exercising, by traveling all over the world, supposedly for his business but really because his temperament required it. He always wanted to get away. I know men are made differently, but he was even more of an escape artist than most men. Why do you think I chased those demons through hotel rooms all over the world?

None of us in that Roundling will ever escape. We should be buried in it together. Because the Roundling is, in fact, a cemetery. It's a sort of pie-shaped burial plot, like the famed Sedgwick Pie of Edie Sedgwick's eccentric Massachusetts family.

> *Arrived at the finish,*
> *Unfrightened, unblemished, free*
> *of craving, he has cut away*
> *the arrows of becoming.*
> *This physical heap is his last . . .*
> *ungrasping,*
> *astute in expression,*
> *knowing the combination of sounds—*
> *which comes first & which after.*
> *He is called a*
> *last-body,*
> *greatly discerning*
> *great man.*

That was the poem the mousy male social worker (with the long gray ponytail) from the palliative care team (I called them the "death squad") quoted to my father in the hospital.

He had studied Buddhism. Detachment? Surely you must be kidding.

"Bullshit!" my father hissed. "Pure, unadulterated bullshit."

"But, Mr. Mann, you would be happier if you turned over the decisions to your daughters and gave them permission to—"

"Bullshit!" Then he wanted the little notebook he carried every-where with him. He had no energy to read aloud, but he drummed on the page, stabbing it with his index finger:

> *I feel like King Lear.*
> *I have three daughters*
> *beautiful and dear,*
> *clever and cute,*
> *already in dispute.*
> *Who gets more?*
> *Who gets less?*
> *What a terrible mess*
> *for an aging Lear*
> *In geriatric stress.*

The social worker was speechless. Nothing—not his MSW, not his Buddhism class—had prepared him for this. He was out of words. We all waited, listening to my father struggle to breathe. "Very nice poem, Mr. Mann," he finally said.

"Bullshit!" said my father. "Get out of here!"

My father started out as a pianist, drummer, bandleader, *tumler*, but *tumler* won. He wound up in business, first as a salesman, then as the founder of his own company.

Because he loved music, worshiped musicians, our house was filled with it. We were dragged to concerts at the Philharmonic every month before we had any idea what a privilege that was. I remember being a bored thirteen and escaping to the ladies' room, where I could practice applying my Powder Pink Revlon lipstick. Bartók or Ives or Beethoven, conducted by Dimitri Mitropoulos or Leonard Bernstein, would be thundering through Carnegie Hall and there I was practicing lipstick. What an ingrate I was! My father sent my younger sister to lure me out. I knew I was being an ingrate and I was guilt-ridden. Yet I have grown up with a love of music that mirrors his. I don't play an instrument and I consider myself a troglodyte for this lapse, but music thrills me more than any other art. He gave me this gift.

Our parents' attachments become our own. Often I've thought that if I could have opened my musical of *Fanny Hackabout-Jones* before he died, he would have been prouder of me than for any book I've written. Which is saying a lot. He was proud of me, but he showed this mostly to other people when I wasn't around. He loved to hector me about everything I was doing wrong with my career. I wasn't doing enough PR. I wasn't hassling my publishers enough. I was too laid-back.

Laid-back? For most of my life, I have been bedeviled by ambition and professional jealousy (which I counter with defiant generosity like a witch trying to break her own spell). I've only recently learned how to love the work itself without expectation—something my father never learned. Perhaps this joy in the work and not the outcome is what is meant by detachment. I achieve it only in rare moments, but when I do my writing flies.

Did he ever know this joy? I doubt it. Nothing was play to him after he became a businessman. Everything was work. Except music.

I started out as a painter, and switched to writing to avoid competing with all the painters in my family. (Probably I also had more talent to write and was freer in using it than if I had gone into the family racket.) But you can't give up seeing the world as a painter does, even if you no longer paint. You are doomed to see kaleidoscopes of color in white eggshells and rainbows in black seas.

My reason for giving up painting was cowardly, and it goes back to my troubled relationship with my mother. In my teens, I began to paint colorful, rambunctious fantasy portraits that were at odds with all the academic traditions my mother and grandfather held dear. While my mother didn't destroy these canvases, she made it very clear that they were *infra dig.*

"We used to draw in charcoal first, then in pastels, in order to win the *right* to even *use* oil paints. And we never drew from the figure ["figger," she said, in the English manner] till we had mastered plaster casts." The inference was clear: I was jumping in without perfecting my craft.

In the 1950s, abstraction was the only permissible language for American art. All the academicians in my family felt threatened. How could I understand that? I was only a kid, looking for my own language in color or words. I wanted to find a language that was neither academic nor abstract, but the world of painting seemed so hemmed in by familial restrictions that I fled to words. Poetry became my refuge. Yet, in writing poetry, I was drawn back to the artist's palette of cobalt blue, alizarin crimson, viridian green. I sought flaming watercolor skies.

It's not unusual for whole families to be painters. Think of Tintoretto and his daughter, Marietta Robusti. Or think of the Bellinis—before they became peach-flavored drinks. Or consider Artemisia Gentileschi and her father. Painters tend to grow up in studios. It's possible to see the making of art as a continuum, rather than a competition. But in my family, competition was rampant. My grandfather had two talented painter daughters whom he carefully trained, then tried to crush. He would have been much happier as Tintoretto when he could have delegated his daughters the painting of angels' wings and folds in satin. In Tintoretto's time, art was still a cooperative enterprise. Many hands were needed to cover immense canvases or ceilings or walls.

By the twentieth century, the idea of the sole genius artist steeped in ego had corrupted everything. By definition, there can be only one genius. The others are reduced to *assistenti*. Especially if they are girls.

We have lost so much by looking at art this way. In fact, all artists stand on the shoulders of their predecessors, just as all writers drown out choruses of the dead.

I was raised to be a fierce competitor, so I must have felt that by competing with my mother, I would kill her. Whatever message I was given, my own interpretation was, *Only one of us can paint and live.* I withdrew from the field. Better to be a writer than to commit matricide. But of course I never kissed pictures of painters, so maybe the drive was never there.

Or maybe I lacked the requisite grit for the physicality of painting or sculpture. My early paintings show promise. They are not bad—

even though I stopped before I discovered a style. If I was hiding from my own matricidal yearnings, I went on to kill my mother with words. Do all writers kill their parents with their work—then try to resurrect them (as Philip Roth has done in *The Plot Against America*)? The tenderness toward his parents in that book erases the earlier caricatures. They have been dead long enough for him to love them.

When I imagine the painter I might have been, I see myself stretching my own canvases, as my grandfather did, and priming them myself. But I imagine much huger canvases than anyone in my family actually painted. What are my subjects? Not horses like Rosa Bonheur's, or giant sexual blooms like Georgia O'Keeffe's, or beheaded men like Artemisia Gentileschi's—though these are all images I love. No. My huge canvases are awash with whirling color like the cosmos at the beginning of time. There are exploding suns, clouds of gases, rings of planets that have disappeared. Perhaps I will paint again when my mother dies.

Here the demon enters.

*Why doesn't she die already?*

*I don't want her to!*

*Yes you do! First of all, you'll be free of those depressing visits she never remembers you made, and you'll get more of her money! Won't that be nice!*

*I don't want her money.*

*Liar! You could use it. You're so extravagant. You could buy a house in Italy. How about that? And you could paint there!*

This is absurd. My mother no longer paints. She lies in bed dreaming most of the day, and she has forgotten that she ever painted. Why can't I pick up her brush, as a tree produces a green shoot? We all grow out of and extend each other. My daughter took to writing as a baby seal takes to swimming. But I think I made her passage easier. I never criticized her work or insisted that she read my own. I never believed that my journey was the only possible journey. I refused to be her critic even when she protested that I was too uncritical, too enthusiastic. I understood that any word of direction from a parent carries the weight of an iron anchor dropping into the sea. It may take the child's enthusiasm with it. A parent can never criticize a child too little. A parent can never encourage too much. Criticism can be found everywhere. The one place you don't need it is at home.

Writing was a way of reinventing my own childhood. I could make it more horrible than it was and heal myself that way. Or I could make it better than it was. Both approaches can be curative. In writing, I had power over the very people who made me feel utterly powerless when I was a child. Even the most horrible childhood can be made tolerable just by writing about it.

I'm thinking of Augusten Burroughs's crazy childhood in *Running with Scissors,* a book I love. Here's a kid whose father deserts him, whose mother is a mad, selfish narcissist and a terrible poet, who is turned over legally to an insane psychiatrist—and yet who thanks his parents at the beginning of the book for giving him the materials of a writer's childhood. He's absolutely right. What would a writer like Augusten Burroughs do with a happy childhood?

Nothing. It could have silenced him. Of course, he is being tortured with a lawsuit for telling his truth. In another age, he might have been burned at the stake.

I think of my own family *mishegoss*, which I have shamelessly milked for three decades. Or Woody Allen's. Or my daughter's. When I'm being honest, I kneel down and thank God for my crazy parents. I've accepted the fact that we only get so much from parents. The rest we have to provide ourselves. Writing is a way of bringing myself up all over again. I could never have done this as a painter. I must have known intuitively that writing was the only way to live my life.

When you're young, your parents cast these huge shadows. Then they shrink and shrink until it's time to put them in a box. How would I have survived these metamorphoses without writing? And how would Molly, my daughter, have survived without it? Her acid humor is her survival tool. It ate through whatever shadow I cast.

My demon thinks I want to murder my mother. Can he possibly be right? I have often wondered why writers are so obsessed with murder. Is it because we all need to murder our parents in order to go on?

Writers are murderers of more than their parents. They murder everyone they love. Time and again I have found that once I have frozen a person in a book, I can hardly remember what the real person was like. While writing, I have the sense of having oversimplified, of having fixed the character with too few complexities and too many exaggerations—because writing must necessarily be more dramatic than life—but years later I can only remember the person who inspired the character through the scrim of my own words. Everything else about the person is lost to me.

My first husband, for example. I wrote him as "The Madman" in *Fear of Flying,* and now that is all I can remember about him. But he was more than just a madman. Who *was* he? The poetry of his schizophrenia was compelling. He thought he was Jesus Christ, but he had done the research. He was a medieval historian, after all. Did I murder the real person for the sake of the fictional one? Is he still alive? Is he still angry with me? We had such a close connection once, and now he is only a character frozen in a book.

Last year I had lunch with my first love from high school, and sometimes I run into him shopping in the New York neighborhood where we both live. When I see him, I hardly recognize him because he looks so unlike the image in my head and his cameo in *Fear of Flying.* He startles me. Do I want him to stay frozen? Not really. But my nostalgia is more comfortable than the reality. I'm sure that in writing about him, I exaggerated to make him more vivid. That's inevitable. But it knocks off the real person.

When I tell a story at a dinner party, my husband always says, "Remember, this is a story being told by a novelist!" He means I have a tendency to embellish, to make the story more dramatic, to buff up the jokes so they are funnier and shine the dilemmas till they seem symbolic. A storyteller does this naturally, without even being aware of it. My tendency to dramatize murders ordinary life and ordinary people. I care more about drama than ordinary people and ordinary life. I'm lucky to be married to a person who knows this about me and finds it amusing.

Don't hang out with novelists unless you can live with their murdering real life in favor of fiction. Don't be a novelist unless you can tolerate this. It's a short jump from murdering real people to murdering your characters. Most novelists can make that jump for the sake of drama. Novelists always lie about how much it hurts them to murder their characters, but don't believe them. The passage from life to death is the most dramatic of passages, and novelists love it no matter what they say about weeping over their pages. Novelists love to weep.

Why is crime so rampant in novels? Why is murder such a hardy MacGuffin for novelists? Because there's nothing more theatrical. Breaking *any* of the Ten Commandments is good for plotting a novel. But murder and adultery are best. In fact, the more commandments you can break in a single novel, the better.

When I look back on my eight novels so far, I find I haven't murdered enough people. Death is a great plot device.

The frequency of brutal murder and dismemberment in fairytales and folk ballads shows us how prevalent these fantasies are. What I fantasize I also fear, because I naturally believe that my foulest fantasies will be turned against me.

Alan Lomax, the folk historian and collector of traditional ballads, noted that more than half of the folk ballads he collected in America recount murder, usually the murder of a young woman by a boyfriend.

The interesting thing about folk ballads and fairytales is that they relate the events of murder with no apologies and no psychologizing. They simply assume everyone will understand that violent behavior is as prevalent as, more prevalent in fact, than loving behavior. When we sing Child Ballads or read fairytales, we are deep in the human unconscious. It's a dark and bloody place.

My grandson was born and my father died within one month of each other. My grandson has my father's father's name. As I watch Max develop, I see in him things I used to see in my father: a delight in clapping his hands as a kind of speech, the soul of a percussionist, a mad desire to climb as high as he can. I don't know what stories Max will tell me, but I have the feeling they will be important ones. I have barely begun to make sense of my father's stories but I believe that if I keep writing about him, I will unravel them. Max is a clean slate, proof that the world is always beginning again. We have complicated conversations in which only two words—"dog" and "car"—are in a common language. Everything else is *lalala* or *deedlee, deedlee.* Yet because I love him so much, I understand him perfectly. If life is a series of intersecting novels, we are only in the prologue. Since I understand everything I love by writing, I will inevitably write about him as I have written about my daughter and as she has written about me. Writing is not a hostile act but an act of understanding—even when it's satirical, even when it's bitter. You only write about the things you care about. Indifference doesn't need to be put into words.

When I was in my twenties, I thought I didn't want to have children because Emily Dickinson and Virginia Woolf didn't have children. What a schmuck I was. I have learned more from Molly than I ever learned from Emily Dickinson and Virginia Woolf. I expect to learn even more from Max, because I've become less self-obsessed.

I had to be dragged kicking and screaming into parenthood, but grandparenthood is easy. I saw him and thought, *Mine*. There was no ambivalence, no anxiety. I always knew he wouldn't stop breathing. I crawl behind him on the rug in perfect bliss. He stops to inspect a toy and I stop to inspect it too. He makes up nonsense words and I make up nonsense words. Hours go by in a sort of trance. It's not that he is so much more interesting than my daughter was at that age, but because my anxiety is gone, I can truly experience him. I can see the world from his point of view. I am in the land of *deedlee*. He has no self-consciousness and I have lost mine.

This was impossible when I was a mother. I was so afraid of being lost in motherhood and angry like my own mother that I fought the dropping of self-consciousness you can experience only with a baby. It's not that I lose my adult mind completely with Max, but I do at moments. When I come back from the land of *deedlee*, I am suddenly struck by his vulnerability, and how the Nazis would have snatched him from his mother's arms and killed him. Or killed him in his mother's arms while I watched. And then killed me. Mercifully—since I wouldn't want to be in a world where he and she were not. My grandson reminds me of the cruelty of the human race. At his bris I worried about letting him be circumcised, for fear a new wave of anti-Semitism would doom him. I wanted his penis to be left alone so as not to mark him. So my joy in him is punctuated by sheer terror. This must be how my grandparents felt. Why else would my grandmother have lathered my little hands between hers, saying she was "washing away the Germans"?

When I look at movies of my daughter as a baby, what I see is the openness of her face. She trusts adults to take care of her. She trusts her mother and father. I watch her nod her head loosely, then learn to steady it, learn to grab things, learn to sit up, learn to walk, learn to run. I see her growing confidence. All the while I know that when she is four, her parents will separate and her whole world will come apart. I wish I could seize the film and change its ending. I wish I could protect the baby frozen on this film. Yet when she was four, I could not change anything. Nor could her father. I am so pained by this that I eject the disk.

Not long after Molly's father and I separated, I wrote a kids' book about divorce in which everything comes out all right. It was called *Megan's Book of Divorce,* and it featured a spunky little girl who never tired of plotting to bring her parents back together. In it, divorce was a sort of lark. The kid got double presents, double toys, double people to spoil her. She was cynical and knowing about the dad's girlfriend and the mom's boyfriend. She played the adults against each other.

I look at the book now and I think it wasn't about Molly at all, but about my own wish fulfillment. If I could have really gotten inside Molly's head and dealt with the divorce, the book would have been very dark. But I was trying to make it okay—as much for myself as for Molly. I was trying to rewrite history under the guise of a children's story.

I often do this in writing and don't realize it until years have passed. I cannot bear very much reality. I often wonder how people who don't write endure their lives. At least I can get through the pain by making up stories. Sometimes my funniest stories have come out of the blackest despair.

When I go over to my daughter's house to play with my grandson, I find him surrounded by educational toys. Everything he touches counts, pronounces the names of colors, oinks, moos, neighs, barks, or sings in an irritating little electronic voice. He is drowning in didacticism.

What are we so afraid of? Are we afraid these kids won't learn, by imitation, the way the rest of us did? Why do we need all these Baby Einstein toys? There is a kind of panic inherent in this endless preaching. It's as if we think our children are in danger of whiling away their early years in fantasy. God forbid. Every moment of their lives must be crammed with counting and spelling. I notice that Max's proudest achievement is in finding the little switches that turn these voices off. He is forever turning toys over to probe their mechanical guts. Aha! Rebellion! This generation will surprise us with their reaction to all this motorized talking. Will he disconnect all the robots in sheer fury and read books instead? Already he loves to sit contemplatively and turn the pages of books. We may be surprised by the reaction of this generation to our cramming didactic toys down their throats. I hope so. Play is far more important than drilling. If kids can't play, who can?

This love for didacticism and mistrust of fantasy invades every corner of our culture. It must stem from America's puritanical origins. But when fantasy does creep into children's lives, they are so grateful for it. This accounts for the success of the *Harry Potter* and *Lord of the Rings* series. Children don't need more cramming. Fantasy is what they need.

In the time I wrote and rewrote *Seducing the Demon,* Max went from six months to nearly two. He now calls me in the morning and says, "Hi Erica, hi Erica, hi Erica. I love you."

Because I have returned from the odyssey I've described here, I am able to give myself to him completely. Margaret Mead, who was one of my mentors—though I only met her once, briefly, and knew her chiefly from her books and articles—thought that the way we raise children was of paramount importance to culture. She studied it all her life—whether in New Guinea or in the United States. Whenever I see Max exploring his world, I think of her extraordinary understanding of children and our bond with them. She once said that instead of complaining that a child cried so much and kept us from our other work, we should say, "The child smiled so much."

I think back on all the dire predictions that were made in the '60s and '70s—*If women have the birth control pill they'll stop having babies; if women work outside the home their children will be criminals; if women earn money they'll scare away men*—and all of them have proved to be absurd. Women are still wanting babies and having babies. Men have been liberated to be fathers. Children are still hypnotizing their mothers and fathers, grandmothers and grandfathers. The world has not stopped. What I have learned is that the fearmongers are usually wrong about change. It's wonderful to have lived long enough to see it.

"How was the Toddler Center?" I ask Max, who now goes to Barnard one afternoon a week to play with other toddlers. We are in my study, where I have a huge toy train set waiting for him. He is engrossed by the toy trains, making them crash and fall all over the floor.

I make long lines of trains and he proceeds to pick them up and drop them as though he were King Kong. He is not interested in talking to me about school or anything that is not here and now. All he wants to do is play with trains. But he is entranced with naming.

"Ok-y-pus," he says, picking up the aquarium car with the octopus inside.

"Zebra," he says, lifting the car with the zebra that pops up.

"Ga-raff," he says, looking at the car with the tall giraffe.

He is naming the animals and then gleefully dropping the trains on the floor. No sooner do I put the trains together than he picks them up and scatters them on the floor.

"Gold," he says of the train with the golden load.

"Apples!" he says of the orchard train with its fruit. And then he tries to bite the plastic apples, as if to tell me that he knows what they are.

"Choo-choo train!" he shrieks triumphantly, dropping the red engine, which goes on whirring even though it's on its back like an insect.

"All done!" he concludes, having wrecked the trains I carefully assembled.

The love of words is clearly in his genes. The story is not over yet.

# The Root of All Evil

*Janice Eidus*

*Y*ou'd never mistake me for a money-hungry woman even now. I dress simply, in T-shirts and jeans or yoga pants, rent a no-frills apartment on an ungentrified East Village block, and plan to send my four-year-old daughter to public kindergarten. Yet the past few years have completely changed my philosophy about money.

My left-wing, proud-to-have-no-bucks parents raised me to be scornful of materialism. Flashing his intense blue eyes, my atheist father used to say, "One thing the Bible got right—money really is the root of all evil! Just look at the Republicans." And my parents weren't keen on buying me things. I never owned a Barbie, a Troll doll, or a Monopoly set, and I didn't have an endless array of dress-up clothes and princess accoutrements to wear as I paraded around our small Bronx apartment. I played mostly with cardboard boxes, strings, and buttons, transforming the boxes into solar systems and galaxies, the strings and buttons into an evolving cast of fantastical characters.

Every December, when my Jewish friends were busily counting their eight Hanukkah gifts and my Christian friends were *oohing* and *ahhing* at the astonishing number of worldly goods piled beneath their opulent, glittering trees, my Jewish parents, true to both their secular and anti-materialistic beliefs, gave me just a dreidel and a couple of pieces of chocolate gelt. But instead of feeling deprived, or envious of my friends, I was proud that we had "bucketfuls of integrity," as my parents put it. Looking back, I don't blame them for being somewhat immodest, since integrity really *was* what they had, instead of a country home or a fancy car, like many of their relatives and friends did. For better and worse, their values took deep root in me.

When I was in my twenties, living by myself in a series of tiny apartments in tenement walk-ups, each with its own distinct set of plumbing problems, I noted how some of my peers, living in highrise buildings with doormen and concierges, were already amassing pretty decent sums of money—some through hard work, but just as many through family and school connections, inheritances, and investments overseen by their savvy parents. Once again, instead of feeling deprived or envious, I felt proud of my genuine lack of interest in the doors money could open and the things it could buy. In fact, I felt sorry for those friends of mine who were still beholden to their parents. It didn't occur to me that my worldview—and the choices I was making—rendered me, in a different, nonmaterial way, equally beholden to mine.

Back then, I had three major interests: publishing my edgy, literary short stories in out-of-the-mainstream magazines (often *way* out of the mainstream) that paid in contributors' copies, as opposed to cash; being an activist for progressive social and political causes, like my parents before me; and engaging in exciting, short-lived sexual liaisons befitting a liberated young woman who didn't believe in marriage or long-term commitment.

After living relatively contentedly like this for a number of years, to no one's surprise greater than my own, I met tall and dark-eyed John, a jazz drummer going for his master's degree in anthropology, who specialized in ethnomusicology and shared my political and humanist values. He also considered himself a pro-feminism male, and, best of all, unlike the men I'd been involved with before, I felt that he truly "got" the intent and essence of my quirky, offbeat writing.

Practically overnight, John and I moved in together, first into my spare West Village apartment, then into his equally spare East Village pad. It was clear to both of us that ours was no wild, short-lived infatuation. The liberated young feminist and the pro-feminism male had fallen in love.

One of our shared and cherished beliefs was that marriage was not only a patriarchal institution but also an embarrassingly materialistic one, as much about expanding bank accounts and Olympian piles of wedding gifts as about true love—perhaps even more so. Nevertheless, after about a year of living together, we found ourselves wanting to legalize and legitimize our romance.

Deep down, to no one's surprise greater than ours, we appeared to harbor some fairly traditional desires.

But we didn't have a traditional wedding with white gowns, tuxes, bridesmaids, flower girls, and presents—nor did we have a lavish three-day hippie fest on some exotic, faraway beach with organic vegan food and aging '60s folk singers specially flown in. Rather, we held hands and stood side by side in our everyday clothes in an impersonal, wood-paneled courtroom that smelled of cleaning solution. The judge was bland and barely audible, and the court's two sensible shoe–wearing secretaries served as our witnesses.

After saying our vows, we walked to a local pizza joint. "So," John said, uneasily, watching me take a large bite of anchovy pizza, "who are we now?"

I chewed and swallowed. "Still radicals," I assured him. "Still anti-materialistic."

We toasted each other with beer, finished our pizza, and returned to the new apartment into which we'd recently moved and that we'd proudly and happily furnished with furniture either found on the street or purchased cheaply in thrift shops. We read only books borrowed from the library. We wore inexpensive, non-trendy clothes that we hoped would last for years.

The only thing I wanted back then, that I didn't yet possess, was the same thing that my parents had spent their lives working to achieve, and had encouraged me to want for as long as I could remember: to live in a harmonious world based on racial and economic justice.

Occasionally, however, the unpleasant subject of money did rear its head. In the early years of our marriage, I was awarded a month-long residency at an artists' colony upstate, which meant I would be provided room, board, and uninterrupted time to write. The bedroom I was assigned was spacious, with high ceilings and an antique bed. The separate studio where I wrote looked out on lovely, dense woods. The colony itself was Paradise, replete with hiking trails, two lakes, and a lush rose garden.

But a few days into this idyll, I discovered the serpent lurking within paradise: There was an informal tradition among the twenty-five artists-, writers-, and composers-in-residence to each purchase, on a designated evening, enough bottles of some exquisite-tasting, extremely expensive wine to satisfy everyone's tastes and needs.

In a panic, I called John from the single, claustrophobia-inducing phone booth shared by all of us at the colony. "What should I do?" I whispered, not wanting to be overheard by anyone who might be lingering outside the booth. "We don't have that kind of money!"

He acknowledged that our budget definitely didn't allow room for me to go on a lavish wine-buying spree. "So what are the alternatives?" His voice was calm and measured.

I grew silent, envisioning myself explaining my financial situation to my new friends at the colony. I sensed that, in the eyes of many of my colleagues, my lack of funds, which was such a great source of pride for me, would be viewed as pitiful. Not because the majority of them were wealthy. Far from it. Yet they seemed able to allow themselves to spend whatever they had on whatever they chose, and to have a good time doing so, without judging themselves harshly.

Grimly, I answered John's question: "There are *no* alternatives. We'll just have to tighten our belts even more."

The next day, I walked into town and found a liquor store. I allowed the clerk to talk me into buying some bottles of pricey vintage bordeaux. I was acutely embarrassed as I paid, and very, very glad that my parents were not around to witness how I had given in to the invariable pressure to keep up with the proverbial Joneses.

Fast forward to a few years later: Our financial situation changed. We finally had some money, because, after putting aside his drums for good and earning a master's degree in anthropology, John was working part-time toward a PhD in sociology, and working full-time for an agency that helped underprivileged foster children obtain social services. I taught creative writing part-time at a university and had by then published a couple of books and was collecting some royalties, and my stories occasionally appeared in "upscale" magazines that paid in cash.

John climbed the nonprofit ladder, and my writing grew calmer and more expansive, less edgy and in-your-face, now tinged with the quotidian details of settled, married life. I received fairly steady invitations to give readings and lectures and to teach at writers' conferences around the country—even around the world.

Our lifestyle was no longer quite as spartan as it had been. We bought art and hung it on the wall; we splurged on fresh flowers for the table; we took an occasional vacation. Now, when I was invited back to the artists' colony, I unhesitatingly supplied my colleagues with good wine. While I realized that we were better off than we had been, we still weren't rich by any means, and while we stuck to a fairly strict budget—our vacations were short and unglamorous, and our clothing was usually discounted and decidedly untrendy—perhaps most important, we continued to believe in our hearts that we were the same nonmaterialistic couple we had always been.

*Would we, could we,* we asked ourselves, *if we needed to, give up all of our things? In a heartbeat,* we answered. It would be no hardship whatsoever for us to do without health club memberships or the original artwork we'd purchased on our last trip to Mexico. I could easily, for my part, never again have a professional manicure, as much as I'd come to love indulging myself at my neighborhood salon on a monthly basis. For that matter, I could stop polishing my nails altogether.

Eventually, into our relatively contented lives came personal tragedy, when my sister died in her thirties of a rare, long-lingering, and devastating cancer. She had been the rebel in my family, becoming a deeply religious, card-carrying, fur coat–wearing Republican. My father died not long after she did, and I was sure that her tragic death contributed to his passing.

Not long after my father's death, John and I began to feel that something was missing in our lives, and gradually we realized that it wasn't a *thing* we were craving—not an iPod or a next-generation Mac computer, not a membership at a fancier health club, not designer clothes—but that we were suddenly yearning for a child.

No one was more surprised by this desire to become parents than we were. Practically from the day we met, we'd agreed that children were not in our future. I believed that all my nurturing instincts went into my writing, my good works, and my doted-upon cats. John and

I were equally turned off by the parents of infants we sometimes met, who spoke rapturously and at great length about their offspring's every poop, and by the parents of older kids, who were all caught up in the competitive world of New York City's status-mad private schools.

Despite all of that, we joined what seems to be a trend in New York City these days when we became middle-aged, first-time parents. The moment we beheld our beautiful daughter, we were instantly smitten, finding her every burp, fart, and squeal evidence of brilliance, precocity, and unlimited creativity. We became typical doting parents, caught up in a whirlwind of love, able to hold passionate discourse on the subjects of poops, strollers, sippy cups, and projectile vomiting.

Our black-haired, black-eyed daughter is now a delightfully verbal and willful four-year-old who loves to play, as her mother did before her, with cardboard boxes and strings and buttons. There's no need for a Barbie when her own body provides her with endless hours of excitement and joy. "Look, Mama," she cries delightedly, "I can shake my buttocks!"

I gaze upon her as she shakes and shimmies, so innocently in love with her own prowess, so open to possibility, and I am overcome by a love so shockingly fierce and primal that I must look away to contain myself. And finally, for the first time in my life, it is for her that I suddenly really want . . . money.

I'm just not satisfied anymore with the amount of money I have in the bank. I now crave what has always been off-limits and taboo to me, the thing that my twenty-something peers wanted long ago—money! Lots and lots of it—and not to purchase Barbies and

American Girls and Bratz for her, but rather to invest and save for my daughter's future.

For the first time, I understand the *true* power of money. I want to be assured that my child will never want for anything crucial to her well-being. Isn't it bad enough that she's destined to inherit a world with shrinking resources, a world riddled with violence and racism and misery and intolerance—things my parents spent their lives fighting against so bravely but failed, just like I have, to stop?

I want money so that she can have all the options in the world open to her. I want to buy her the best healthcare, the best education, the safest apartment in the safest building on the safest block in the city. I want the world to embrace her, to be kind to her. I want her world to be a fair and equitable place. And I think money may be able to help all that happen.

My father may have been right. Money may be the root of all evil. I'm still not sure what part money plays in my life or will play in my child's.

But I do know for sure that, right now, I want it. I want it for the freedom and peace of mind it brings. And perhaps, when I finally get as much of it as I want, when I feel that my daughter is truly safe in the world, I may even blow some of it on pure pleasure. Perhaps she and I will go out to celebrate, first by indulging together in manicures and pedicures at some very, very elegant and chichi salon, and then by hitting that extremely expensive, trendy toy store on Fifth Avenue, the one she doesn't even know exists, and I'll let her run wild.

# Neighborhood of Desire

*Cathryn Hankla*

*A*ttired for church in a white suit and white gloves, the large black woman in the yard next door to us worked her way prayerfully around the house with the bright yellow siding. There, between our houses, before resuming her ritual, she closed her eyes tight in meditation.

For sale signs were planted in both front yards. Our house, a high Victorian with stained glass, a two-story bay window, and plenty of gingerbread, had already sold to newlyweds from Florida, but the house next door had sat idle for a year, ever since the family renting it had been invited to vacate. Their sister, aunt, and landlord, who had bootstrapped her way from community college to the Ivies, held an academic position out of state. Right then, the full professor was standing in the yard with the Christian witch doctor.

The big woman in the suit undertook solemn, emphatic work, praying at the corners of the property, to the north, south, east, and west. "Oh, Jesus, take off the curse from this house," she chanted in the side yard, her voice finding its strength and rising. "Jesus, we're asking you to lift off the curse from this nice home. Oh, gentle and supreme Jesus, in your name we pray."

At her next stop in the front yard she repeated the ritual, then continued on to the porch, into the house, and through each room. She finished with the upstairs back porch while my partner, Ann, stood pruning the roses in our front yard, trying not to stare.

The owner of the house next door, whose recent scholarship examined U.S. nationalism as an economic and racial divide, had obviously hired the woman to pray, although Ann said she looked askance and rolled her eyes as she explained that her sister's family had hexed the house. When they left they declared that no one else would ever live there again. So far it had proved a heady curse. The professor had spent many thousands of dollars renovating the mess her family had made, and she needed the house sold.

We had had our house blessed after moving in—by a defrocked gay Methodist and my Unitarian universalist minister. I had beat a drum room to room while the ministers prayed by turns, burned some sage, and sprinkled some water around. So we really were not that skeptical, but I thought it might take more than a Christian witch doctor to lift the spell off the house next door. The family that had cursed the house might have been cursed themselves—even their own family member had given up on them—yet Ann and I had felt our own hex loosen a bit when the tenants packed up, and gradually the house next door was turned inside out in renewal. Loads of abandoned appliances, trash, and a car were hauled from the backyard, and every fixture was replaced within. The old mattress that had haunted me with nightmares of fire, so close was it stored to our bedroom window, finally came off the second-story back porch, thrown to the ground in one motion. Mangy carpet was torn out, floors refinished, a new kitchen installed; a new roof covered all. Flowers and shrubs took root in sculpted, mulched beds where before there had been nothing but weeds and shoots of onion grass so tall that several bent metal folding chairs had been immured, as if in kudzu chokers.

The only disturbance since the tenants' departure had been on a late summer night when one of the teenage former tenants—the brother not yet in jail—and his friends had vandalized the renovated house, poking the garden hose through the mail slot and throwing potted plants at the windows until some glass broke and some neighbors woke up.

In less than a month Ann and I would be gone from here, if only to literally a few blocks away. We were moving into what would be our second home together, a new space in an old building downtown that we had designed and had built: an ideal space for our shared and different realms. Our first house together was another story, as charming a house as you could ever imagine, we thought, even as we struggled against its century-old arrangement daily, which paved the way for many more arguments between us than I could have believed possible without a breakup. We desperately wanted our gamble on each other to pay off.

For more than a year, Ann converted the front parlor into her studio. The room was large enough but totally inappropriate for oil painting. For one thing, the walls had been drenched in Christmas green by a former owner, and we had not yet decided where to go with that; the horsehair plaster chunked out if Ann nailed in a picture hanger. The amazing walnut and mirrored mantel, carved with vines and a green man and faced with matching ceramic tiles hand-fired by a German craftsman, had to be covered with a drop cloth while canvases were stacked against its base and its delicately spindled shelves became cubbies for brushes and supplies. A treasure was rumored to be hidden behind the living room mantel, stashed there after a convenience-store robbery. All we actually found was a crumbling Roanoke newspaper from the 1930s. On one of the little, brittle pieces was printed my ex-husband's father's name. Some omen.

I felt as if I was living in a paint can. My sinuses killed me, my head throbbed from the second I woke up, and I complained mightily, while Ann was "just trying to make a living."

"At least," she would shout, "you can go to your office." My office at school was housed in a 19th-century building with a creek running beneath it, right below the oak floor, when it rained. All of the plaster had fallen in or cracked away over the years, replaced by wallboard furry with black mold. My bookcase was sinking through the floor.

Some refuge. I felt more like a refugee.

All the while we were struggling just as much against the neighborhood surrounding us. It was the same place that we had thought would be funky and chic, after attending a potluck held by one of

Ann's art friends who had long lived on the street and wanted us to join the club. Built-in friends. Like Joe, from Kansas, who had followed his ex-wife to Virginia to stay in his children's lives, and had moved in directly across the street right before we did. Good food and drinks spread out on the table. How bad can it really be? we had reasoned, when considering the area's reputation for crime. It's only Roanoke, not Richmond or, for God's sake, L.A., where Ann had lived for ten years. The white-bread suburbanites must be exaggerating, elitist, or both, although ours was a part of downtown that never failed to produce in my academic colleagues a raised eyebrow when I said where Ann and I had moved.

Our neighborhood was a cauldron of mixed desires, desires for friendship, money, drugs, sex, and music, but most of all for respect. The volume was up so loud on the mayhem that sometimes I could not remember why I had wanted to live there. I think it was for love. Ann and I wanted to live together, two women in search of someplace to make a home where we could halfway fit in, or at least not inspire any active hatred of the cross-burning kind. We were in danger of becoming lesbian lost causes, at forty-five and fifty-three. Both of us childless, married and divorced once in the conventional sense, and in the long interval bent on experience, with little relational stability. We needed to reinvent ourselves as people who could be part of something larger, something like a couple. For our transgression of a life together in the state of Virginia (not for lovers like us), we chose a transitional neighborhood; we chose the most economically and racially diverse street in town. At one end of our block was a known crack house of prostitution owned by one of the three most notorious slumlords in town, who were all "property investors" on our one short block, and at the other end was a large eyesore of brick apartments housing mostly Latino families that had to vie for control with pimps and druggies.

Ann said she thought our house was the most beautiful house in Roanoke before she'd even seen the inside. She took me across Elm Avenue one fateful night, when we were still fresh in our house-hunting, to the other side of Old Southwest, Roanoke's large historic district. Crossing Elm was like crossing the railroad tracks to the wrong side. A side in the painful process of renewal or gentrification, another troubling subject clarified to my satisfaction only by the sheltered distance that afforded a perfectly moral judgment: structural and institutional racism and economic inequality. I had one of those academic, liberal minds, and I didn't particularly want it challenged with too much reality on top of my politics. Like all of my friends, I mused on social problems while reading the newspaper and living somewhere else—someplace quiet and more, well, more privileged, or at least farther removed from the action.

For twelve years I had lived alone in a small house on fifty acres. It took me a while to see, through her painter's eyes, that high Victorian Painted Lady that Ann thought was so beautiful. Its sixteen exterior hues had been chosen by an informal neighborhood commission of willing opinions that had cajoled Bob, the former owner, the one responsible for the renovation of our house, into accepting their suggestions. Bob didn't know what colors he liked, so the neighbors began to volunteer ideas about the colors that Bob often wore. The khaki, white, black, and several oscillating trim shades of red and orange and yellow, as well as the multicolored columns around the porch, were a little much to take in all at once, but since I think Ann is the most beautiful woman in Roanoke, I didn't really have to love the *house*. And luckily, when Ann first drove me past it, the house was not for sale—yet later, miraculously, it was.

Even if the house had a Chinese red bathroom flanked by a dark teal bedroom, the kitchen was large enough, quaint enough, with a black-and-white tile floor, and tasteful in comparison to the many aberrant decor schemes we had tried to imagine remedying without having to knock down the house. I would finally have a library, with enough bookcases and more than three thousand square feet of high ceilings, period details, hardwood, and stained glass—more than enough space for living and entertaining. As a bonus, there was a shed in the back for potting or framing.

Just down the alley, a few houses away from ours, there was a house with twelve cars parked behind it in the mud. Mexican polka music cranked on the weekends, and when I went outside to hang my clothes—because our dryer was one of the first victims of an old-house power surge—the volume made me wince. If I went out the front door I was going to hear rap or hip-hop. In our backyard, someone had rammed into our chainlink gate so hard that the center pole had bent and the lock had broken off. From the front porch we observed a man kicking a kitten, and when Ann could not help but object, he told us he could do what he wanted: "It's my cat."

Early on we learned that entertaining on the wraparound porch could be interesting. During our inaugural lesbian fete a pair of folks started walking down the sidewalk; a woman, twenty feet ahead of a man, chorused, "Get off my dick!" The man then shouted, "You bitch!" While our party looked at each other in stunned silence, the call-and-response of "Get off my dick" followed by "You bitch!" continued for several long minutes, until the couple had walked to the far end of the block. But Ann and I shrugged it off and absorbed "Get off my dick!" into our mock-fighting vocabularies.

Adjusting to the neighborhood, I tried to remember how interesting I had found it when I learned that our house had been built by one of the original investors in the railroad in Roanoke. William Williamson had lived there until his death in the late 1930s and was responsible not only for the original 1890 house, but also for the addition of 1917, when the back porches were converted into two baths, up and down, and a kitchen and upstairs room were added.

After all, as we liked to joke with our neighbor Joe from Wichita, we were not in Kansas anymore.

One morning, as Ann and I sat across from each other at the stainless steel cook's table where we drank our coffee and solved the world's ills in the room farthest from the street, I read in the paper about an attempted robbery at nearby Sparky's convenience store, one block over, on Elm.

"O'lando Jones," I read aloud, "of the 500 block of Day Ave. is accused—"

"That's our neighbor!" Ann interrupted.

"Which one?"

"The teenager next door. The long-faced one."

I remembered who he was then. O'lando had been out in the street just a few months earlier, during an August full moon, threatening to kill himself after his girlfriend dumped him. Not more than a week before, he had introduced himself to us when we were out walking. "Hi, I'm your neighbor," he had said. "I live next door." He smiled at us; he was happy, out strolling with his girl. We were strolling, too, walking the dogs to the park and back in the cool of the evening.

The intervention team carted O'lando away the night he couldn't stop wailing, "Just love me, just love me." And in the next breath it was, "Hate that bitch." While he stumbled around in the middle of the street, his mother watched from the front yard. She had already lost one son to suicide.

O'lando's breakdown marked the culmination of an active week for social and emergency services. A young child had been escorted from the upstairs apartment of the rental house across the street. It was the same apartment where pit bulls were being bred. When we had called Frank Roupas, one of the notorious trio of slumlords, about the pit bull problem, he had demurred in his way. We could always call Animal Control, he said. Frank was well-practiced at quick footwork; he was a ballroom dance instructor and had owned the rental house for forty years. Frank liked to call us his "neighbors," but he lived across the bridge, in a decidedly middle-class neighborhood, while trolling the courts for the tenants who would become our neighbors.

This time someone else had beaten us to 911, and had informed Social Services about the probable condition of the apartment where the toddler lived. The dogs barked with regularity through the banisters of the upstairs balcony, but we had never seen them walked. As we watched the child be carried out, Ann called up Frank, as she had many times before. "I thought you'd want to know what's happening at your property."

Earlier in the week, O'lando's family dog had been taken away and put down by Animal Control. Their chained dog, which we fed and tried to water through the fence, was finally removed when it broke free and fatally chomped a little yipping dog at the pink house down the street. Everyone was out for blood over that one. The white folks in the pink house were yelling the "n-word," while their children cried over the bloody Pomeranian.

The two little children being raised in the house next door, O'lando's nephews, scattered their grade school papers in the gutters, leaving the A's on homework for urban anthropologists like me to pick up, as I tried to imagine how I would save them from their circumstances, offer them the possibility of a college education, which would of course solve everything, as it had for their great-aunt, the Ivy League–educated professor. The children would never speak to us when we tried to address them. We were strangers who lived next door. The professor's sister, their grandmother, was raising them, along with O'lando and another son of her own; she drank and suffered from manic depression, the professor later told us. Unlike her grandchildren, she would comment to us through the chain-link fence separating our backyards. That's how we learned the dog's name was Poochie.

"They said O'lando used a hammer," I paraphrased the short article for Ann. "They recognized him at the store, and the police have picked him up already."

"Poor O'lando."

Ann and I sang our little ironic chorus from *Mister Rogers' Neighborhood*: "It's a beautiful day in the neighborhood, a beautiful day in the neighborhood . . . ."

The gallows humor had grown a bit stale, just as embellishment of fact into fiction had become more than unnecessary in the year and a half we had lived on the street. There wasn't much left to say about it, and we didn't know what to do except continue what we were doing while we drew up plans for our exit. We showed up on biannual cleanup day and donned gloves to help remove the accumulated tons of litter and plain old garbage that kept blooming in the alleys, yards, and gutters that surrounded us, just beyond our black iron hoop-and-spear fencing—although not one of the "property investors" ever showed up to help. We thought about that especially when we were picking up soiled plastic diapers.

I had taken to leaving out the details when speaking with my family. All of the things I left out added up to a horror tale that elderly relatives didn't need to hear. It was uncomfortable to hear about, and more so to live with. There was the day I saw a thin young man breaking the glass of the back apartment window of the house to the right of us. There was the time an officer tackled a man with a gun in the side yard to the left, just seconds after I had pulled the laundry from the line. And there was the afternoon I saw a pickup truck slow down just enough for one of our favorite hookers to expel a dubious substance from her mouth.

I feel kind of bad writing down stuff like this, yet I am, because for us it was fairly relentless and much louder and more intrusive than a representation on canvas or in print can ever convey. I wanted to keep my sheltered academic perspective intact, along with all of the liberal views I had long fostered before having to deal with the street. We were annoyed to distraction by the spillover from the lives in survival mode and disarray that surrounded us. It made us feel even more dysfunctional than we were. We fought with each other out of frustration. The noise depressed and freighted us with anger of all kinds, the sort we heard in nearly constant streams of obscenities when we went outside, and the kind we felt in response when our peace was shattered again and again. All we had wanted was a home together, not this constant assault of lives in turmoil rolling through our own.

And yet every time Ann painted the scene through the kitchen window to the backyard—cut roses in blue vases in the foreground, with garden beyond—it was a hit that kept bread and butter in the bank. Everyone wanted to buy these still-lifes; they fought over them. The picture without the sound. Or the motion. Still life. Like the light in the afternoon, strung across the facades of the multicolored houses on our block—the pink and the acrid green, the gray and the mint julep— all glowing together. Pink azalea bushes framed our front porch, fennel as high as your hip teemed in the south-facing back garden, and roses of pink and yellow continued to bloom during the mild winters. Children tossed balls in front yards wearing Indian headdresses, children of every color who studied in public school together. Our crazy street in a certain cast of light sometimes looked, for an hour or an evening, the way an American neighborhood was supposed to, and gave us a little demonstration of the promise of democracy.

One evening a stranger knocked at Kevin's front door, just down the street. Kevin loved the neighborhood, became president of the association, took citizen police training, and got involved. His parents had moved to the neighborhood from northern Virginia and started renovating a house a couple of streets over. Flipping on his porch light, Kevin opened his front door to an unfamiliar white face that had been recently split by a knife, the knife visible now only as a handle sticking out of the man's sinus cavity. Judging from the length of the handle, it looked to be a long knife. With blood pouring down his face from the wound, the man asked for help. Kevin set him on the stoop, made the emergency call, and waited with him for the paramedics.

The paper reported, in a follow-up article, that the knife blade almost severed the man's upper spine. It was the man's live-in partner who stabbed him, and he refused to press charges. They still lived together afterward. The only thing that changed was the victim's face.

All of these lives in proximity, all of these people trying to live together without pressing charges, filled with rage and love, scarring each other with desire. The gay mixed-race couples, the ex-cons, and Ann and me.

Even though, after three and a half years, we have sold the most beautiful house in Roanoke and retreated to a quiet space where we can work undisturbed, our deepened bond is more dependent for its strength on the annealing pressures of the neighborhood we left behind than we can explain. Neither of us was particularly sad to leave, but in our minds it will always be our neighborhood.

# My Lover, My Home

*Jenny Siler*

$\mathcal{I}$ have a confession to make: I have a lover. No one knows this;
at least, not really. My husband probably has his suspicions:
He's heard me talk, sensed the passion in my voice, the excitement I
can't quite hide. He has to know there is something going on, some
part of my life that remains inaccessible to him.

I think about my lover all the time. Sometimes when I'm falling
asleep at night I'll go over and over the details of a past rendezvous. I'll
recall the physical sensations, the goose bumps, the chills, the breath-
taken bodily joy I feel when we are together. Other times I'll spend
hours daydreaming about a certain small attribute—a particular ripple
or fold, say—unable to re-create it perfectly in my mind. Sometimes
my longing is so fierce, it is like a sickness.

There was a time when I saw my lover every day, when we spent
entire days together. My lover was a constant presence, visible when

I woke in the morning and when I went to sleep at night. You might think this kind of proximity would be a destructive force, but it was not. Just being close to my lover has sustained me through some of the darkest periods of my life. Now that we are apart, I am like an addict without her drugs, thinking constantly about the succor of the last fix and the possibility of a future one.

The most unexpected things will trigger my desire: a newspaper article, a movie, a picture in a magazine, the unexpected sound of the wind in a stand of trees. Or someone—a stranger in a restaurant or an unthinking friend—will mention my lover's name, and the rest of my day will be consumed by visions of what we once had. Occasionally, someone will allude to having spent time with my lover. When this happens I find myself becoming fiercely jealous, enraged even. I cannot tolerate the idea that a stranger could know my lover as I do, that they could have shared the kind of intimacy that is ours alone.

My husband tolerates all of this with remarkable patience. And I imagine he has his own unspoken longings, a lover or lovers to whom he will always be drawn, by whose allure I am baffled. I have my suspicions, but I am not worried. After all, we have a strong marriage and a good life. Despite our affairs, there are certain things—love, companionship, intimacy, sex, to name a few—that we can get only from each other.

The first time I saw my lover, I was five years old. I have no real recollection of that initial glimpse, though I've been told the story enough times to have crafted my own memory. It was January, twenty below zero, with a Great Plains wind whipping snow ghosts across the high-way. Montana, the place to which I would find myself forever tethered by longing, must not have looked like much through the back window of our yellow Ford Pinto. Certainly, this could not have been an instance of love at first sight; I've been back to that lonely stretch of interstate enough times by now to know that. But there must have been something, the first embers of love, a genetic predisposition to utter desolation passed down by my ancestors, who were themselves not unfamiliar with the more barren places on this earth. The ferocity of my feelings leads me to believe there is a part of me that has always been in love with Montana, that I loved it even before I knew it.

Like all great affairs, my relationship with this state has been a complicated one. The landscape of my childhood was not a forgiving place. People froze to death, or were eaten by grizzly bears, or simply lost their way and were never found. These perils were a fact of life. But if danger was omnipresent, so was beauty. Growing up I experienced moments of grandeur that were almost mythic in their power, and to which I am still able to return with fearsome clarity: a snowbound stream in the Sapphire Mountains, the ice punched through to reveal the water flowing beneath, a brook trout flashing against brown stones; sunrise, a frigid September morning in the high sage desert, a hunter emerging from beneath a frost-covered tarp, his bearlike form silhouetted against the pastel-washed crags of the continental divide. Though I wouldn't realize it until much later, until I had left Montana and gone back again more than once, these experiences were the bedrock upon which I would build all my notions of beauty.

I first endured the heartbreak of separation at age fifteen, when I left for Massachusetts to attend boarding school. Until then, I hadn't understood the extent to which my soul was tethered to the landscape of the West. Amid the lush hardwood forests of the East Coast, with no visible horizon with which to orient myself, I felt smothered and claustrophobic, unable to get my bearings. I was not simply homesick, but profoundly heartsick. In the evenings I would sneak out of my dorm and jog across the school's empty playing fields, searching for the illusion of open space. Weekends or holidays I would hop a bus to Boston, then take the train out to Revere Beach and stare for hours at the Atlantic's gray horizon. But as vast as the ocean was, it lacked the vertical grandeur of the Rocky Mountains, and these pilgrimages rarely provided more than small comfort.

My summers at home, like all seasonal love affairs, were brief and ecstatic. I spent long stretches of time in the car, driving the state's empty, two-lane highways, usually at night. I hiked to back-country hot springs and immersed myself, literally, in the mountains I loved so much. I passed endless afternoons on the river I had known since childhood, memorizing each trout-filled pool or rocky bend.

My twenties were characterized by a kind of restless torpor. I can see now that my feelings had everything to do with a deep need to find my way back to the place from which I had exiled myself. But at the time I assumed that I, like everyone else my age, was just trying to find myself. In my quest to do just that, I dedicated myself to wandering—from place to place, job to job, and man to man— always, ultimately, looking for the same thing.

The places I chose to visit or call home over the next decade testify to my desire to be overcome by the physical landscape around me. New York City, Alaska, Key West, Morocco, the French Pyrenees, the windswept northern islands of Scotland—all are places in which the individual is incidental; all veer in some way or another toward the outer boundaries of the human environment. In the looming Manhattan skyline I found echoes of my beloved Rocky Mountains. On the bald plains of the Sahara I was reminded of my own Great Plains. In all of these locations, I found solace in the stark and the magnificent.

In my relationships I invariably selected partners whose indifference was a metaphor for the harsh landscape of the American West. I was drawn to men whose egos were bigger than mine, who needed me much less than I needed them and were quick to remind me of that fact. Confusing cruelty with power, and power with beauty, I fell for mean men. I allowed myself to be mistreated, even reveled in it, as if the ferocity of these relationships could somehow make up for what I had lost in leaving the wilderness of Montana behind.

I liked my religion equally overwhelming. I desired a god that would subsume me, something vast and dreadful into which I could merge entirely. I traveled for days to visit mountaintop monasteries, spent weeks in painful and penitent silence. I prayed and fasted and wept. I contemplated shaving my head and donning a nun's habit.

I wanted my life to be hard, and when it wasn't, I made it so. I took the worst jobs and worked the worst hours, as if comfort itself was an unpardonable sin, as if through misery I could commune with my beloved.

And then, finally, I went home.

I was in my early thirties when I made the decision to go back. My first novel had just been published, allowing me to quit my day job and focus on writing full-time. For the first time in my adult life, I had a career that made it possible for me to support myself while living in the place I loved, and I jumped at the chance to return to Montana.

I arrived in the spring, limping across the mountains from Seattle in a U-Haul to the promise of paradise. By the time the last of the snowpack had melted, I had reacquainted myself with the person I had always known I was supposed to be. My first summer home, I went to the mountains almost every day. When I was not in them, I was thinking about them, gazing up toward the secret drainages of the Bitterroot Range, planning my next foray into the fairyland of glacial cirques and alpine lakes.

After years of searching, I had finally reclaimed the larger portion of myself, and I was physically and mentally at ease in a way I had never thought possible. I ended a doomed relationship I had been in for years; I began to look at life as something to be enjoyed, not suffered. I even started to think of myself as physically attractive, an idea I had never before considered. In short, I was ecstatic and in love.

And then, at the tail end of my second summer home, I met the man who would become my husband, and for whom I would eventually choose to leave Montana yet again. The irony of the situation is not lost on me. Had I not gone back, I would never have met my husband. Had I not blossomed in that place, I might never have fallen in love. But each of these things happened, and I cannot be anything but grateful that they did.

Montana may be beautiful, but it has a terrible economy. "You can't eat the scenery," people there always say. While my writing career was highly portable, my husband's ambitions were not. He tried valiantly to stay on, but in the end it became clear to both of us that while my happiness was tied to the West, his was being slowly and steadily compromised by the lack of opportunities there. As much as I dreaded the prospect of another exile, I knew I could not ask the person I loved to surrender his happiness for my own. Besides, I told myself, Montana would always exist, and I could come back whenever I wanted or needed to.

As I write this, I am at the end of a three-year stint in Virginia's Shenandoah Valley. It is a beautiful place, stunningly so, a swatch of green farmland dotted with quaint settlements, watched over by the benevolent presence of the Blue Ridge Mountains. A cozy place, I might say, a gentle place, a place in which people belong, a landscape, with its snug hollows and loamy fields, that shelters and nourishes. In the summer, the hills are lush with the thick canopy of the hardwood forests. In the winter, snow sugars the rooftops and the fields—just enough white to be beautiful—before melting compliantly in the afternoon sun.

It is a place where other people come to refresh themselves, to forget their own exiles. It is a place of fantasy, of wide porches and small-town parades, of carriage rides and stone walls and hillside cemeteries. There are no June snowstorms here, as there was on the day of my wedding in Montana. Spring comes in March, a glorious blizzard of daffodils and dogwood. In short, Virginia is everything Montana is not: a craven suitor, eager to please and quick to show its affection, bearing flowers and a warm smile. Is it any wonder I have come to loathe this place?

In just a few months we will move again, north this time, to Maine. I have high hopes for my new home. At the very least, there is real weather in that part of the country, nor'easters and the like, storms that can claim a person's life. There is the Atlantic again, that old flame into whose arms I ran as a teenager. And there are mountains, though not of the scale to which I am accustomed. But I believe I will make do.

I do go back to Montana, as I promised myself I would, but it's hard to recapture the magic. As with all lovers who have been apart and will be again, there is an awkwardness to be bridged, a period of adjustment in which the place and I must learn each other all over again through touch and smell and taste, each of us holding something back in the hope that our reticence will make the next inevitable separation easier. I am not only a wife, but a mother now as well, my love divided three ways, my heart tugged this way and that by forces I cannot control. *Someday,* I tell myself, *when all the other commitments of my life have been met, I will go back.* And when I do, it will be for good.

# Acknowledgments

*T*hanks to Brooke Warner at Seal Press for asking me if I had a book in me, and to Camille Cusumano and Stephanie Wilkinson for giving me the assignments that led to Brooke's asking.

I also want to thank all the writers who contributed to the anthology, in spite of the request for total disclosure and the small remuneration. It was wonderful getting to know you all!

Thanks to Jenny Siler for her enthusiasm for the original project, even though it didn't get off the ground at that time.

Thanks, always, to the Virginia Center for the Creative Arts, where my writing and my soul have been nurtured for many, many years.

Thank you to Michael, my new husband, who came into my life about the same time as this book, and who kept assuring me I would meet my deadline.

And all thanks to Margo, my sister, who never let me give up my writing. Ever.

# About the Contributors

CONNIE BAECHLER'S work has appeared in *Kalliope, Pearl,* and *The Hurricane Review*. She holds both an MFA in poetry and a PhD in literature and women's studies and is a member of Zona Rosa, a writing workshop series facilitated by author Rosemary Daniell. Baechler's writing also appears in Daniell's most recent book, *Secrets of the Zona Rosa* (Henry Holt and Company, 2006).

MAGGIE BUCHOLT has an MFA in writing from Vermont College and was recently awarded a fellowship to the Virginia Center for the Creative Arts to work on her novel. A contributing editor to *Hunger Mountain: The Vermont College Journal of Arts & Letters,* she had an essay on craft published in *The Writer's Chronicle*. She is the editor of *An Insider's Guide to Southern Vermont* (Viking/Penguin).

RACHEL KRAMER BUSSEL (www.rachelkramerbussel.com) is senior editor at *Penthouse Variations,* hosts the "In the Flesh" erotic reading series, and wrote the popular "Lusty Lady" column for *The Village Voice.* She's edited more than a dozen anthologies, most recently *Best Sex Writing 2008; Cross Dressing; Hide and Seek: Erotic Stories; Caught Looking; She's on Top; He's on Top;* and *Naughty Spanking Stories from A to Z 2.* Her writing has been published in more than one hundred anthologies, including *Best American Erotica 2004* and *2006, Single State of the Union,* and *Everything You Know About Sex Is Wrong,* and she's contributed to *Bust, Curve, Diva, Gothamist, The Huffington Post, Mediabistro, Memoirville,* the *New York Post, Penthouse, Playgirl,* the *San Francisco Chronicle, Time Out New York,* and *Zink.*

ROSEMARY DANIELL, living legend and noted author of *Sleeping with Soldiers* and *Fatal Flowers: On Sin, Sex, and Suicide in the Deep South,* among other books of poetry and prose, has been called "one of the great writing teachers I have seen at work in this country" by author Pat Conroy. She runs the famous Zona Rosa workshops and retreats that have been featured in such magazines as *People* and *Southern Living.* She lives and works in Savannah, Georgia.

DEBORAH MAGPIE EARLING teaches fiction and Native American studies at the University of Montana. Her first novel, *Perma Red,* was published in 2002. Her publications also include stories in *The Last Best Place: A Montana Anthology; Talking Leaves: Contemporary Native American Short Stories; Circle of Women: Anthology of Western Women Writers;* and *Wild Women: Anthology of Women Writers.*

JANICE EIDUS, short-story writer, novelist, and journalist, has twice won the O. Henry Award for fiction. She is also the recipient of the Redbook Prize and a Pushcart Prize. She teaches at the University of Victoria.

S. S. FAIR cut her teeth as a roll 'n' roll critic for *The Village Voice, Rolling Stone,* and *Sounds* in London, back when such things were cool. She has written movie reviews, book reviews, and fashionista ravings for publications ranging from *Psychology Today* to *Ms.* to *Esquire* and has interviewed A-list celebrities and done pop-culture essays for the *New York Daily News Magazine.* Currently she writes for Neiman Marcus's "The Book" and is the "Samurai Shopper" columnist for *The New York Times Magazine.* She is at work on a book.

ZOË FAIRBAIRNS is a journalist, novelist, and short-fiction writer and has published her work in such British magazines and newspapers as the *Guardian, The Independent,* the *Times Literary Supplement,* the *New Statesman,* and *Cosmopolitan.* She published her first novel at age seventeen and her second while still at university. *Here Today,* an exploration of feminist themes in a crime setting, won the 1985 Fawcett Society Book Prize.

MYRA GOLDBERG is on the faculty at Sarah Lawrence College and runs writing workshops for teachers and students in New York City public schools. Her collection of stories, *Whistling and Other Stories,* was a *New York Times Book Review* notable book. She has published a novel, *Rosalind,* and her short story "Who Can Retell" was reprinted in the National Public Radio anthology *Hanukkah Lights: Stories of the Season.* She lives with her daughter in New York City.

San Francisco–based performance poet DAPHNE GOTTLIEB stitches together the ivory tower and the gutter using just her tongue. She is the award-winning author of four books of poetry (*Kissing Dead Girls, Final Girl, Why Things Burn,* and *Pelt*), as well as the graphic novel *Jokes and the Unconscious* (with artist Diane DiMassa). She is the editor of *Homewrecker: An Anthology Reader* and is currently working on a new anthology about sex and identity. She teaches at New College of California.

Poet, fiction, and short-story writer and painter CATHRYN HANKLA is a professor of English at Hollins University and poetry editor of *The Hollins Critic.* Her novels are *Blue Moon over Poor Water* (Ticknor and Fields) and *The Land Between* (Baskerville). Her books of poetry include *Afterimages* and *Texas School Book Depositor* (published by LSU Press), which was one of three finalists for the 2000 Library of Virginia Prize. Honors include the PEN Syndicated Fiction Award for short story and a Virginia Commission for the Arts Grant in poetry.

VICKI HENDRICKS is the author of noir novels *Miami Purity, Iguana Love, Voluntary Madness,* and *Sky Blues.* She lives in Hollywood, Florida, and teaches writing at Broward Community College. *Cruel Poetry,* scheduled for publication in 2007, is her darkest novel yet, entwining sex, drugs, and murder with an obsessive "love pentagon" involving a prostitute and the men and women who love her or want her dead.

ERICA JONG'S book *Fear of Flying* has sold 18 million copies worldwide and was one of the first novels to deal frankly with women's
sexuality. Jong is the author of seven other novels, including *Fanny,*
*Inventing Memory,* and *Sappho's Leap,* as well as six volumes of poetry
and five volumes of nonfiction, including her most recent, *Seducing*
*the Demon: Writing for My Life* (Tarcher/Penguin). She has been
honored with the United Nations Award for excellence in literature and has received *Poetry* magazine's Bess Hokin Prize for poetry
and the Deauville Award for literary excellence in France, among
other awards.

Born in 1933, JANE JUSKA is an old person but a new writer. After
forty years teaching English in high school, college, and prison, she
embarked on the fulfilling adventure of finding men with whom to
have sex. Those adventures appear in *A Round-Heeled Woman,* published in 2003 and followed in 2006 by *Unaccompanied Women.* In
between, her articles have appeared in various anthologies and magazines. At present she is working on a novel. Jane's four-year-old grand-
daughter, bemused by all these goings-on, wonders, "Isn't Grandma
old?" "Not yet," says her dad.

MYRNA KOSTASH, a native of Edmonton, Alberta, works full-
time as a nonfiction writer of magazine articles, books, and radio
documentaries. Her publications include *The Next Canada: In*
*Search of the Future Generation* (Toronto: McClelland & Stewart),
*The Doomed Bridegroom: A Memoir* (Edmonton: NeWest), and *No*
*Kidding: Inside the World of Teenage Girls* (McClelland & Stewart).

She has been the recipient of the Queen's Jubilee Medal for contribution to the arts and won *Canadian* magazine's Silver Medal Award, among others.

SHARON LEITER writes poetry, fiction, essays, and literary criticism. Her latest book is *A Critical Companion to Emily Dickinson: A Literary Reference to Her Life and Work* (Facts on File, 2006). She is the author of the literary study "Akhmatova's Petersburg" (University of Pennsylvania Press, 1983) and a volume of poetry, *The Lady and the Bailiff of Time* (Ardis, 1974). She won a 1990 Virginia Prize for fiction and has published stories and poems in such journals as the *Georgia Review, The Virginia Quarterly Review, Cimarron Review,* and *Atlanta Review.* A long-time resident of Charlottesville, Virginia, she serves as poetry editor of *Streetlight,* a regional journal of arts and letters, and teaches in the Bachelor of Interdisciplinary Studies program at the University of Virginia.

JOYCE MAYNARD, who first achieved acclaim with her memoir *Looking Back,* published when she was nineteen, is the frequent contributor to many magazines, including *The New York Times.* She has been a syndicated columnist and radio commentator and is the author of five novels, including *To Die For* (which was made into a critically acclaimed film starring Nicole Kidman), *Baby Love,* and *Where Love Grows.* She is also the author of novels for children and young adults. Her newest book is the nonfiction *Internal Combustion: The Story of Marriage and Murder in the Motor City* (Jossey-Bass).

K. W. OXNARD, a finalist for the Sarabande Books Mary McCarthy Prize in Short Fiction and a semifinalist for the Pirate's Alley William Faulkner Novel Prize, has been published widely in literary journals and magazines and has been the recipient of several fellowships to the Virginia Center for the Creative Arts.

MELISSA PRITCHARD is a Pushcart Prize winner and O. Henry Prize winner. Her novel *Late Bloomer* was named a 2004 Best Book by the *Chicago Tribune*. She has won countless other awards and citations and served as one of three judges for the 2005 PEN/Faulkner Award for Fiction. She is associate professor of English at Arizona State University.

JULIA SERANO is an Oakland, California–based writer, spoken word artist, trans activist, and biologist. She is the author of *Whipping Girl: A Transsexual Woman on Sexism and the Scapegoating of Femininity*, a collection of personal essays that reveal how misogyny frames popular assumptions about femininity and shapes many of the myths and misconceptions people have about transsexual women. Julia's other writings have appeared in anthologies (including *BITCHfest: Ten Years of Cultural Criticism from the Pages of Bitch Magazine* and *Word Warriors: 30 Leaders in the Women's Spoken Word Movement*) and in feminist, pop culture, and literary magazines, and have been used as teaching materials in college-level gender studies courses across the United States. For more information about all of her creative endeavors, check out www.juliaserano.com.

RUTH KNAFO SETTON is author of the novel *The Road to Fez.* Her fiction, poetry, and creative nonfiction appear in *The Schocken Book of Modern Sephardic Literary, Best Contemporary Jewish Writing, NAR,* and many others. Her awards include fellowships from the NEA, Pennsylvania Council on the Arts, and PEN. She is the writer-in-residence for Jewish studies at Lehigh University.

JENNY SILER, who also writes under the pseudonym Alex Carr, is the author of five novels and numerous short stories and essays. Her first Alex Carr novel, *An Accidental American,* was published by Random House in spring 2007. Her second, *The Prince of Bagram Prison,* will be available in spring 2008. Jenny lives in Maine.

# About the Editor

*F*ormer journalist Lisa Solod Warren published her first newspaper story at age seventeen. In the past twenty-five years she has been an editor at *Boston* magazine and with Whittle Communications, and she has written for *The Boston Globe,* the *Boston Herald, Brain, Child,* the *International Herald Tribune,* and *The Roanoke Times & World News,* among other publications. Warren's seminal interview with Edward Gorey (which she wrote under her maiden name) is published in *Ascending Peculiarity: Edward Gorey on Edward Gorey.* Her fiction has been published in a dozen literary journals and anthologies and has won several awards. Also under the name Solod, she has recently published essays in *France, A Love Story* and *Matzo Balls for Breakfast.* Under her new name, she has stories just out in LiteraryMama and *Meridian.* She lives in Virginia with her husband, the writer Michael Warren, and her teenage daughter.

# Selected Titles from Seal Press

For more than thirty years, Seal Press has published groundbreaking books. By women. For women. Visit our website at www.sealpress.com.

*Indecent: How I Make It and Fake It as a Girl for Hire* by Sarah Katherine Lewis. $14.95, 1-58005-169-3. An insider reveals the gritty reality behind the alluring façade of the sex industry.

*Single State of the Union: Single Women Speak Out on Life, Love, and the Pursuit of Happiness* edited by Diane Mapes. $14.95, 1-58005-202-9. Written by an impressive roster of single (and some formerly single) women, this collection portrays single women as individuals whose lives extend well beyond Match.com and Manolo Blahniks.

*Confessions of a Naughty Mommy: How I Found My Lost Libido* by Heidi Raykeil. $14.95, 1-58005-157-X. The Naughty Mommy shares her bedroom woes and woo-hoos with other mamas who are rediscovering their sex lives after baby and are ready to think about it, talk about it, and DO it.

*Inappropriate Random: Stories on Sex and Love* edited by Amy Prior. $13.95, 1-58005-099-9. This collection of short fiction by women writers takes a hard look at love today—exposing its flaws with unflinching, often hilarious, candor.

*Unruly Appetites: Erotic Stories* by Hanne Blank. $14.95, 1-58005-081-6. Erotic fiction with sensual lyricism and dynamic characters that titillate and inspire.

*Shameless: Women's Intimate Erotica* edited by Hanne Blank. $14.95, 1-58005-060-3. Diverse and delicious memoir-style erotica by today's hottest fiction writers.